HILLARY

A BIOGRAPHY OF HILLARY RODHAM CLINTON

Karen Blumenthal

BLOOMSBURY

LONDON · OXFORD · NEW YORK · NEW DELHI · SYDNEY

Bloomsbury Publishing
An imprint of Bloomsbury Publishing Plc

50 Bedford Square
London
WC1B 3DP
UK

1385 Broadway
New York
NY 10018
USA

www.bloomsbury.com

BLOOMSBURY and the Diana logo are trademarks of Bloomsbury Publishing Plc

First published in 2016 in the USA by Macmillan Publishing Group, LLC, New York
First published in Great Britain 2016
This paperback revised edition published in 2017

British Library Cataloguing-in-Publication Data
A catalogue record for this book is available from the British Library.

ISBN
PB: 9781408889664
ePub: 9781408873830

2 4 6 8 10 9 7 5 3 1

Printed and bound in Great Britain by CPI (UK) Ltd, Croydon CR0 4YY

This book is produced using paper that is made from wood grown in managed, sustainable
forests. It is natural, renewable and recyclable. The logging and manufacturing processes
conform to the environmental regulations of the country of origin.

To find out more about our authors and books visit www.bloomsbury.com.
Here you will find extracts, author interviews, details of forthcoming events and the o
ption to sign up for our newsletters.

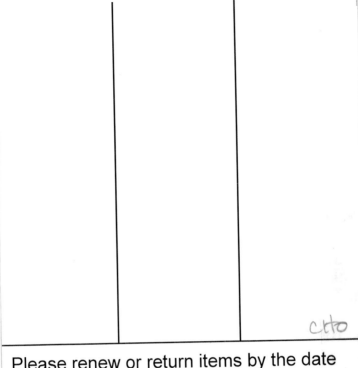

c/to

ALSO BY KAREN BLUMENTHAL

STEVE JOBS:
The Man Who Thought Different

To Abby

CONTENTS

During the blistering primary battles against U.S. Senator Barack Obama, Hillary drew an enthusiastic crowd in Fort Worth, Texas.

A NOTE ON NAMES

Generally, the subject of a biography is referred to by last name throughout. But keeping Hillary Rodham Clinton and Bill Clinton distinct from each other in a text is tricky because they share a surname. Adding titles is also messy: Mrs. or Ms.? President? Senator? Secretary? Too often, this challenge is resolved by calling a woman by her first name and a man by his last, but that is a poor solution that isn't acceptable here.

As a result, for simplicity and clarity, Hillary Rodham Clinton is called Hillary on second reference and Bill Clinton is called Bill. No disrespect is intended.

INTRODUCTION

In losing, Hillary Rodham Clinton gave perhaps the best speech of her life.

For more than a year, she had debated, glad-handed, flown, phoned, conferenced, preached, pleaded, promised, speechified, scraped, and scrambled in her quest for the Democratic nomination for president of the United States. She had started out as the front-runner and then lost ground to a youthful and charismatic senator from Illinois—Barack Obama. She had won close to 18 million votes.

But that wasn't enough. Obama had finally clinched the nomination.

On 7th June 2008, the former First Lady stood before a jam-packed audience to say thank you to her supporters and to endorse her opponent. "This isn't exactly the party I'd planned," she told them, "but I sure like the company."

She told the crowd that she had run "because I have an old-fashioned conviction that public service is about helping people solve their problems and live their dreams."

She counseled her supporters not to wonder "what

if?" "Every moment wasted looking back keeps us from moving forward," she said. "Life is too short, time is too precious, and the stakes are too high to dwell on what might have been."

And though she fell short of her goals, she urged her followers to pursue their own. "Always aim high, work hard, and care deeply about what you believe in," she said. "And when you stumble, keep faith. And when you're knocked down, get right back up, and never listen to anyone who says you can't or shouldn't go on."

Supporters from around the country fill the National Building Museum in Washington, D.C., for Hillary's 2008 concession speech and final rally.

Throughout her campaign, she had avoided talk about her historic role as the first woman in American history to win a binding primary and the first to come oh-so-close to the nomination. She would say that she was running as a candidate, not as a woman. But not today.

"When we first started, people everywhere asked the same questions. Could a woman really serve as commander in chief?" she asked. "Well, I think we answered that one."

She acknowledged that women still face barriers and bias because of their sex. But she hoped that in future campaigns, no one would marvel at the idea that women could compete and win.

"Although we weren't able to shatter that highest, hardest glass ceiling this time," she told them, "thanks to you, it's got about eighteen million cracks in it."

Following that rough race, Hillary did something else: She turned a painful and very public loss into a win. Obama was so impressed with her smarts, her toughness, and her tenacity that he sought her for secretary of state after he was elected president.

It was a dramatic conversion—but not an unusual one. For much of her life, Hillary Rodham Clinton had been defying conventional wisdom, breaking barriers, and baffling even her closest friends with a bundle of personal contradictions.

As a promising young lawyer on the cusp of the women's movement, she chose a traditional path, following her future husband, Bill Clinton, to Arkansas. Once there, she broke new ground as a law-firm partner and as a most untraditional First Lady, first in the state and then in the White House. After the humiliation of Bill's embarrassing sex scandal, she transformed herself again, becoming a senator from New York—and the first First Lady to run for and win political office.

Since becoming First Lady of the United States in 1993, she has been the Gallup Poll's most admired woman in the United States a record twenty times in twenty-three years, losing only to Mother Teresa (twice) and First Lady Laura Bush (once). As an advocate for international women's rights, she is admired around the world.

Hillary's husband, Bill Clinton; mother, Dorothy Rodham; and daughter, Chelsea, join the candidate before her 2008 concession speech.

Yet this supremely confident and strong woman has also made her share of very visible mistakes, giving her a reputation as secretive and arrogant. She is controversial and divisive—as reviled by some as she is respected by others. She turned into a fund-raising powerhouse for Democrats, and then—in that strange business that is politics—her name became a powerful fund-raising tool for Republicans who despise her.

For more than two decades, she has been in the public eye as much as any movie star, yet she remains intensely protective of her private life. She has never developed a good rapport with the media, but reporters cannot write or talk enough about her, her ambitions, her marriage, her trouser suits, and her hair. No other woman has been on as many covers of *Time* magazine as she has.

In 2016, at sixty-eight years old, she broke one more barrier. In July, she officially became the Democratic nominee for the nation's highest office, the first woman ever to be a major party's presidential candidate.

After more than forty years in politics and public life, one question still remained: Who is she?

PART ONE

BEGINNINGS

"I have an old-fashioned conviction that public service is about helping people solve their problems and live their dreams."

Hillary as a toddler, in 1950.

1

ROOTS

The first child of Hugh Ellsworth Rodham and Dorothy Howell Rodham entered the world at more than eight pounds, a bigger-than-average bundle of joy.

"Very mature upon birth," her mother joked.

Born 26th October 1947, the good-natured little girl was part of the baby boom that followed the end of World War II. Her parents named her Hillary Diane, a daring choice, since *Hillary* was generally considered a boy's name at the time. Her mother liked it because it was unusual and sounded exotic.

After little brother Hugh arrived, the growing family moved from Chicago to the suburb of Park Ridge, known for its fine public schools, parks, and nice-sized houses. Her father paid cash for a two-story home in a neighbourhood swarming with children all about the same age. When the weather was good, the streets brimmed with games of cops and robbers, hide-and-seek, or the more elaborate chase-and-run, as well as pickup softball or kickball.

As a newcomer, Hillary was tested by the other kids, especially a girl named Suzy, who had four brothers. Suzy was used to getting into scuffles, and her physical play often sent Hillary running home in tears. Finally, her mother told her, "You have to stand up for yourself. There's no room in this house for cowards." She gave her young daughter permission to hit back if Suzy hit her.

While her mother peeked out from the curtains, Hillary went back outside. Threatened again by Suzy, the four-year-old threw a punch.

The bullying stopped. And Hillary proudly reported to her mom, "I can play with the boys now!"

Hillary's mom wanted Hillary, Hugh, and their baby brother, Tony, to have more opportunities and a better family life than she had. As a child, Dorothy had often been pushed off on relatives or left at home by herself for hours at a time. Her parents divorced when she was eight, and she and her three-year-old sister were sent alone on the day-long train ride to California to live with her father's parents. Her grandmother was unusually strict, and once, Dorothy was grounded for months as punishment for trick-or-treating on Halloween. At fourteen, she escaped by getting a job as live-in help for a family.

Never able to attend college, she had returned to Chicago after high school and got a job. Through her work, she met Hugh, a travelling salesman who was eight years older. She was twenty-two years old when she married him in early 1942, just after the United States entered World War II.

As a full-time homemaker and mother, Dorothy cooked, washed, cleaned, and served. When Hillary came home from school for lunch, as kids did then, she fed her canned tomato or chicken noodle soup and grilled cheese sandwiches, cut into triangles. Dorothy also shared life lessons. Once, she showed her kids a spirit level, with an air bubble floating in the centre, as an example of how to stay centred and balanced. "You try to keep that bubble in the centre," she told them. "Sometimes it will go way up here," she demonstrated, "and you have to bring it back."

The growing Rodham family in the early 1950s: Father Hugh, Hillary, younger brother Hugh, and mother Dorothy.

Though the family had a television set, it wasn't on much—nor was there much on television in those years. Free family time was spent playing card games like war, slapjack, or pinochle or board games like Monopoly and Cluedo. Dorothy took her bright and curious daughter to the library every week for new books and encouraged her to pursue her own interests.

"She was kind of an exasperating little girl because she was right most of the time," her mother recalled later.

Dorothy felt boxed in by restrictive women's roles during the 1950s, and in response, she encouraged her oldest child to be her own person. "I was determined that no daughter of mine was going to have to go through the agony of being afraid to say what she had on her mind," she told an interviewer later.

While Dorothy was affectionate, Hugh was gruff, demanding, and hard to please. If Hillary or one of her brothers left the cap off the toothpaste, her father would toss it out of the bathroom window. The offender would be sent to find it in the bushes, even in the winter. When she struggled in neighbourhood baseball games, her father, who had been a physical education major in college, took her to the park day after day, throwing pitches until she mastered hitting.

Hugh ran a drapery-fabric business and had a small silk-screening shop for printing designs. It was mostly a one-man operation, with help from temporary workers and family members. As a salesman who wanted to make a good impression, he insisted on driving a Cadillac, considered the fanciest car around at the time.

At home, however, he was notoriously tightfisted, a reflection in part of growing up poor during the Great Depression. He turned off the heat at night and turned it back on in the morning. The children were expected to do chores and help out, but weren't paid an allowance for it. "We'd rake the leaves, cut the grass, pull weeds, shovel snow," remembered Tony, the youngest Rodham. But when the kids would ask for some money to join their friends at the movies, their dad would "flop another potato on your dinner plate and say, 'That's your reward.'"

Hillary and her mother had to negotiate for special clothing purchases. "Do you want us to end up in the poorhouse?" he would say.

He was also tight with praise. When her brother Hugh completed ten of eleven passes to lead his high school football team to a 36-0 rout, his father was short on enthusiasm. "I got nothing to say to you," he told his son, "except you should have completed the other one." And when Hillary brought home a report card filled with As, her father was unimpressed. "That must be an easy school you go to," he would tell her.

Hillary was a good student from early on, but not always a perfect one. Her third-grade report card in January 1956 noted that she needed some help in a couple of areas: "keeping belongings neat" and not reading aloud "too rapidly." She did, however, get extra credit that spring for a book report and for being a class librarian.

For Hugh and Tony, she was a hard act to follow. "At school, people sure expected a lot from Hillary's brothers," Hugh said later. But she was an attentive big sister, taking her brothers with her and her friends to Hinkley Park for hot dogs. "When she wasn't studying, she was a lot of fun," Tony said. "But she was always studying."

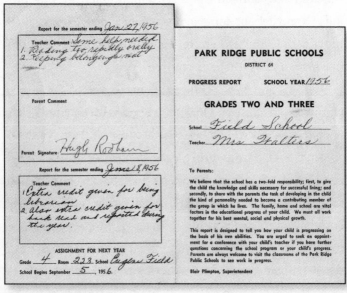

Hillary's third-grade report card.

Along with her father and two brothers, she was a serious sports fan and was especially fond of baseball. Though her favourites were Ernie Banks and the Chicago Cubs, "she also knew all the players and stats, batting averages—[New York Yankees] Roger Maris, Mickey

Mantle—everything about baseball," recalled a school friend, Rick Ricketts. She quizzed him on obscure trivia, like whether he knew about the Bums, the nickname for the Brooklyn Dodgers, or could recite the 1927 Yankees' batting order.

From an early age, she also was interested in the broader world and in history. Ricketts remembered her as a good debater, even at nine. They would discuss politics and current events on the way home from school, or sitting on a wooden fence outside her house. Once they engaged in a long discussion about what would have happened had the South won the Civil War.

At home and in Park Ridge generally, the politics were Republican. Hugh was a believer in self-reliance and drilled into his kids that people succeed because of their personal initiative and hard work. Assistance from government wasn't necessary—and, like many Park Ridge residents, he strongly opposed communism, a political system prevalent then in Eastern Europe, the Soviet Union, and parts of Asia where a powerful central government, rather than private owners, controlled all the property. Amid the sometimes-heated conversations around the kitchen table, Hillary said she learned that "if you believed in something, you had better be prepared to defend it."

Her mother was a closet Democrat, more open to the government helping those with fewer opportunities. But since her husband was dead certain about his opinions, she mostly kept her own views to herself.

To make his point, Hillary wrote later, her father periodically drove the family to a poor area "to see what became of people who, as he saw it, lacked the self-discipline and motivation to keep their lives on track."

His oldest child had little trouble with motivation—or ambition. As a Brownie and then a Girl Scout, she sold cookies, helped with food drives, and joined in with other activities, earning a mass of badges and pins. (She wasn't so good at getting them on her sash, however. "I'm still working on my sewing badge," she joked years later.) She organized neighbourhood games and carnivals and even a mock Olympics, both for fun and to collect nickels and dimes for charities such as the United Way.

In school, she was elected co-captain of the safety patrol, a prestigious position for especially well-behaved older students, who helped younger kids safely cross streets to and from school. Towards the end of sixth grade, she and a friend tried to convince their parents that they should be allowed to wear stockings instead of ankle socks to their graduation. When their parents pushed back, they tried a political ploy, circulating a petition among their friends. But their parents, being more like dictators than elected officials, refused to give in.

For fun, she and a friend saw double features on Saturdays at the Pickwick Theatre for twenty-five cents—with buttered popcorn costing another quarter. She was fond of the Robin Hood restaurant and its spicy spaghetti, which may have helped develop her affection for spicy foods. (As an adult, she liked jalapeños in her scrambled eggs and travelled with a bottle of Tabasco sauce in her purse.)

To earn money, Hillary babysat in the neighbourhood, and starting at thirteen until she went to college, she worked during the summers. In the early years, she ran a children's programme at a nearby park, dragging a wagon full of sports equipment from her home so that kids could play games and jump rope.

In a lengthy essay she wrote in sixth grade, titled "My Future," she wrote of an interest in education and plans to work outside the home, a rarity for adult women in Park Ridge in the 1950s. "When I grow up I want to have had the best education I could have possibly obtained. If I obtain this I will probably be able to get a very good job," she wrote.

Her different career interests reflected the times. In October 1957, the Soviet Union launched the first satellite into orbit, raising the possibility that similar technology could be used to send missiles much longer distances than ever before. In the urgent Cold War space race that followed, schools began to identify smart students who could become scientists. In her essay, Hillary was seemingly torn between a traditional female career and the new national obsession: "I want to either be a teacher or a nuclear physics scientist," she wrote.

A few years later, after President John F. Kennedy challenged America in 1961 to put a man on the moon by the end of the decade, Hillary sent a letter to the National Aeronautics and Space Administration to inquire about becoming an astronaut.

NASA's answer: We are not accepting women into the programme.

It was Hillary's first face-to-face encounter with discrimination, and she was angry and hurt to realize that her own hard work and initiative wouldn't make a difference. Over time, she also realized that her poor eyesight, which required her to wear thick glasses, would have disqualified her anyway. And as she moved towards high school, her interests and passions were already shifting in another direction.

My Future

When I grow up I want to have had the best education I could have possibly obtained. If I obtain this I will probably be able to get a very good job. I want to either be a teacher or a nuclear physics scientist.

Sometimes people ask me why I would want to be a teacher. The way I figure it though, is that the government and adults are always talking about how the children of today are the citizens of tomorrow. With this thought in mind you have to have teachers to train the young citizens or

Sixth grader Hillary spells out her future plans in a neatly written essay.

2

GROUNDWORK

The 1960 presidential race was close and hard fought, pitting the youthful-looking Democratic senator, John F. Kennedy, against the Republican vice president, Richard Nixon. Hillary's father supported Nixon, of course, and so did she.

Kennedy won, but the race was a close one, with only 119,000 votes separating them out of 68.3 million cast. Nixon actually won more states, but Kennedy won more Electoral College votes. In Illinois, Kennedy beat Nixon by just 9,000 votes out of nearly 5 million. Many Republicans believed the Democrats had cheated—especially in Chicago—by stuffing the ballot box with votes from people who didn't exist or were dead.

When one of Hillary's like-minded friends heard that local Republicans needed people to look into irregular voting, Hillary jumped at the chance to help. Without asking their parents, she and her friend took a bus downtown the Saturday after the election and volunteered. A couple dropped thirteen-year-old Hillary in a poor neighbourhood on the South Side, with a list of addresses and registered voters.

Dutifully, she knocked on doors, waking up some residents and hearing "Go away!" from others. She discovered that the address for several voters was a vacant lot. Others supposedly lived at the site of a local bar. Hillary went in to see whether anyone lived there, but the men drinking inside weren't interested in answering questions from an eighth grader.

When she got home, she couldn't wait to tell her dad that his suspicions about ballot stuffing were right.

Her father responded angrily—not at the apparent fraud, but because his young teen had gone downtown and to the city's South Side on her own. Though he didn't resort to the physical punishment he sometimes used on her brothers, he went into "a yelling fit" about her lousy judgment, she remembered. He made it clear to her that "Kennedy was going to be president whether we liked it or not."

Her father's reaction didn't diminish her political interests, which were soon stretched and challenged both in school and at church.

In ninth grade at Maine East High School, Hillary landed in Paul Carlson's history class. Then in his mid-twenties, Carlson taught by telling lots of stories. He took a personal interest in his students, especially inquisitive

Hillary in 1960, on the edge of her teen years.

and overachieving ones. A conservative like Hugh
Rodham, Carlson was staunchly anti-communist. Once,
he brought in a refugee from the Soviet Union to share
frightening tales of living under communist rule, supporting Hillary's own anti-communist views.

Carlson encouraged her to read Senator Barry
Goldwater's *The Conscience of a Conservative*, a skinny book
that was a must-read manifesto for early 1960s conservatives. The book defines conservative politics as "the art of
achieving the maximum amount of freedom for individuals

that is consistent with the maintenance of social order." Goldwater believed the federal government should have limited powers, such as ensuring a citizen's right to vote. But he thought it should stay out of other issues, like education. So while he personally believed that black and white children should attend the same schools rather than segregated ones, he believed it was up to southern states like Mississippi, not the federal government, to decide whether to end racial segregation. "That is their business, not mine," he wrote.

Goldwater's book so inspired Hillary that she wrote her term paper that year on the American conservative movement. It was memorable, Carlson recalled, as much for its length as its content: Hillary turned in seventy-five pages, accompanied by a thick stack of note cards and a sheaf of bibliography cards. She dedicated the paper to her parents, "who have always taught me to be an individual."

Republican Senator Barry Goldwater, who helped define conservatism in the early 1960s.

Still, she had her teen moments. Carlson was obsessed with President Harry S. Truman's decision—ill-advised, he thought—to dismiss General Douglas MacArthur in

1951, and he played the general's farewell speech to Congress for his class several times. In the speech MacArthur addressed how he thought America should respond aggressively to communism, sometimes called the "red scare," a reference to the Soviet flag.

Moved by MacArthur's words after one playing, Carlson urged his class, "Remember, above all else, 'Better dead than red!'"

Ricky Ricketts, sitting alphabetically in front of Hillary Rodham, was amused enough to turn around and crack, "I'd rather be alive!" The comment gave them both uncontrollable giggles—and got them kicked out of class that day.

While Carlson held court in the classroom, Hillary was getting another education at the First United Methodist Church of Park Ridge. She attended Sunday school and Bible school there, participated in the youth group, helped prepare the altar for Sunday services, and was confirmed in sixth grade.

The church had a strong bent toward social justice. She was taught: "Do all the good you can, . . . at all the times you can, to all the people you can, as long as ever you can," and "Be doers of the word, and not hearers only." On the cusp of the civil rights movement, the church hired a new youth minister with a red convertible and some unusual ideas about reaching out to impressionable teens.

Don Jones was thirty years old and just out of divinity school. He was eager to relate pop culture, art, and contemporary thinking to Christianity and share those connections with the bright, ambitious, and sheltered young people of Park Ridge.

His Sunday and Thursday night youth-fellowship sessions were dubbed "the University of Life," and they changed the way Hillary saw the world. Jones would share short excerpts from T. S. Eliot and Fyodor Dostoyevsky's *Brothers Karamazov*. The group looked at Vincent van Gogh's *Starry Night* and discussed the relationship between God and nature.

One day, he handed them an e. e. cummings poem. Hillary was so moved by it that, years later, she recalled its first lines from heart:

dying is fine)but Death

?o
baby
i

wouldn't like

Death if Death
were
good. . . .

Encountering those words as a fifteen-year-old "was just mind-blowing for me," Hillary said, a religious as well as an intellectual experience. "I just felt like there was this whole other world out there that was exciting and challenging that he linked to our faith."

Jones wanted his charges to connect their faith with social action, and he took them to Chicago's tougher neighbourhoods, where they visited with blacks and Latinos in their church basements and learned about the impact of poverty and crime. In one discussion, he put up a print of Pablo Picasso's powerful painting about war, *Guernica*, named after a Basque town bombed during the Spanish Civil War. Jones asked the teens to suggest music that might go with it. Then he asked them if it reminded them of any experiences they had.

The Park Ridge kids were quiet. But one inner-city teen was moved to tears recalling how her uncle had been shot and killed just the week before in a disagreement over a parking space.

Jones also introduced Hillary to the growing civil rights movement, taking the group to Chicago's Orchestra Hall in April 1962 to hear the Reverend Martin Luther King Jr. speak. In the South, blacks were forbidden from eating in many restaurants, shopping in some stores, staying in hotels, and even using the same water fountains as whites. In the summer of 1961, groups of blacks and whites calling themselves Freedom Riders had travelled through the South, trying to end segregation in bus terminals along the way. They were attacked and brutally beaten by angry white mobs and jailed for trespassing.

The young people of Park Ridge knew so little about King and this struggle going on outside of their essentially all-white and mostly Christian town that they might as well have lived in a foreign country.

King's speech "Remaining Awake Through a Revolution" was a true wake-up call to Hillary, her first introduction to racial discrimination and the battle against it. Afterwards, Jones took them backstage and introduced each of them to the man who would become the civil rights movement's most prominent leader. Years later she told Jones that the moment had meant a lot to her.

The youth group had some fun too, swimming at lakes and skiing in the winter, but the adults mostly noted Jones's more controversial programmes. Once, he brought in an atheist to debate the existence of God, and another time, he riled the congregation with a discussion about teen pregnancy, a scandalous topic in the early 1960s.

Hillary often stopped in to chat with Jones. He introduced her to philosophers and theologians, like Reinhold Niebuhr and Paul Tillich, and encouraged her to read J. D. Salinger's *The Catcher in the Rye*. "She loved to have her mind stretched, and she loved to read difficult material," he said. (She didn't, however, like *The Catcher in the Rye* until she reread it in college.)

Inspired by the "university," Hillary began to embrace social service, joining a group of girls who babysat the small children of migrant workers who harvested crops in their somewhat rural community. Without babysitters, the children would have been put to work in the fields or been left with other children.

Inevitably, the newcomer Jones knocked heads with the Park Ridge traditionalists. After two years, he left Park Ridge, ultimately returning to his alma mater, Drew University, to earn his PhD and teach. But he had made a friend for life: Hillary Rodham wrote to him regularly through college, and later he became a trusted adviser during some difficult times in her life. For now, however, she would have to navigate the rest of high school without her spiritual mentor.

3

PARK RIDGE

As a sophomore, Hillary jumped into a number of activities—student council, the school newspaper, the spring musical, a variety show, and speech and debate.

In her speech class, she was the only sophomore girl in a room full of senior football players who thought the class would be an easy one.

When the brainy and serious young Rodham gave her speeches, the boys would "sit up front and insult me and rattle me," she remembered. There was an upside: The hazing turned out to be excellent preparation for a political career in Washington, she said later.

As Hillary was exposed to the broader world, she began to challenge some of her father's views. Each summer, her family joined her father's family at a modest cabin on Lake Winola in northeast Pennsylvania. There, Hillary would hear all the prejudices her father grew up with—biases against Democrats, blacks, Jews, Catholics, and anyone else who wasn't a working-class Anglo Protestant. Over time, she grew frustrated with it and would simply announce that she was planning to marry a Catholic Democrat, which, to her paternal relatives, would be a disastrous fate. (Her father's views, she said later, softened and shifted quite a bit over time.)

Hillary in her senior-year yearbook photo.

Though just modestly rebellious, Hillary was in many ways a typical 1960s high school student. She adored the teen heart-throb Fabian and formed a small fan club with two friends. Her favourite Beatle was Paul McCartney, and she was thrilled to get tickets to a Rolling Stones concert in 1965. She played in a summer softball league throughout high school, wearing the pink and black colours of the team sponsor, the Good & Plenty candy distributor. And she found time for slumber parties and hanging out with friends.

Hillary was interested in boys and had dates to homecoming and proms, but didn't have a boyfriend. Nor did she consider skipping college or putting aside career aspirations to get married, like some of her classmates. "None of my kids dated much, until they were older," her mother Dorothy said later. "And Hillary always valued herself very highly. I liked that about her."

Her mom gently encouraged her high school daughter to wear makeup. But Hillary wasn't the least bit interested. "I think she thought [makeup] was superficial and silly," Dorothy said. "She didn't have time for it."

Hillary's teachers remembered her as unusually articulate and intellectually curious, and her classmates saw her as unusually assured and ambitious. Art Curtis, who became class valedictorian, recalled that Hillary once told him that she was the smarter of the two. In one class, he remembered, the subject of "whether you could live by an absolute code of right and wrong" came up. Hillary, who herself had a strong sense of right and wrong, believed one could live that way.

Some classmates thought she was conceited, but "she was just very self-confident. She was very comfortable with herself. She wasn't afraid to go against the crowd over something she believed in," one of her closest friends, Betsy Johnson Ebeling, told an interviewer later.

Park Ridge was growing quickly as new houses sprang up on vacant lots, and more than 5,000 teens crammed into Maine East High School. In the virtually all-white and Christian school, there were many cliques: athletes and cheerleaders; brains and student-government types; and "greasers" and "hoods," the terms used for tough guys who spent more time on cars than schoolwork; and hoodlums, or troublemakers. In Hillary's junior year, fights broke out among the different social circles at games and in the school car park. In response, the principal created a Cultural Values Committee and asked her to be on it with representatives of other groups.

There, she got to know kids she otherwise would have avoided. The committee was urged to come up with ways to reduce the disagreements and improve relationships between the groups—or at least promote tolerance. The approach was novel enough that Hillary was among a few students invited to appear on a local television show to talk about their work.

That year, Hillary also began to spread her leadership wings. Active in the student council, she chaired the Organizations Committee, which (as the name suggests) organized many of the school activities. She was vice president of the junior class, and sometimes ran the meetings when the class president was at football practice.

The autumn of her junior year was marred by one of the nation's most tragic events. Hillary was in geometry class in November 1963 when a teacher came in to say that President Kennedy had been shot. All the students walked in stunned silence to the auditorium, where they were dismissed early. Years later, Hillary told students during a speech in Park Ridge that "our world changed dramatically" that day. "That was an absolute turning point in the lives of anybody who was there," she said. "It was the kind of thing you just couldn't imagine happening."

Hillary arrived home to find her mother watching the breaking news on television and mourning for the president's family. In her grief, Dorothy also confessed that she had voted for Kennedy. Hillary remembered feeling terribly sad for the country as well as the Kennedy family, though she didn't know how to help. Later, she would see it as one of several "shocks to the nervous system" that challenged her generation's sense of complacency.

Between her junior and senior year, officials split the giant Maine East High School and sent half the students—including Hillary—to the new Maine South. Ahead of the split, she and another girl ran for president of the new student council, a daring move for girls at the time. They both lost.

During the election, one of the boys told her that she was "really stupid" if she thought a girl could win. Tim Sheldon, the football-playing junior class president who won the student council election, admitted later to wondering why Hillary was in the race. "We thought, 'What's she doing? She should be running for secretary.'"

Immediately after his victory, Sheldon asked her to again run the Organizations Committee her senior year. Though it was a secondary role, that position allowed her to help establish Maine South's first traditions by putting together the first homecoming dance and parade, pep rallies, prom, and student council elections.

Despite Hillary's exposure to Reverend Jones's teachings and her mother's liberal leanings, she remained a committed conservative. She was active in the Young Republicans. And as the presidential race in 1964 heated up, she was a Goldwater Girl, supporting and campaigning for Arizona Senator Barry Goldwater, the Republican candidate, including helping at a Youth for Goldwater office in Park Ridge. She had a Goldwater Girl sash and even a cowgirl get-up and a straw hat with the slogan "AuH_2O," the chemical compounds for gold and water.

She helped organize a mock election, complete with posters, buttons, and a debate. Her government teacher, however, insisted that Hillary argue on behalf of President Lyndon B. Johnson, the Democratic nominee, while a Democrat friend took Goldwater's position.

"Both of us went ballistic" over the assignment, she said later. But the teacher refused to back down. So "with our teeth gritted," they headed to the library to spend hours researching the candidates and party platforms. It was that assignment that may have propelled Hillary toward adopting her mother's politics.

Despite her efforts, she was less than successful in winning votes for Johnson. In the staunchly Republican enclave, 55 per cent of her classmates went for Goldwater in the mock election, only a bit less than how their parents voted a few days later.

Park Ridge, however, was wildly out of step with the rest of the nation. President Johnson won in a landslide, with 61 per cent of the popular vote and the electoral votes of forty-four states.

While Hillary remained active in politics, school activities, and church, she also occasionally took a turn at theatre. Her singing voice was so bad that she was asked to lip-synch during the school musical, but she brought the house down in a variety show with a hammed-up skit about the temperance leader Carrie Nation. While girls behind her pretended to drink, she dramatically sermonized about the evils of alcohol.

She also continued to do very well in school—though she had a sense of humour about it. Before an Advanced Placement English exam, she arrived early to hang a homemade banner with a warning from Dante's *Inferno:* "All hope abandon, ye who enter here."

A member of the National Honor Society, she was an alternate on Maine South's *It's Academic* team, which competed against other schools on a local television quiz show. She was one of eleven National Merit finalists at Maine South, meaning her scores on the National Merit Scholarship standardized test put her in the top tier of all graduating students across the country. She got mostly As and was ranked around fifteenth in her class out of more than 500 seniors, which put her within the top 5 per cent. Her classmates elected her as the girl "most likely to succeed."

In a spoof interview in the student newspaper, she looked back on her high school experience from the perspective of her career as a "prosecuting attorney." "What was your ambition in high school?" she was asked. Her

Hillary *(back row, second from left)* served as an alternate on Maine South's *It's Academic* team.

prescient answer: "To marry a senator and settle down in Georgetown."

In the senior issue, a satirical story made predictions for graduates. Two boys would become clergy, it said, and debate the beauty of certain nuns. "Sister Frigidaire, the former Hillary Rodham, appears to be the most favoured at this point," the story said, apparently noting the ability of a smart, ambitious girl to intimidate her classmates.

Hillary won so many awards when graduation rolled around—including the social science award and the Daughters of the American Revolution Good Citizenship Award—that her mother remembered being "slightly embarrassed."

With top-notch schools like Northwestern University

we now enjoy.

For it is this small group, less than three per cent of the student body, the very group Mr. Gerald Baker spoke about in his speech on school spirit, that makes us have restrictive regulations.

Let each of us, the students of Maine, set our goals, our standards of work and play so high that the phrase "That is the way our school really is" becomes the rallying cry of our highest integrity, exuberant spirit, our searching excellence.

Lawyer Hillary Reviews Career

"Excuse me, I'm from **Time** magazine. I'd like to get an interview from you about your high school career. You've had such a famous career, and . . ."

"Well, yes, I'm very busy, you know," replied Hillary Rodham, prosecuting attorney for Harrington versus Harrington. The

Hillary Rodham

case has been going on literally for years. "What would you like to know?"

"That in my senior year so many years ago this month I received the DAR Award for citizenship? Or that I served on student council for three years? Or that I worked for Goldwater, Percy, and other Republican nominees in a mock political convention? Or that I was a National Merit Semi-Finalist?"

"Well, yes—"

"I was also a member of the Cultural Values Committee my junior year. What an experience! We re-evaluated teenagers' ideas in relation to dress, etc. We tried to unite opinions of different factions of the school — and what a difference."

"Can you give me a few words on vandalism?"

"Oh, yes, in high school I was a co-chairman of an Anti-Vandalism Committee. We worked to raise money for damage done to the school building by vandals. I was very disappointed that vandals would ruin the wall, but I hardly think it was representative of all the students."

Snow Blankets

Sukie Askew

The snow comes down in blankets of white.

They turn the darkness into light.

Your steps are softened in the night.

What a wonderful feeling to be alive.

In looking around there's peace at your feet

The soft, pale lights along the street

Lighting the way where all paths meet

In the wonderful feeling of being alive.

But the night is short and the air is cold,

And tomorrow will make tonight seem old,

For life goes on, and spring unfolds

"What was school spirit like back in those days?"

"School spirit improved my senior year for a number of reasons. The school was new, and the student body was smaller. A combination of many things brought about improved spirit. (To the side) Just a minute, Rodney."

"I see. One last question. What was your ambition in high school?"

"To marry a senator and settle down in Georgetown."

Eveyone'

Clark Weichmann '65

It was a hard winter that year and the nights around Debir were cold enough to kill a man who was without the benefit of shelter. Such an occurrence was indeed sustained by a nomad called Amel-Shir.

The corpse was survived by its two brothers, Amel-Kahr and Amel Meda, who sat around a fire near a mound of freshly worked earth. Retaining an expression mournful enough to satisfy the strictest of his ancestors, Amel-Meda broke the silence.

"Dear Brother, it is a shameful thing that one with a soul as kind as our departed kin's soul should suffer such a cruel fate. And just because he was poor."

"Yes, surely, if we were in possession of wealth enough to provide shelter every cold night, such tragedies would never come to pass. By the gods should my words be heeded!"

Seemingly angered by Amel-Kahr's oath, the wind executed a howling reprisal which thoroughly chilled Amel-Meda's weathered body. His rejoiner was more coherent.

"The gods never listen to poor wanderers such as we are. They do not even protect this grave. Lo, no mortal knows what I would sacrifice for a god that would care for poor men.

"How I wish that there were some symbol of a god's power that I could now place upon this mound of frozen soil to consecrate it, and do so without fear

Shoppers Arise! Fight on! Fight!

Ken Winiarski, '65

To the tune of "Jingle Bells" on a treble bass clavichord)
Fight on with a will, bludgeon all you see,

All is fair in shopping now so smile sadistically.

All our manners gone; we run and hit and bite,

While the shrieking Christmas songs urge us to the Christmas fight.

The orchestras crash on, with spirit and with verve

(Let's happily compare it to stepping on a nerve.)

Unheeding we shop on — to an accompanying din.

Hypersonics reverberate as we grow pale and thin.

Refrain:
Jingle bells, jingle bells, roar on without cease,

While "Silent Night" and "Bethlehem" help blast away the peace.

Store owners' smiles show their wiles; thinking every buyer

Is lured into their store by

A spoof in the school newspaper envisions Hillary Rodham as a busy lawyer who had a notable high school career.

and the University of Chicago nearby, as well as the University of Illinois down the road, most of Hillary's classmates applied to schools in Illinois or in neighbouring states. Hillary had visited Michigan State, but hadn't expanded her list until two young government teachers suggested she look at women's colleges in the East. At the time, most Ivy League schools like Yale, Princeton, and Dartmouth were for men only. Women wanting a similar experience looked to one of the Seven Sisters schools. One teacher had attended Smith College in western Massachusetts, and the other had gone to Wellesley College, in a Boston suburb. Inspired by their recommendation, Hillary applied, though she had hardly ever been far from home on her own.

Her father was willing to pay for college, but not if his daughter headed west or went to Radcliffe, then the all-women counterpart to Harvard in Cambridge, Massachusetts. He thought that Cambridge was a hot spot for radicals and beatniks, young people who rejected traditional social rules in favour of self-expression. He hadn't heard of Smith or Wellesley.

She was accepted to both, but chose Wellesley after seeing photographs of its campus, which included a small lake that reminded her of Lake Winola. Her father paid the tuition, room, and board of $2,800, about $21,000 in today's dollars. (Tuition would rise to $3,100 her junior year.)

When the time came, her father and mother packed up

the Cadillac and drove her there, where they all saw the campus for the first time. Her father was relieved that there weren't any beatniks in sight.

"It was really, really hard to leave her," her mother, Dorothy, remembered. "After we dropped her off, I just crawled in the backseat and cried for eight hundred miles."

Far from her family and the comfort of Park Ridge, Hillary, too, had some challenging adjustments ahead.

4

WELLESLEY

The school that Hillary Rodham arrived at in autumn 1965 was full of tradition and strict rules. The almost 1,800 women were required to wear skirts to dinner. They were encouraged to dress up and don white gloves weekly for afternoon tea and wear white gloves into town. Freshmen were given green beanies and required to take a physical education class called Fundamentals of Movement, which taught good posture and how to get in and out of a car gracefully.

Men were allowed in their rooms only on Sunday afternoons—and the door had to be open, with at least two feet visibly on the floor. All the students had to be back in their rooms by either a midnight or 1:00 a.m. curfew.

Many young women arrived at college with the primary goal of finding a good husband and becoming a wife and mother. Seniors aimed for a "ring by spring." Another tradition: In May, seniors used sticks to roll wooden hoops down Tupelo Lane; the winner, legend had it, would be the first to marry.

More young women were beginning to go to college, but many dropped out, often to marry. Those who finished their degrees expected to work only until they married or had a child. Just three of every hundred lawyers at the time were women, and just six of every hundred doctors.

Women were just beginning to speak up for equal rights, and in 1965, Wellesley still seemed tied to the status quo. Princeton's guide to coeds, or female students, said Wellesley girls were "strikingly traditional." *Time* magazine wrote that August that Radcliffe students were known for their "breathless brilliance" and Bryn Mawr women were "muscularly athletic," but those at Wellesley didn't fit a particular stereotype. "They tend simply to be wholesome girls who make normal, well-adjusted housewives and civic-minded citizens," the magazine said.

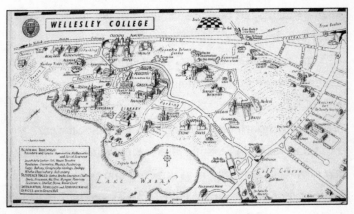

The Wellesley campus in the mid-1960s.

The school motto was *Non Ministrari sed Ministrare*, a call to service translated as "Not to be ministered unto, but to minister." In the restrictive 1960s, some joked that it actually meant "not to be ministers, but to be ministers' wives." Hillary, who would soon help upend some of Wellesley's long traditions, saw it differently: "as a call for women to become more engaged in shaping our lives and influencing the world around us."

Over the next four years, the tumultuous upheaval that would sweep through America—the fight for racial equality, the beginnings of the women's movement, and the exploding opposition to the Vietnam War—would touch Wellesley as well. But in the early weeks of her first semester, Hillary mostly felt lonely and overwhelmed.

For the first time in her life, she seemed out of her league. Her classmates were at least as accomplished as she was, but many of them were also more worldly and sophisticated. Some had lived abroad or spoke other languages fluently. The closest she had come to foreign travel was crossing the border once into Canada. Her foreign language in high school had been Latin. Her French professor suggested, "Mademoiselle, your talents lie elsewhere." She struggled with maths and geology.

About a month into school, she called her parents and told them she didn't belong there. Her father, who missed her, gave her permission to come back home. But in a role reversal, her mother took a hard line. Dorothy told her, "I don't want you to be a quitter."

Hillary gradually found her bearings. She enjoyed political science, which became her major, but began to lobby against a list of required courses, including ones on the Old and New Testaments. She joined the Young Republicans, becoming the president in her freshman year. In that role, she organized a panel discussion titled, "Why be a Republican?"

In the autumn of 1966, she encouraged classmates to campaign for Republican candidates, especially the Republican candidate for Senate, Massachusetts Attorney General Edward Brooke. (He would become the first popularly elected African American senator.) "The girl who doesn't want to go out and shake hands can type letters or do general office work," she told the school newspaper.

At the same time, she tried to step out of her comfort zone. She had never had a classmate or friend who was black. Wellesley had been admitting black students since the 1880s, but only six of the more than 400 members of the class of '69 were black. Until Hillary's year, the school had never put black and white room-mates together—and when it finally did, officials considered the move an experiment. (The school also paired Jews with Jews and Catholics with Catholics.)

Early on, Hillary became friends with an African American classmate, and the two decided to go to church together. When she told some of her friends in Park Ridge, they accused her of trying to make a political statement by challenging a white church rather than acting from good intentions.

Later, Hillary acknowledged that she felt "self-conscious about my motives." If she had seen someone else doing that while she was still in high school, she wrote to her former youth minister Don Jones, she would have thought, "Look how liberal that girl is trying to be going to church with a Negro."

But, she said, "I was testing me as much as I was testing the church."

She developed friendships with the other black students in her class and became a supporter of the black student group they formed called Ethos. Among other things, Ethos pushed Wellesley to drop its segregated room assignments.

A classmate remembered that many white students were afraid to talk about discrimination and racial issues. "But Hillary's attitude was, 'What's so embarrassing? If we're not willing to talk about it, how are we going to get past it? If prejudice exists, let's talk about it.'"

Hillary poses for a photo taken for the Wellesley yearbook.

Race was also an ongoing topic of discussion with Geoffrey Shields, a Harvard junior from another Chicago suburb, whom she started dating early in her freshman year. The two met at a

Harvard party and found common ground talking about politics and social issues. One of Shields's room-mates was a black student who was active in racial issues, and the three of them discussed integration at length. "It was a time of awakening" for the two Midwestern white kids, Shields said later.

Hillary and Shields saw each other most weekends during her freshman and sophomore years and into her junior year, talking, hanging out, and attending parties, often at Harvard. They danced to Elvis, the Beatles, and the Supremes. They took long walks around Wellesley's Lake Waban while discussing writers and philosophers. After one of those walks, Hillary gave him a copy of Henry David Thoreau's *Walden*.

As her Republican roots were challenged, her politics began to shift, but she remained intensely pragmatic. Even in the middle of an impassioned debate, she would point out to him, "You can't accomplish anything in government unless you win."

She wasn't just about ideas. On occasion, they took hiking trips to Vermont and visited Cape Cod. She also took in some Harvard football games with Shields, a former all-state high school football player, and tossed around Frisbees and footballs.

"I thought she was attractive, interesting to talk to, and she was a good dancer," Shields said later. More than anything, she loved the back and forth of a meaningful discussion. "The time when she seemed to light up the most," he said, "was when there was a good interesting, heated debate about issues, particularly issues that had a practical impact on the world—racial issues, the Vietnam War, civil rights, and civil liberties."

How serious they were as a couple isn't clear. In an interview years later, he called the relationship "healthy" and "normal in every way." Hillary has never written or spoken about him by name, saying only that she had two boyfriends serious enough to meet her parents. She and Shields saw each other over the summer and met each other's families, but in extensive correspondence with others, she didn't mention him. At some point after he graduated, they reverted to being friends. (He also ended up in her law-school class, though neither of them seems to have spoken publicly about that.)

On campus during the week, Hillary engaged in equally intense discussions with her classmates. She would read the *New York Times* over breakfast and then debate with her friends how to solve the world's problems until the dining hall was empty. The world around them was in turmoil, and there was much to talk about. In addition to the African American fight for civil rights, women were beginning to clamour for fair treatment. The National Organization for Women formed in 1966 to fight for fair-hiring practices at a time when help-wanted ads frequently listed jobs for men only or women only.

The war against communist North Vietnam began to escalate the year Hillary went to college, and a small anti-war movement began on college campuses soon after. As students at a women's college, Hillary and her classmates were less directly affected than the men who faced a mandatory draft into military service. As the protests escalated and grew much louder through the later 1960s, Hillary had "long conversations about what we would do if we were men." Of course, nearly all the men they knew were affected. "It was agonizing for everyone," she said later.

She was also reflective, trying to find her true beliefs now that she was far from home, and she shared her thinking in letters with old friends.

In April 1967, Hillary wrote to her former youth minister Don Jones, saying that her sophomore spring semester had been one of experimentation with different identities. Early in the new year, she had committed to dig intensely into her studies in every free minute. But "after six weeks of little human communication or companionship, my diet gave me indigestion. The last two weeks of February here were an orgy of decadent indulgence—as decadent as any upright Methodist can become," she wrote. The next month, she got involved in campus activities, and in April, she had a flower painted on her arm and tried out a little bit of a "hippie" personality.

They also corresponded about the intersection of religion and politics. Could one be a realist about history and, at the same time, be idealistic enough to push for social justice? Wrote Hillary: "It is an interesting question you posed—can one be a mind conservative and a heart liberal?"

In letters to a high school friend, John Peavoy, she

Hillary urges her Wellesley classmates at a 1967 rally to challenge the school's strict course requirements.

expressed frustration with her father, who had restricted her travel privileges. She described a "miserable weekend" spent arguing with a friend who believed "acid"—the drug LSD—"is the way." Hillary wasn't interested. (Friends say she didn't drink to excess or smoke marijuana, though it was widely available at the time.)

In another letter, she encouraged Peavoy to choose a life of civic action, rather than merely reacting to what was around him. "Man is born to live, not prepare for life," she told him, quoting *Doctor Zhivago*.

She also detailed a February funk in her sophomore year: She couldn't get out of bed and skipped classes, which made her feel terrible about herself.

The funk apparently didn't last too long. At the end of February, Hillary was one of seven speakers at a rally in a campus car park challenging Wellesley's extensive course requirements and arguing for more opportunity to take classes pass-fail, rather than for a specific grade. "If we get this going," she told the 400 students who had gathered, "maybe we'll see a change before we graduate."

As Hillary began to define her own role, her interests expanded. She went into Boston weekly to tutor a seven-year-old in reading. And she pushed back against her father's rigid views. She opposed the Vietnam War and concluded that she was no longer a Republican, turning over the leadership of the Young Republicans to a friend.

Still, she remained engaged on campus. She was elected to the student government and won a spot as a Vil Junior, a prestigious position for responsible upperclass-men, who acted as counsellors and resources for fresh-men. She served not only as the Vil Junior for her dorm, but as chair of all Vil Juniors.

A former room-mate recalled that Hillary sought the position, in part, for political reasons. She knew she wanted to have more involvement in student government, the roommate said, and the position "would connect her to younger students coming in."

As a junior, Hillary was poised to take on new leader-ship roles. But she couldn't have possibly imagined the waves she would make well beyond Wellesley's Lake Waban.

5

MAKING POSSIBLE

In early 1968, the second half of Hillary's junior year, the three candidates for president of Wellesley's student government met with the student newspaper—Hillary Rodham, Francille Rusan, and Nonna Noto. After hearing their positions, the editors of the paper decided that each of them wanted a greater student voice in both social and academic issues. "But," they wrote in an editorial, "all three were equally vague as to exactly *how* they would implement the change in the power structure."

The paper declined to endorse any of them, saying students essentially had a choice among different personalities and experience.

Hillary did have a strong endorsement from her dorm's freshmen, who shared a song they had written for her birthday, to the tune of "Wouldn't It Be Loverly" from the popular musical *My Fair Lady*:

All we want is someone who will
Help us out 'til we've made a kill;
Now, who could fit that bill—
Why, wouldn't it be Hillary?
Lots of questions we've got to ask
About our schedules, a grueling task;
The answer girl unmask:
Oh, so Hillary's solving problems for the freshman class;
She's spent so much time; we just hope that Hillary's
  going to pass!
So, if everything else goes wrong,
Our faith in Hillary still is strong:
Who else could stand this song?
Why, no one else but Hillary!

She had another edge: Hillary had campaigned door-to-door in Wellesley's dorms.

She won—to her surprise and pleasure. She pulled aside one of her professors to tell him. "I can't believe what has just happened. I was just elected president of the government. Can you believe it?"

During her time in student government, many of the restrictions she had challenged were finally changed. Rules that had Wellesley acting like a strict parent were lifted, such as the limits on men in dorms, and the course requirements were relaxed. She also urged Wellesley to offer a summer Upward Bound programme for low-income kids.

Hillary, between Nonna Noto and Francille Rusan, at a candidates' forum for Wellesley student government president.

But there was also some pushback. At one point, the school newspaper took her to task for overseeing the appointment of two students to a key committee rather than holding an election. It called for an end to "back room politics," saying, "The habit of appointing friends and members of the 'in' group should be halted immediately in order that knowing people in power does not become a prerequisite to officeholding."

On 4th April 1968, Martin Luther King was assassinated in Memphis. Hillary was devastated. The eloquent man she had heard speak as a teenager had been a powerful leader, insisting on non-violent protest. Her roommate, Johanna Branson, remembered her bursting into their room yelling and crying. "Her book bag flew across the room and slammed into the wall. She was distraught," Branson said. "She said, 'I can't stand it anymore. I can't take it.'"

The next day, Hillary joined a protest march in Boston and came back wearing a black armband. On campus, students were in turmoil over racial issues and the war, and a conversation in the chapel turned into something of a shouting match. In the aftermath of the assassination, Ethos threatened a hunger strike if Wellesley didn't agree to admit more black students and hire more black faculty and staff; Hillary, as student government president, backed the black student group's demands. The administration agreed to changes, and the following year, fifty-seven black students enrolled in the class of 1973.

Hillary met weekly with Wellesley President Ruth Adams, who found her student-government president to be a determined advocate. Hillary was "not always easy to deal with if you were disagreeing with her. She could be very insistent," Adams recalled.

Still, while other young people at the time wanted to tear down walls, Hillary was willing to negotiate and compromise. "She was liberal in her attitudes, but she was definitely not radical," Adams said. "She was, as a number of her generation were, interested in effecting change, but within rather than outside the system. They were not a group that wanted to go out and riot and burn things.

They wanted to go to law school, get good degrees, and change from within."

Hillary would say as much that autumn, in a talk to incoming freshmen, with her thoughts handwritten and edited on notebook paper. Recognizing that they were in "a year of confrontation politics from Chicago to Czechoslovakia," she told them that Wellesley was different: "On some campuses, change is effected through non-violent or even violent means. Although we too have had our demonstrations, change here is usually a product of discussion in the decision-making process."

For all her focus, ambition, and intensity, Hillary also knew how to relax with friends and was considered funny and fun loving, with a huge belly laugh that resonated down the dorm hallway. Rather than put on a formal dress for a dance junior year, she wore bright-orange culottes—wide-leg pants that look like a skirt—and adorned her outfit with feathers. "She was not overly bookish, or interested in grades, or committed to studying too hard," recalled Alan Schechter, a political science professor and adviser for Hillary's honours thesis. "She was a warm, friendly, outgoing, smiling, relaxed person."

In keeping with the rebellious times, she also wasn't concerned about her appearance. In addition to her thick glasses and a ponytail, she sported ragged jeans, a navy-blue pea coat, heavy boots, sweater vests, and wrinkled work shirts. "I look like hell and I could care less," she once wrote to Peavoy.

Politically, Hillary had become more liberal. Ahead of the March 1968 primary, she had campaigned in New Hampshire for Eugene McCarthy, an anti-war Democrat from Minnesota. McCarthy urged his young supporters to be respectful and neat, to cut their hair and be "Clean for Gene."

Still, she found herself back with the Republican Party that summer as part of a Wellesley internship in Washington, D.C. Schechter, who oversaw the internship programme, placed her with the House Republican Conference, which handles party matters for Republicans in the House of Representatives. She protested, but he insisted. There, she worked under House Minority Leader Gerald Ford, who would later become president, and Conference Chairman Melvin Laird of Wisconsin, who would become Richard Nixon's secretary of defense. She helped with speeches, wrote position papers, and occasionally tangled with her bosses over the Vietnam War. Once Laird spoke with the interns and called for more military force in the war. Hillary challenged him, asking why he thought "this strategy could ever succeed." They disagreed, but he took the time to explain his position—and she appreciated being taken seriously.

"She was very, very bright, very dedicated," Laird said later. "She presented her viewpoints very forcibly, always had ideas, always defended what she had in mind," he told another interviewer.

She came home with two Washington acquisitions. One was a photograph of herself with Republican leaders, which her father hung in his bedroom. The other was a new boyfriend, David Rupert, a Georgetown University student who had also interned for a Republican congressman. The two met one evening at a mixer for Republican interns and then headed to Georgetown for a drink. It didn't take long for a pair of bright and intense college

Hillary's father treasured this 1968 photo of his daughter with Republican leaders, including future President Gerald R. Ford (*third from right*), taken during her summer as a Washington intern.

students to realize that neither was all that Republican at heart.

They continued a long-distance relationship her senior year. She spent a weekend in Washington, and he came to Wellesley, staying in her suite. A good friend described the dark-haired Rupert as an "arrogant, sneering, hard-to-please" man, much like her father, and characterized their romance as somewhat rocky.

Still, they dated for quite a while, and after they attended a wedding in Kansas, she introduced him to her parents in Park Ridge. In a rare interview with Hillary biographer Gail Sheehy, Rupert said he was drawn to Hillary's character, her intellect, and the laughs they shared, and he found her physically attractive. But they never had a formal commitment: "Ours was a primary relationship but not an exclusive one."

Towards the end of her internship in 1968, Hillary and a few other interns were invited to the Republican National Convention in Miami to answer phones and deliver messages to those trying to help the moderate Nelson Rockefeller win the Republican nomination over the more conservative Richard Nixon. She got to stay in her first hotel, sharing a room with four other women, and there were some heady moments, including meeting crooner Frank Sinatra and seeing actor John Wayne. She also had her first encounter with room service, which impressed her with a large peach, delivered in a napkin, with her cereal.

The experience in Miami would be her last dalliance with Republican politics, which she began to see as more than just fiscally conservative. "All of a sudden you get all these veiled messages, frankly, that were racist," she said later. "I may not have been able to explain it, but I could feel it."

Hillary returned to Park Ridge for a few weeks before school started, just as the Democratic National Convention was coming to Chicago. Inside the convention centre, the delegates wrestled over candidates: President Johnson had decided not to run, and Senator Robert Kennedy had been assassinated in June after winning the California primary. Hubert Humphrey, the vice president, had sat out the primaries but was winning support over Eugene McCarthy. Meanwhile, protesters, many of them young, gathered in Grant Park to oppose the Vietnam War and call for substantial political change.

As the protests grew, violence broke out, with police firing tear gas and beating demonstrators with clubs. The last night, Hillary and one of her best friends from high school decided to witness history for themselves. They headed the seventeen miles to Chicago's Grant Park in her friend's family station wagon, and were unnerved by what they saw.

The park smelled of tear gas, and the police response was shocking. "We saw kids our age getting their heads beaten in. And the police were doing the beating," Betsy Johnson Ebeling recalled later. "Hillary and I just looked at each other. We had had a wonderful childhood in Park Ridge, but we obviously hadn't gotten the whole story."

With assassinations, protests, and the intense opposition to the war, some people feared the United States was on the verge of a revolution. Hillary doubted that—and she knew she would never participate in an uprising. But the experience also deepened her commitment to working as an activist for change. (Not yet as a voter, however. Hillary wouldn't turn the voting age of twenty-one until after the Illinois deadline for registering, so she couldn't vote in the 1968 election.)

Back at Wellesley, she pushed on with French and tried courses in psychology, sociology, and economics, but political science remained her true interest. She decided to focus her honours thesis on a Chicago community organizer and activist, Saul Alinsky, evaluating his views on how to lift the poor out of poverty. She had met Alinsky in Chicago the previous summer and then interviewed him for her project. In a thoughtfully written and well-argued ninety-two-page paper, she saw some value in Alinsky's efforts to organize the poor and empower them through confrontation. But she concluded that power and access to resources alone wouldn't end the plight of the poor or allow for truer equality. Instead, fixing poverty was more complex than that, requiring help and participation from others, including government.

Alinsky "believed you could change the system only from the outside," she said later. "I didn't."

In cheeky acknowledgments she noted, "Although I have no 'loving wife' to thank for keeping the children away while I wrote, I do have many friends and teachers who contributed to the process of thesis-writing." The paper earned an A, and Alinsky was so impressed with her that he offered her a job.

Hillary considered it, but she already had her sights on law school as a way to pursue her growing interest in helping others. She took the Law School Admission Test at Harvard, and quickly got a bitter taste of the gender divide that she had avoided at a women's college. The men taking the test started harassing the few women. "What are you doing here?" they said. "You shouldn't be here." Then they got more pointed: "Why don't you go home and get married?"

She was rattled, but not deterred. Professor Schechter wrote a recommendation saying, "She has the intellectual ability, personality, and character to make a remarkable contribution to American society." Her father told her that she would have to pay for law school, and she won a prestigious Vida Dutton Scudder Fellowship of $2,500 from Wellesley for graduate study. (The fellowship covered about a year of tuition. She would also take out low-interest, government-backed student loans and work to help pay the roughly $4,000 a year in tuition, fees, and housing.)

She was accepted to both Harvard and Yale, and while she was weighing her options, she was invited to a cocktail party at Harvard Law School. A male friend introduced her to a famous law professor, saying she was "trying to decide whether to come here next year or sign up with our closest competitor." The professor responded dismissively, "Well, first of all, we don't have any close competitors. Secondly, we don't need any more women at Harvard."

She chose Yale.

Though many women at Wellesley were standouts, Hillary's energy, charisma, and leadership separated her from the crowd. Although she didn't talk about becoming a future political candidate, others saw the potential— maybe because politics seemed more accessible to women at the time than other professions. "A lot of us thought Hillary would be the first woman president," remembered Karen Williamson, a good friend.

As Wellesley's graduation neared, some classmates began to lobby President Adams for a student speaker at graduation. Wellesley had never had a student commencement speaker before, but then, there had rarely been a four-year period of such upheaval and social change. Adams initially said no.

Hillary went to see if she could mediate a resolution. Adams told her she didn't want to break tradition—and she didn't know whom the students wanted to speak. When Hillary told the president that her classmates had asked her to be the speaker, Adams agreed to think about it.

Just a couple of days before graduation, Adams gave in. While Hillary scrambled to draft a speech under the tight deadline, her classmates offered suggestions and dropped off poems and favourite sayings at her dorm room. Most of all, they told her, they wanted her to talk

Hillary at graduation, with *(from left)* John Quarles, chairman of Wellesley's board of trustees; Wellesley President Ruth Adams; and U.S. Senator Edward Brooke.

about trust—or rather, the intense and growing distrust between young people and adults in charge who couldn't see eye to eye on the war, civil rights, protest, or where the world should be headed.

Hillary's mother was having some health problems and couldn't travel. But after learning that his daughter would be speaking, her dad made plans to fly in the night before and leave after graduation.

At the graduation ceremony at the end of May, Edward Brooke, the Republican senator from Massachusetts—the man Hillary had supported in 1966—gave a speech that seemed to support President Nixon's policies. He began by noting, "Wellesley has even more admirers than its girls have beaux." He didn't mention Vietnam or the angst it had caused or recognize the simmering concerns of the graduating class. He noted that the percentage of Americans living in poverty had declined, and he argued that "coercive protest" was misguided and unnecessary. "Let us not mistake the fire of protest for the value of accomplishment," he said.

The speech received polite applause from the 2,000 people in attendance.

Hillary was next. President Adams noted some of Hillary's academic and extracurricular achievements, and called Wellesley's first-ever student speaker "cheerful, good humoured, good company, and a good friend to all of us." But the Hillary who came to the microphone hardly seemed so good-natured.

Bristling at the senator's speech, she began with an impromptu response, saying that her generation wasn't interested in the percentage of people living in poverty, but in the human reality. She defended her generation's right to speak up, saying they had "that indispensable task of criticizing and constructive protest."

She noted that her classmates weren't interested in an "acquisitive and competitive corporate life." Instead, she said, "We're searching for more immediate, ecstatic, and penetrating modes of living."

They also were looking for a different kind of politics. "For too long, our leaders have used politics as the art of the possible," she said. "And the challenge now is to

As Wellesley's first student commencement speaker, Hillary gives a memorable—and stinging—speech.

practise politics as the art of making what appears to be impossible, possible."

She concluded with a poem written by a classmate, ending, "You and I must be free / . . . to practice with all the skill of our being / The art of making possible."

Hillary's speech—especially her rebuttal of a U.S. senator—stunned the older members of the audience. Alumnae from the early 1900s to 1954 sat in awkward silence, wrote *Washington Post* reporter Judith Martin, a Wellesley alum. Younger graduates applauded graciously, while recent and current graduates exploded in support, jumping to their feet and giving her a long, thundering ovation.

The impact lasted much longer. The *Boston Globe*—in the first of thousands of articles that would mention her hair—reported that the "blond, bespectacled honour student" upstaged Senator Brooke. The *Chicago Tribune* scolded her in an editorial for being unjustifiably rude in response to a sound and timely speech. A *Chicago Daily News* writer noted that just a few days before, "she was just another uncommonly pretty girl in the ranks for this year's legion of college graduates." *Life* magazine featured her in a special article on notable graduation speeches nationwide.

Years later, the poet Robert Pinsky, then a young Wellesley professor, wrote that hearing her on that day was "like hearing a very young, uniquely gifted musician play." He had only heard of Hillary around campus, but he was moved by her ability to improvise, to articulate, and to rise to the occasion. "I saw a gifted, electrifying natural in action, calling for something better than what we had," he said.

Back in Park Ridge, the phone was ringing off the hook with requests for television appearances and interviews. Some were enthusiastic—"she spoke for a generation"—and some were intensely critical—"who does she think she is?" People either loved her words or hated them.

Not long after, Hillary would head to Alaska to travel and work before diving into law school. Though she was going to Yale with the hope of embarking on a career of action, her time there would lead her in completely unexpected directions.

6

YALE

Even at Yale Law School, among the elite of the elite, Hillary Rodham stood out.

For starters, she was a woman, one of just thirty-six in a law school class of 237. Though its graduate programmes had long accepted a few women, the university had admitted its first undergraduate female students that autumn. On top of that, Hillary's appearance in *Life* magazine meant that many classmates already had heard of her before she arrived.

Because of her Wellesley speech, she was invited to participate in a national League of Women Voters youth conference in October 1969 looking for ways to better involve young people in the political process. Among other things, the group supported lowering the voting age to eighteen from twenty-one, reflecting the belief that people old enough to go to war were old enough to cast a ballot. (The Twenty-Sixth Amendment to the U.S.

Constitution, adopted in 1971, made eighteen the official voting age.)

Through that work, Hillary began to connect with people on the national political stage, including Peter Edelman, a lawyer and former staffer for Robert Kennedy, and Vernon Jordan, a prominent African American lawyer with deep political connections.

Hillary during a photo shoot for *Life* magazine's spread on notable graduation speeches.

In contrast to Wellesley, the Yale campus and the surrounding city of New Haven, Connecticut, were a hotbed of political activism in 1969. That autumn, there were protests and teach-ins—unstructured lectures and workshops—in the Yale Law School quad on the Vietnam War and poverty in New Haven. In October, an estimated 50,000 people crowded into the nearby New Haven Green to protest the war.

In an already emotionally tense city, tensions grew as nine members of the Black Panther Party, a group of black revolutionaries, were charged with torturing and murdering a nineteen-year-old man who was believed to have been a police informant. Among the accused was Bobby Seale, a Black Panther co-founder and leader, who had come to speak at Yale and was alleged to have ordered the young man's murder.

A First Amendment professor encouraged students to monitor the court proceedings, looking for violations of the Panthers' civil rights, and to write papers on them and discuss them in class. Hillary took on the task of creating a schedule to be sure someone was at every court hearing, classmates said, though she has never spoken publicly about the case. The Federal Bureau of Investigation was known to be tracking and trying to infiltrate the Black Panthers to break them up, and the Yale students monitoring the trial were certain that the federal agency was noting their own movements as well.

Even Yale's president, Kingman Brewster, expressed concerns, saying, "I am appalled and ashamed that things should have come to such a pass in this country that I am sceptical of the ability of black revolutionaries to achieve a fair trial anywhere in the U.S."

As the trials neared, a massive three-day rally in support of the Black Panthers was planned for the nearby New Haven Green beginning on 1st May, a Friday. Anger simmered as the May Day rally drew near.

Early in the morning of 27th April, the international law library in the basement of the law school erupted in fire. Hillary was horrified when she heard, and she and other students and faculty rushed to form a bucket brigade to extinguish it. The police sergeant on the scene was impressed with the quick work, noting that "some girls also took part."

Five hundred books were destroyed, and students and faculty alike were appalled that someone would burn books. Though the cause of the fire was never determined, some students believed the law school was being punished for not sufficiently supporting the Black Panthers. Hillary and other students agreed to form a security team to patrol the library around the clock to prevent more damage.

Then, to add more fuel to the blazing emotions, President Nixon expanded the war at the end of April by sending American troops into Cambodia.

Worried about violence and riots, New Haven retailers closed up shop and boarded up their windows before May Day. Trash barrels were removed to prevent bonfires, and a flagpole above a World War I monument was greased to protect the American flag. About 3,000 National Guard troops were brought in. Yale suspended classes and agreed to feed all comers in its dining halls. It offered brown rice and beef stew for lunch and a breakfast of tea and *familea*, a granola-like concoction of "oats, dates, matzoh, sunflower seeds, peanuts, prunes, raisins, corn flakes, and fat-free milk." One revolutionary took a taste and was unimpressed, saying, "You're going to start a riot with this stuff."

Between 12,000 and 15,000 mostly young people converged on New Haven Green. Given the fear and the build-up, the rally was relatively peaceful. Tear gas was fired just once, and the gathering petered out in two days, instead of its scheduled three.

But the turbulence wasn't over. A growing number of students and activists around the country were protesting the expansion of the war in Vietnam. That Monday, 4th May, the National Guard opened fire on unarmed protesters at Kent State University in Ohio, killing four young people.

Hillary cried when she heard the news.

In their grief and fury, students at hundreds of colleges began to strike to protest the war.

That night, Yale's law students crammed into a lecture hall to decide whether to join the strike. Sitting on a table at the front in bell-bottom blue jeans, moderating the intense and heated discussion, was Hillary Rodham. Though just a first-year student, she had established herself as someone to talk to if there was a law-school problem. She had a good enough relationship with the dean, a classmate remembered, that she could speak to him "in a way that nobody else could. She was somehow able to transmit the message without getting overly confrontational or hysterical."

She applied the same calm at the student gathering. As students vented their frustrations, she kept the discussion moving.

"It was almost like being a translator," remembered Kristine Olson Rogers, who was a classmate at both Yale and Wellesley. Someone would erupt with a burst of rhetoric. "She would say, 'I hear you saying this,' or 'If you could be in a room with Professor So-and-So, is this what you would say?'" Rogers said. Hillary was like an international negotiator, "flying back and forth between both sides."

The students voted 239-12 to go on strike.

It seemed at the time, Hillary said later, "that our government was at war with its own people."

Just a few days later, on 7th May, Hillary was in Washington, wearing a black armband in memory of the Kent State students and giving one of two headline speeches for the fiftieth anniversary of the League of Women Voters. There, she shared the dais with Marian Wright Edelman, a Yale Law graduate, who was the first black woman admitted to practise law in Mississippi and the wife of Peter Edelman. Just thirty years old, Wright Edelman had already made an impact as a civil rights activist in the South; later, she would found the Children's Defense Fund to speak up for disadvantaged children and families and would also become a mentor to Hillary.

That night in Washington, Wright Edelman spoke of the frustrations of black people, and worried aloud about the future of a country where, she said, "we sacrifice law . . . to achieve order."

Hillary took direct aim at the Nixon administration and especially the expansion of the war. She said students felt "mute rage" over the war in Cambodia, which she called illegal and unconstitutional. Moreover, she said,

Hillary at the League of Women Voters' fiftieth-anniversary banquet with the League's president, Lucy Benton Benson.

"We are being governed by an elected dictatorship that acts and then claims ex post facto support from the silent majority."

She challenged the women in attendance to push companies to be accountable for their actions. And she urged them to help stop "the chain of broken promises" that her generation had endured.

Both women got loud and frequent applause.

Hillary had met Wright Edelman at Yale earlier in the school year and asked her for a summer job. Wright Edelman was happy to have her—but couldn't pay her. Needing income to supplement her scholarship and loans, Hillary found a grant for law students working on civil rights.

That summer, working for Wright Edelman's Washington Research Project, Hillary was assigned to research the health and education of children of migrant workers, children like the ones she had babysat for as a teen in Park Ridge. She attended a Senate committee hearing on large companies' poor treatment of farm workers who travel from harvest to harvest for work. Hillary realized that children and their families often still lacked decent housing or even basic sanitation—and that few people were speaking on their behalf.

The experience became a "personal turning point," she said later. She returned to Yale with a growing commitment to speak for the rights of children, especially those who were poor or disadvantaged. She sought out professors who could help her develop expertise and began working on legal issues involving children at Yale-New Haven Hospital. After so many years studying government and politics, she had found a clear direction, something that would become a lifelong passion. Soon, she would discover another one.

7

BILL

On the first day of her second year of law school, Hillary spotted her old friend Robert Reich, a new Yale Law student, and walked over to say hello. When she had been a freshman at Wellesley, Reich had been a sophomore at Dartmouth, and they had once had a date of sorts, remaining friends afterwards.

Selected as a prestigious Rhodes Scholar, Reich had spent the two years after graduation studying at Oxford University in England. When Hillary walked up, he was visiting with a fellow Rhodes Scholar and first-year law student, a big, gregarious classmate named Bill Clinton, who, at six feet, two inches, towered over the much-shorter Reich.

Reich said later that he introduced Hillary to Bill then—but apparently it wasn't a very impressive first meeting. Neither of them remembered it.

While Hillary's second year wasn't as eventful as the

first, she was busy. She worked part-time, jumped into her newfound interest in children's rights, and volunteered with New Haven's legal services office, which helped people who couldn't afford legal advice. A friend remembers she also enjoyed heading to Clark's Dairy for milkshakes "because they were supposed to be good for you" and going to the gym to work out.

One day in the student lounge, Hillary overheard a bearded and bushy-haired fellow carrying on. With his thick reddish-brown hair, he looked something like a Viking, and he was boasting, "We grow the biggest watermelons in the world!"

"Who *is* that?" she asked a friend.

"Oh, that's Bill Clinton," her friend replied. "He's from Arkansas, and that's all he ever talks about."

Bill recalled first noticing Hillary that spring in a class called Political and Civil Rights. Reich, who was also in the class, remembered that when Bill actually attended, he seemed to answer every question correctly. Hillary was "an active and enthusiastic participant" in the class. (Future Supreme Court Justice Clarence Thomas was also in the class, but sat in the back and didn't join in, Reich said.) Bill was taken with the woman with thick dark blond hair and big eyeglasses who had "a sense of strength and self-possession I had rarely seen in anyone, man or woman." He started to catch up with her after class, but backed off. "Somehow I knew that this wasn't another tap on the shoulder, that

Hillary and Bill Clinton during his bushy-haired "Viking" stage.

I might be starting something I couldn't stop," he said later.

Not too long after, Bill spotted her studying in the Yale Law library while he was chatting with another student. He kept looking at her. She tried to look at him, while not looking like she was looking. Finally, Hillary walked over to him, saying, "If you're going to keep looking at me, and I'm going to keep looking back, we might as well be introduced. I'm Hillary Rodham."

Briefly stunned by her introduction, Bill took a few seconds to spit out his own name. They chatted for a few minutes and went their separate ways. (While Bill and Hillary have similar memories, they have disagreed on exactly where they were in the library at the time. Reich calls it a "wonderful, charming story that I'm sure is absolutely correct"—except, he says, "I don't remember Bill spending a minute in the Yale Law library.")

Close to the end of the semester, Hillary ran into Bill again as she headed to register for autumn semester classes. He said he was going that way, too. They chatted as they stood in line. But Bill's cover was blown when they reached the front of the line, and the surprised registrar asked why he had returned after already registering.

From there, they went on a walk, ending up at the Yale Art Gallery, which was closed because of a strike. Bill sweet-talked a guard into letting them in by offering to pick up litter and branches that had accumulated in the courtyard while the workers were gone. They walked through the empty museum, talking about an exhibit by the abstract artist Mark Rothko and ending up in the courtyard, still talking. Bill cleaned up, as promised, and Hillary settled into the lap of a Henry Moore sculpture of a woman, continuing the conversation until the sun went down. It was their first date.

There was a hitch. Hillary was still dating David Rupert, her boyfriend from her junior year summer in Washington. Rupert had worked in Alabama during her first year at Yale, and they didn't see each other much. But once he relocated to Vermont, she drove to see him most weekends, wrapped up in a horsehair blanket because her car didn't have heat.

In fact, she was headed to see Rupert that weekend. But the relationship was already on the rocks. She wasn't moving to Vermont, and Rupert, disdainful of her interest in government, wasn't moving to New Haven, either.

When Hillary returned, she was sick with a cold, and Bill brought orange juice and chicken soup to her apartment. They picked up their conversation where it had left off. Though the semester was coming to an end and exams were looming, they became—in their own words—"inseparable."

Bill was living in a beach house in Milford, Connecticut, with three room-mates, and over the next several days, Hillary and Bill hung out there or drove around in his 1970 burnt-orange station wagon. They talked, and talked some more. Bill shared his dream: He wanted to return to his home state to run for office; Hillary was less certain about her path.

They also talked about her upbringing in Park Ridge and about his childhood in Arkansas. While Hillary had grown up in a stable and somewhat sheltered suburban community, Bill's childhood was turbulent. His father,

William Jefferson Blythe Jr., died in a car accident in southern Missouri three months before Bill was born in August 1946 in Hope, Arkansas. His mother, Virginia, was just twenty-three when he was born. Though she had trained as a nurse, Virginia wanted to be a better provider for her son, William Jefferson Blythe III. So when he was about a year old, she left Bill with her parents for months while she moved to New Orleans to train as a nurse anesthetist.

His grandmother, a private nurse, was loving but demanding, feeding him well, but also pushing him to learn to count and read. His grandfather was kind and generous. He ran a small grocery, and though many stores in the South were segregated, his store was not. Bill remembered that he treated all his customers the same, and Bill played with their children, black and white.

When his mother returned, she was dating a new man, Roger Clinton, a handsome, hard-partying car dealer, who was twice divorced. Virginia married Clinton in 1950, and soon after, Bill began to call himself Billy Clinton, though he didn't formally adopt the name until he was a teenager.

After first grade, Bill and his family relocated to Hot Springs, and in 1956 his half-brother, Roger, was born.

Bill's "daddy," as he called his stepfather, loved him, but he often drank to excess. When drunk, he could be irresponsible, and abusive and threatening to Bill's mother. Once, when they were still living in Hope, a drunken Roger argued with Virginia and then pulled out a gun and fired it. The bullet pierced a wall between Virginia and Bill. Virginia and Bill escaped to a neighbour's house, and Roger spent a night in jail.

Bill's daddy would straighten up for a while and then drink heavily again, at times going after Virginia. When Bill was fourteen, he finally had enough. When he heard Roger attacking his mother in their bedroom, he grabbed a golf club, and barged in to see Roger hitting her. Bill threatened to beat him if he didn't stop. Roger backed off.

Not long after, Virginia finally moved out with her boys and divorced Roger. But the separation lasted only a few months. He pleaded for her to take him back, and she did.

Bill; his mother, Virginia; and his younger brother, Roger, around 1958.

Like Hillary, Bill excelled in school and school activities, finishing fourth in his high school class. He was a talented saxophone player and active in the marching band and concert bands, as well as a dance band and a jazz trio. But he was also fascinated with politics. In 1963 he participated in Boys State, which engages high school juniors in the political process, complete with mock political parties and elections. There, he was selected to represent Arkansas at Boys Nation near Washington, D.C. During a visit to the White House, Bill actually got to meet his hero, President Kennedy, and shake his hand.

That year, Bill decided he would to go into public service as an elected official.

Like Hillary, he travelled halfway across the country to college, attending Georgetown University in Washington and serving in student government there. By the time they met at Yale, Bill and Hillary had much in common beyond their college choices and student government roles: enormous energy, exceptional intelligence, ambition, fascination with national politics, commitment to public service, natural curiosity, and a fondness for a good argument.

But there was also, as Hillary biographer Carl Bernstein called it, "a fitting of gears" in the way their differences meshed and complemented each other. Hillary was direct and to the point; Bill was a storyteller, a raconteur. She could have sharp elbows. He was charming. She was decisive. Bill, who was eager to please others, was not.

He appreciated her confidence and depth. "Hillary was a straight shooter," said a Yale classmate. With Bill, "she saw right past the charm and saw the complex person underneath. I think he found that irresistible."

Even more, they enjoyed each other's company. "They were very funny together, very lively," said one of Bill's roommates.

As the summer approached, Hillary prepared to work for a small Oakland, California, law firm that had represented some Black Panthers and that was known for its civil rights work. (Once again, she landed a grant for those working on civil rights.)

Bill was committed to helping Senator George McGovern's upcoming presidential campaign for the Democratic nomination get off the ground in the South. Bill was planning to move to Miami, completely across the country from Hillary, and travel across the South, working for McGovern's campaign manager, Gary Hart. For a twenty-four-year-old, the job offered "the political experience of a lifetime."

He and Hillary had been together only about a month. But as the separation date drew closer, Bill had a change of heart—or rather, a tugging of the heartstrings. He didn't want to lose her. He asked Hillary if he could go to California with her. Though surprised he would give up such a great opportunity, she was thrilled for him to come along.

Hillary stayed in a small apartment not far from the

University of California at Berkeley. Bill drove out with her and then returned to the East Coast for a few weeks to tell the McGovern folks that he wouldn't be joining them. He also spent some time signing up supporters in Connecticut before returning to California.

Hillary's summer employer, Treuhaft, Walker and Burnstein, was considered a radical law firm. Some partners there either belonged or had once belonged to the Communist Party. Critics later tried to paint Hillary as having communist leanings because she worked there. But her boss, Mal Burnstein, remembered her as a "classic liberal," not a revolutionary seeking to overturn the system.

Hillary recalled spending most of the summer working for Burnstein on a child custody case. But lawyers who were there at the time say she most likely worked on cases where men were asking for conscientious objector status, allowing them to opt out of the draft and avoid Vietnam. In addition, two other cases were active that summer. In one, a law school graduate was denied admission to the California bar because of his previous participation in protests. And in the other, two medical students were asked to sign an oath saying they weren't communists in order to work at a Veterans Administration hospital.

Choosing such a firm seemed out of character for someone who preferred to work within the system— but as a female law student in 1971, she may not have had many options. Many top law firms and government agencies, including the Oakland public defender's office and the federal public defender, simply refused to hire women lawyers. "Even in the public interest world, it was hard to find a job," recalled a female classmate of Hillary's. Treuhaft, Walker had a record of hiring female Yale Law students.

While Hillary worked, Bill read and scouted out restaurants, parks, vintage stores, and other attractions in the San Francisco Bay area. They went to a Joan Baez concert and tried their hand at cooking.

When the summer ended, she officially ended her relationship with Rupert. Her former boyfriend described the ending as painful, but he understood. "If you care for him, then go for it," he told her.

Hillary and Bill decided to live together in New Haven for the 1971–72 school year, renting a small apartment with a sagging floor. Hillary also made an unusual decision: Rather than finishing law school in three years, she would do extra research on child development and child advocacy, and spend a fourth year at Yale so that she and Bill would finish at the same time.

Their love was growing. Next would come the tricky task of winning the support of their very different families.

8

COURTSHIP

As Dorothy Rodham tells it, Bill Clinton showed up at her door in Park Ridge the day after Christmas to visit for a few days. Her greeting was as frosty as a Chicago snowstorm.

"Hello, my name is Bill Clinton," he said.

"That's nice," she said. Then she called out to tell Hillary that she had a visitor.

"To tell the truth," she told an interviewer later, "I would have preferred that he left. He had come to take my daughter away!"

The young man with the long sideburns was sent up to see Hillary, but he would spend the night in her brother Tony's room, and Hillary's parents kept a close eye on him. Within a day, he began to win over Dorothy. When he saw her reading a philosophy book for a class she was taking, he engaged her in a long conversation about it—the first time she'd been able to discuss the subject at length. "From that moment, I loved him immediately," she said.

At one point, Dorothy asked him about his future plans. He told her the same thing he had already told Hillary and legions of other people: He was going back to Arkansas, and in time would run for office.

Hugh was a tougher nut to crack. Never one for big conversations, he wasn't sure what to make of this Southern liberal who loved to talk about Arkansas and where the nation was going. Slowly, they began to break the ice watching football and playing cards. But it was hard for Hugh to accept that anyone would be good enough for his only daughter. It would take a while for him to come around.

Back at Yale, Hillary spent her third and fourth years learning more about children, child development, and children's rights. She did research on children's legal rights for the Carnegie Council on Children and helped with research on a book, *Beyond the Best Interests of the Child*, by Yale Law Professor Joseph Goldstein, children's psychoanalyst Anna Freud, and Albert J. Solnit of the Yale Child Study Centre.

At Yale–New Haven Hospital, she helped draft legal procedures for handling cases of suspected child abuse and saw first hand children who had been beaten or burned or who had been left alone for days at a time. She also worked on children's issues at the New Haven Legal Assistance Association. In one case, a woman wanted to

Hillary and Bill make their case—and an impression on their classmates—at the 1972 Prize Trial.

adopt her foster child of two years. But state rules prohibited foster parents from adopting. Hillary lost the case, and the young child was moved from the only mother she had ever known to another family. The experience hardened Hillary's resolve to change the system.

At the Yale Child Study Centre, a part of the medical school, she observed and played with children, helped nursery school teachers, sat in on diagnostic meetings, and participated in a seminar on child development readings. With children, she was "very natural, playful, laid-back," Solnit said later. "Even before she became prominent, we used to think of her as a model of what a law student could get out of the programme."

Her relationship with Bill continued to evolve, and in

the spring of 1972, they competed together in Yale's mock trials. Hillary and Bill won in the semi-finals and were assigned the role of prosecutors in the law school's closely watched Prize Trial, which brought a former Supreme Court justice and other attorneys to campus.

Hillary and Bill's assignment was to convict a police officer of beating to death a young person with long hair, a case based on a recent trial in the South. But the scripted case included plenty of reasonable doubt, making their job challenging.

Bill recalled that he had a bad day. Hillary had a bad fashion day, wearing a blue suede jacket with pop-your-eyes-out orange flared pants. Bill worried that the judges would see only her clothes. Their classmates saw something else:

Both Hillary and Bill *(back row, far right)* participate in moot court, a student organization, in 1973.

their powerful partnership on display for the first time. He was folksy and engaging, playing to the jury. She was sharp, composed, and intellectually shrewd. Still, they lost the case, and another student won the top prize. But they left a memorable impression on those who saw them.

After a busy school year together, Bill went to work on the McGovern presidential campaign and then to the Democratic National Convention in Miami Beach. Hillary headed back to Washington to work for Marian Wright Edelman gathering information about so-called white-flight schools.

More than fifteen years after the U.S. Supreme Court ruled in *Brown v. Board of Education* that segregated schools were not constitutional courts were ordering public school districts to desegregate—that is, to end white-only and black-only schools. When public schools began to integrate, however, new private schools sprang up, especially in rural areas, apparently to offer parents an all-white option. Segregated private schools weren't supposed to get a break from federal taxes, but the Nixon administration wasn't enforcing that rule.

Hillary travelled to Atlanta to collect information from civil rights workers and lawyers to highlight the problem. She also went to Dothan, Alabama, where she pretended to be a newcomer looking for a school for her child. In a meeting with a private-school administrator, she was promised that the school would be all white.

In Miami, McGovern won the Democratic nomination. Shortly after, the campaign sent Bill to Texas to help coordinate the campaign there. Bill invited Hillary to join him when her summer job ended. She lined up a job registering Texas voters, especially young people, who could now vote at age eighteen, as well as blacks and Latinos in South Texas. Though still enrolled at Yale, both she and Bill put their studies on hold.

A McGovern win in Texas against incumbent President Richard Nixon was a long shot at best. Fervently antiwar, the candidate was seen as too liberal, and his campaign was disorganized. But the team based in Austin hoped—naively—that if enough young people and minorities registered and voted, McGovern might have a chance.

Bill meets up with Democratic presidential candidate George McGovern *(centre)* during a campaign swing in 1972.

As co-coordinator of the campaign with Taylor Branch, who would become a Pulitzer Prize–winning chronicler of the civil rights era, Bill had a high profile. But Hillary got plenty of attention, too, especially from other women working with them. After long discussions with Hillary about women and politics, Betsey Wright, an experienced political organizer in Texas, said she became "obsessed with how far Hillary might go, with her mixture of brilliance, ambition, and self-assuredness."

Hillary came across as intense and "terribly serious," Wright said. But she also liked spontaneity and a good time, which was obvious when she burst out with her "fabulous" guttural laugh.

Bill seemed to tap into her fun side, and the two spent time together when she was in Austin. But they had their roller-coaster moments. They argued with as much passion as they pursued politics, and they saw other people, according to a Bill biographer, David Maraniss. At one point, they nearly broke up, but a union organizer who had worked with Hillary in South Texas helped keep them together.

When voter registration ended thirty days before the election, Hillary was asked to help with the campaign in San Antonio, about an hour away from Austin. There, Hillary worked for Sara Ehrman, a member of McGovern's legislative staff in Washington, who had taken a leave to work for the campaign. Ehrman remembered Hillary as a voracious reader who frequently carried a Bible with her, a liberal Christian who seemed to be trying to line up her politics with her religion. She also went at campaigning with an almost-religious fervour, tramping through tough neighbourhoods and relentlessly knocking on doors. Ehrman nicknamed her "Fearless."

To no one's surprise, McGovern was trounced in the November election, taking just a third of the vote in Texas and winning only Massachusetts and the District of Columbia nationwide.

Hillary and Bill took a short holiday to Mexico before heading back to New Haven. To their advantage, Yale Law classes were graded pass/fail. Despite missing most of the semester, they managed to catch up and pass.

As the two prepared to finish up that spring, their future together was uncertain.

Later in her life, Hillary would tell an interviewer that she was attracted to Bill because "he wasn't afraid of me."

But Bill had a different view. "But I was afraid of *us*, I tell you that," he said. He knew they would have to make hard choices. He had told her early on, "You know, I'm really worried about falling in love with you, because you're a great person, you could have a great life. If you wanted to run for public office, you could be elected, but I've got to go home. It's just who I am."

He landed a job teaching law at the University of Arkansas in Fayetteville.

"I wanted nothing to do with that," Hillary said in a 1991 talk. "I had never been to Arkansas and, like many people who grew up in Chicago, wasn't even sure where it was."

After graduation, Bill took her to England and Wales to show her places he had seen during his time as a Rhodes Scholar. One evening, overcome with emotion as the sun was setting, he asked her to marry him.

She loved him. But to her, marriage was for life, and she wasn't ready for that commitment yet. She said no.

They shared a love of politics and a dedication to public service. But, she said later, "We also realized that a marriage between two people like us was never, ever going to be easy, if it could happen at all."

When they returned, she agreed to visit Arkansas—and take the Arkansas bar exam just in case she changed her mind. (She also took the Washington, D.C., exam and, later that year, she learned that she'd passed in Arkansas, but failed the D.C. exam, along with a third of the D.C. applicants. She would take the results as something of a sign.)

Despite the summer heat, her welcome in Hot Springs was just as chilly as Bill's had been in Chicago.

Bill's mom, Virginia, was an outgoing woman who didn't leave the house without her hot-pink lipstick and false eyelashes and who kept the original grey streak through the centre of her hair and dyed the rest around it. Bill had always dated good-looking women, including a former Miss Arkansas, and Virginia hadn't been impressed with Hillary when she met her briefly in New Haven.

This time, she was completely put off by what she saw: "No makeup. Coke-bottle glasses. Brown hair with no apparent style." It was an instant clash of big city versus small town, North versus South, dolled up versus dressed down.

Bill was so appalled at his mother's response that he herded her and brother Roger into the kitchen and gave them a lecture. "Look," he told them, "I want you to know that I've had it up to *here* with beauty queens. I have to have somebody I can talk with. Do you understand that?"

Virginia said she did—but like Hillary's father, it would be a while before she could warm up to the woman who might take her cherished son away.

Hillary wasn't ready to give in yet, either—but she braced herself to accept that she and Bill might ultimately go their separate ways. "This was one of those relationships that can't really stand the test of time because we are so different," she reasoned. "We have career paths that probably cannot be reconciled, and so it's been a very important experience, but it's probably finished."

She took a job in Cambridge, Massachusetts, with Marian Wright Edelman's new Children's Defense Fund. For now, she and Bill would live far apart.

9

CHILDREN

Hillary rented the top floor of an old house and, for the first time ever, had a place all to herself. As a staff attorney for Wright Edelman's fledgling organization, she was doing what she had studied for, looking after the rights of children.

That November, her first scholarly article, "Children Under the Law," based on work she had done at Yale, was published in the *Harvard Educational Review*.

Jay Katz, one of Hillary's professors, who taught a course in family law, called the piece "a pioneering article" that pointed out how "children need greater protection by the law." In writing it, he said, Hillary "was amongst the first" legal scholars to attack the issue.

The subject was still evolving. "The phrase 'children's rights' is a slogan in search of a definition," Hillary wrote.

But, she said, more adult rights—such as one's right to representation when accused of a crime—were being extended to people under the age of eighteen or twenty-one. In addition, she wrote, assuming that the age of eighteen was a dividing point between childhood and adulthood was simplistic. Obviously, a six-month-old is wildly different from a sixteen-year-old. And already, the same states that said children couldn't speak for themselves in some situations had granted various rights to young people in other situations, such as the right to drive, get a job, or drop out of school at a certain age.

Hillary also argued that the unique needs of children entitled them to certain rights. For instance, children who were subject to neglect or caught in custody battles might need a representative or lawyer to speak for them apart from their parents or the state—and their voices should be heard.

In a 1979 article, she would take a stronger stance on behalf of young people. She noted that a fifteen-year-old in the nineteenth century could have left home or run off to sea without getting into legal trouble. But in modern times, adults made many more decisions for young people. She argued that the law shouldn't assume that children aren't capable of making decisions; rather, children should be considered competent unless they are proven otherwise. And, she wrote, competent children should have a say in their own future when it comes to issues like schooling, employment, or whether they will become mothers or have an abortion.

Later, those articles would kick up storms of

controversy about her politics and parenting approach. But at the time, she was able to put her ideas into action through her new job. The Children's Defense Fund dispatched her to South Carolina to interview teenage offenders who had been put in jail cells with adults. The Children's Defense Fund would work to make sure that juveniles were separated from adults and that their cases were handled more quickly.

Hillary was also sent to investigate communities like New Bedford, Massachusetts, where the census data indicated that many kids weren't enrolled in school. Again knocking on doors in tough neighbourhoods, she met children who had to stay home to babysit younger siblings and kids who were in wheelchairs or were deaf or blind and weren't welcome in their public schools. Armed with that knowledge, she helped prepare the Defense Fund's first major report, *Children Out of School in America*. That, in turn, helped lay the groundwork for a new federal law requiring education for disabled children.

Though her work energized her, Hillary missed Bill, who was enjoying his first semester of teaching in Arkansas. He came to visit at Thanksgiving, and after Christmas, she went to visit him.

Itching to dive into Arkansas politics, Bill was mulling over a plan to run as a Democrat against Republican John Paul Hammerschmidt, who was in his fourth term in the U.S. House of Representatives.

While Hillary and Bill were immersed in their new

jobs and their relationship, the nation was immersed in a new crisis. Nixon had all but ended American participation in the Vietnam War in 1973. Now the focus was on a new crisis. During Nixon's 1972 campaign against Hillary's and Bill's candidate, George McGovern,

Professor Bill Clinton, at the University of Arkansas in the mid-1970s.

five men had been caught trying to plant a wiretap in the Democratic National Committee headquarters at the Watergate office complex, even though Nixon had a huge lead in the polls.

Over several months a scandal unfolded: Top Nixon aides had used campaign money to spy on and sabotage opponents—and then tried to hide the whole messy affair after the men were arrested in the Watergate burglary.

Nixon repeatedly denied any knowledge of the spying or the cover-up. But one of his former top advisers, John Dean, testified that he had discussed a cover-up with the president dozens of times. Another top official revealed that the president had taped all his conversations—so there might be proof. In a rare move, the three broadcast networks at the time took turns broadcasting Senate hearings into the break-in during the summer of 1973. A fascination with the unfolding Watergate case gripped the nation.

Though Bill was only twenty-seven years old and had never held any office, he thought the scandal would hurt the Republicans and give him a chance to win.

It also opened up another opportunity. The House Judiciary Committee had asked John Doar, a noted civil rights lawyer, to lead an investigation into whether President Nixon should be impeached. Under the U.S. Constitution, a president can be removed for "treason, bribery, or other high crimes and misdemeanors." (Today, a misdemeanor is a minor infraction, but at the time the

Constitution was written, it meant an offense against the state or an abuse of power.)

The Judiciary Committee would recommend to the full House of Representatives whether to impeach the president—in plainer language, to charge him with wrongdoing. If it did, the Senate would try the president on the charges, with a conviction removing him from office. Only one other president, Andrew Johnson, had ever faced an impeachment inquiry, for removing his war secretary without informing the Senate. He was impeached, but was acquitted.

Doar had met Bill and Hillary the previous spring at Yale Law's 1973 Prize Trial. After his House appointment, Doar called a Yale professor to ask for names of a

Marian Wright Edelman, founder of the Children's Defense Fund and an early mentor to Hillary.

few young lawyers willing to work around the clock. Both Bill and Hillary were recommended.

Bill got the first call, while Hillary was visiting after Christmas. He declined, saying he planned to run for office. But he put in another good word for Hillary.

When the call came to her, she accepted. She got Marian Wright Edelman's approval to take the job and packed up to move to Washington, D.C., to work on the biggest legal case of the day. The up-and-coming young woman, a student leader who had once spoken for a generation of frustrated college students, would once again have a spot on the national stage.

10

NIXON

As the Watergate scandal gained steam in 1973, President Nixon famously declared to the American people, "I am not a crook!" But it was up to John Doar and his team of lawyers to help Congress decide that.

Hillary was one of the first staffers to arrive in mid-January 1974. She and another young lawyer, William Weld, a future Republican governor of Massachusetts, were quickly called into Doar's office and given an assignment.

"We have a research project here," Doar told them. "We have to find out what constitutes grounds for impeachment of a president, and there doesn't seem to be any case directly on point.

"So let's see. It's Friday afternoon. I don't want to ruin your weekend. Why don't you have the memo on my desk Tuesday morning?"

Months later, Weld said, the group was still trying to figure out exactly what "high crimes and misdemeanors" meant. Did the president have to commit an actual crime that was on the books? What if he had moved to a foreign country and started a life there? Wouldn't that be an impeachable offense? At the same time, violations of other laws might not be serious enough to remove a president from office.

The group was divided into teams. One pieced together every detail of the Watergate burglary and another looked into other Nixon administration missteps. Hillary was assigned to the constitutional and legal-research team and given several other projects, from the fascinating to the intensely tedious.

To keep politics out of the process as much as possible, a Democrat often shared an office with a Republican, and staffers were told to keep political viewpoints to themselves. To show respect for the process, they were told to refer to Nixon only as "the president," rather than by name.

Doar, a moderate Republican, barred all of them from talking to the press; the process was so secretive that some staffers didn't even tell their spouses what they were working on. For extra security, the office had separate wastebaskets for sensitive documents. Clerks collected the sensitive trash daily and drove it directly to a rubbish dump.

There were only three female lawyers on the staff, and they sometimes had to remind the male lawyers that they had been hired to do legal work. To make their point, someone added a sign to the office coffee machine: "The women in this office were not hired to make coffee. Make it yourself or call on one of these liberated men to do so." A list followed.

When she started, Hillary didn't think much about appearance, showing up in blue jeans and blue work shirts. But since a member of Congress might drop in at any time, she learned to dress more professionally.

As part of her job, Hillary was asked to research American impeachment cases, which often involved federal judges who drank too much. Another staffer researched British cases.

Computers at the time were big and complicated, and Doar didn't trust them much. So rather than creating computer databases, Hillary worked with her boss, Joseph Woods, to create a way to organize important facts and make them available.

For instance, when Nixon learned that the Watergate burglars had been caught, he threw an ashtray across the room. Hillary and Woods worked out a method where information like that was typed up on a small index card with enough carbon paper to make seven copies. Each of those copies could be filed in a different place. Then they devised punch cards, where someone could punch out certain holes for certain categories. When the cards were lined up, someone could run a long knitting needle through the open holes and pull up all the information in a certain category.

It was a crude method, and ultimately it didn't work all that well, though the total number of index cards eventually exceeded 500,000. It was "essentially grunt work," Woods said later.

She also worked with Woods on a memo that outlined the procedures the House Judiciary Committee would follow. Because the options were open, they asked committee members about their ideas for the rules and based the memo on what they learned.

For a twenty-six-year-old just out of law school, it was a heady experience to work on a staff composed of some of the country's best young lawyers, helping to determine the fate of a sitting president. "I felt like I was walking around with my mouth open all the time" in amazement, Hillary said later. She approached the work with great determination, "as absolutely the most important thing in the world," recalled Tom Bell, who shared an office with her. "I saw it as important, but also as a job. To her it may have been more of a mission."

She was also winning over her more-experienced colleagues. "She was obviously extremely bright and capable, and she pretty quickly made herself indispensable," said Richard Gill, who was in his early thirties at the time. If someone had a task "and you wanted it done right and quickly, you gave it to Hillary to do," he said.

She was such a standout that Doar began to treat her as more than a rookie lawyer, including her in big-picture discussions. "On occasion, he would call her in and bounce something off her," Bell recalled.

Lawyers on the staff were expected to work day and night, returning to their desks after a quick dinner, and to show up on Sundays. Because they spent so much time together, many of them formed close friendships, but they had almost no social life. Hillary was staying in a spare bedroom in a townhouse owned by Sara Ehrman, from the Texas McGovern campaign. Sometimes they caught up over yogurt in the kitchen at midnight.

Hillary ran up big phone bills talking to Bill in Arkansas and offered daily advice on his fledgling campaign for the House. Colleagues say she fretted when she didn't hear from him and worried that he might be seeing other women while she was in Washington. Many young women were working on his campaign, and they found Bill very attractive; the politician-to-be returned the attention. Still, Hillary lit up when he came to visit.

Because Hillary didn't have a car, Ehrman dropped her off at her office at 7:00 a.m. Bernard Nussbaum, who was one of the oldest lawyers on the team at thirty-seven, often drove young lawyers home so they didn't have to take a train late at night.

One night, Hillary was the last to be dropped off, and she told Nussbaum she wanted him to meet her boyfriend, who was coming to visit. Nussbaum said he'd be happy to meet Bill and innocently asked what law firm he was going to work for.

"Oh, no, he's not going to a firm; he's going into politics," Hillary told him. In fact, she told him, he was going to run for governor of Arkansas and "he's gonna be president of the United States."

Perhaps it was exhaustion, or the endless pressure, or simple frustration, but Nussbaum exploded at what seemed like a ridiculously silly comment from an inexperienced kid. "That's the stupidest thing I ever heard," he screamed at her. "What kind of child are you that your boyfriend's going to be president of the United States?"

His anger ignited hers. Glaring, she responded with a few unprintable words, then added—before slamming the car door—"you haven't even met him and you're just a big jerk!"

The next day, Nussbaum went to apologize, and Hillary beat him to it. They made up, and he took care to be cordial when he met Bill, wishing him luck with his campaign.

As the inquiry progressed, the evidence began to pile up against Nixon, especially as the group transcribed the tapes the president had made. Hillary teamed with another colleague to dissect how the White House worked, who gave orders, and who followed them. To figure that out, she spent time in a soundproof room with big headphones on, listening to what became known as the "tape of tapes."

"It was Nixon taping himself listening to the tapes, making up his defenses to what he heard on the tapes," she said. "So you would hear Nixon talk, and then you'd hear very faintly the sound of a taped prior conversation with Nixon" and his top aides. As he heard his own conversations, she recalled, he would say, "What I meant when I said that was . . ."

"It was surreal, unbelievable," Hillary said later.

In May 1974, the House Judiciary Committee began hearings on whether to recommend impeachment. In late July, the U.S. Supreme Court ordered the president to release additional tapes that he had refused to provide to the House of Representatives. Just a few days later, the House Judiciary Committee adopted three articles of impeachment, setting the impeachment process in motion. The president, it concluded, had misused his power in violation of the oath of office, had interfered with the Watergate investigation, and had failed to comply with its subpoenas for tapes.

Though Nixon had said he knew nothing of the break-in, and had only learned of the cover-up in 1973, his future was looking grim. In early August, in response to the Supreme Court ruling, the White House released a transcript of a tape showing that Nixon had discussed how to cover up the mess back in the summer of 1972 and had even tried to interfere with the Federal Bureau of Investigation's inquiry into the burglary. Though many Americans still supported Nixon, his advisers told him that his chance of surviving an impeachment trial was slim.

As a member of the Judiciary Committee legal staff, Hillary aids John Doar *(centre)* at a 1974 hearing on Capitol Hill.

On 8th August 1974, the thirty-seventh president of the United States told the American people that he would resign from office at noon the next day, the first and only president in American history to do so.

For Doar's staff, the end was quick and almost anti-climactic. They watched Nixon's speech on an old black-and-white television, and true to their efforts to be impartial, no one made a sound. But suddenly, their work was over.

As the mountain of evidence grew, Hillary had considered what she would do next. At one point, she told a senior lawyer, she wanted to be a trial lawyer like him.

"Impossible," he told her.

"Why?" she asked.

"Because you won't have a wife," he said. A good trial lawyer, he explained, needed a wife at home to take care of grocery shopping and other personal needs, "like making sure I had clean socks for court." Whether he was kidding wasn't clear—but the legal business obviously wasn't yet used to female lawyers.

She had another plan, anyway. When she visited Bill in Fayetteville, she met the dean of the law school. He was so impressed that he told her to call him if she ever wanted to teach there. In the spring, she made the call and managed to get away for a few days to interview. She was offered a job—and by the time Nixon had resigned, she had accepted it.

Nussbaum tried to talk her out of it, telling her she should join a law firm in New York or Washington. Sara Ehrman also opposed the decision. She offered to drive Hillary, her boxes, and her bike to Arkansas. About every twenty minutes along the way, she asked Hillary if she knew what she was doing, and she told Hillary exactly what she thought.

"You are crazy," Ehrman said. "You're going to this rural remote place—and you'll wind up married to some country lawyer."

Ehrman had worked to help women get opportunities, and she felt Hillary was throwing her big chance away. Ehrman finally stopped her pestering when Hillary said simply that she was going because she loved Bill Clinton.

They pulled into Fayetteville on a football Saturday. Young men crowded the streets and hung from the lampposts. Many were wearing pig hats and shouting the Razorback cheer: "Wooooooo, pig, sooie!" It was like seeing Hillary dumped in a trough.

"And that," Ehrman said, "is when I started to cry."

But when she saw Bill Clinton speak the next day, she had a change of heart. "I didn't question her judgment anymore."

Later Hillary confessed, "My family and friends thought I had lost my mind. I was a little bit concerned about that as well." But, she said, "It was clear to me, as much as I would have liked to have denied it, that there was something very special about Bill, and there was something very important between us."

Bill campaigned aggressively for a seat in the U.S. House of Representatives—but it wasn't enough to defeat the Republican incumbent.

One of them had to give, and Bill's determination to serve Arkansas was more defined than her desire to try to do some good in the world. Part of her wanted to stay on her career path and work on behalf of children. But ultimately, she decided, "I had to deal with a whole other side of life—the emotional side, where we live and where we grow and, when all is said and done, where the most important parts of life take place."

An ad for a budding politician's first race.

So in late summer 1974, she rented a place in Fayetteville to see if she and Bill could live that side of life together. They were two young, bright, extremely talented people with their adult lives still to come. Who could possibly predict what was ahead?

PART TWO

ARKANSAS

"Every moment wasted looking back keeps us from moving forward. Life is too short, time is too precious, and the stakes are too high to dwell on what might have been."

11

FAYETTEVILLE

Just a couple of days before school began, Hillary was assigned to teach criminal law and trial advocacy, though she had never actually tried a criminal trial.

Bill had taken a leave from teaching. Earlier in the year, he had secured the Democratic nomination for the U.S. House seat held by Hammerschmidt. If Bill somehow won the election, he could quickly be headed to Washington. There was still a chance that Arkansas might be just a stopover for Hillary.

While Hillary was in Washington, Bill had won the primary with help from—of all people—Hillary's dad. In May, Hugh Rodham and his youngest son, Tony, showed up in Arkansas in Hugh's Cadillac and stayed for several weeks. "Hillary told me I ought to come down here and help you out," her father told a campaign worker.

Though Hugh remained a Republican, he was quick to tell people who called the campaign headquarters that they should support Bill. He and Tony also plastered Clinton signs all over the district's rural areas. "We'd go out and nail 'em on anything that didn't move and some things that did," Tony said. As they made their way around northwest Arkansas, the campaign got calls asking about the Yankees with the Illinois license plates.

They may also have been there for another reason: Some on the campaign believed Hillary wanted them to keep an eye on Bill, who reportedly was romancing a college-student volunteer. The young woman only truly disappeared from the campaign after Hillary showed up that autumn.

Despite running against two opponents, Bill took the lead in the primary election, and then won the run-off in June. He made headway, but without Nixon still in place as the bad guy, his Republican opponent held on. The election was close, but in the end, Bill got just 48 per cent of the vote. They would stay in Fayetteville.

By then, Hillary was establishing herself as a tough, demanding teacher. In the classroom, Bill was conversational, rambling, and easy to distract. Hillary was aggressive, quizzing her students and staying on subject. Bill already had a reputation as a generous grader who gave mostly As and Bs—when he got around to it. While he was campaigning during the spring, he brought exams with him and managed to lose a few. Horrified, he offered the students the chance to retake the exam or to pass the class without an actual grade; the sloppiness didn't win

Hillary and Bill during the first campaign.

him any new fans. Hillary, by contrast, wrote challenging tests and didn't mind giving Cs.

As part of her job, Hillary was asked to lead the university's legal aid clinic, which handled civil cases, and a prisoners' assistance project. To get support for the clinic, she had to win over local judges and lawyers, who worried about losing business to a free clinic. To win backing, she agreed to take criminal cases for poor people who were entitled to a court-appointed lawyer. Under her direction, the clinic worked with 300 clients in her first year.

In the spring of 1975, a judge assigned her to represent a factory worker accused of raping a twelve-year-old girl. The man specifically asked for a female lawyer, and

Hillary was plucked from the handful practising in the county. Hillary didn't want to take the case and initially tried to back out, but defying a judge's request was tricky business.

Hillary's forty-one-year-old client insisted he was innocent, and Hillary put enormous energy into representing him. She helped him get out on bond, visited the crime scene, sought independent testing of his clothing, tracked down experts, and demanded reams of information.

She also took a more controversial step: Drawing on her background in child development, she questioned the girl's credibility and emotional stability and requested that she be given a psychological evaluation. That approach was an established tactic in defending rape cases, but one that women's advocates protest because it tries to place blame on the victim—in this case, a child—rather than the offender. That seemed inconsistent for someone who considered herself a supporter of women

Professor Hillary Clinton at work at the University of Arkansas.

and children. At the same time, she had a duty to her client to present the best defense possible.

"She was vigorously advocating for her client. What she did was appropriate," a legal expert told a newspaper later. "It would have been hell on the victim. But that wasn't Hillary's problem."

Hillary's approach poked holes in the case, and later that year, the prosecution agreed to a plea bargain. Her client pleaded guilty to unlawful fondling of a minor, which carried a five-year sentence, rather than first-degree rape, which carried a penalty of thirty years to life in prison.

During the plea hearing, the judge asked Hillary to leave the room before he discussed explicit details of the crime, saying, "I can't talk about these things in front of a lady."

Hillary had to convince him that she was a lawyer, representing the accused.

The judge sentenced her client to a year in jail and four years' probation.

In the coming months, she and some women friends and colleagues helped form a centre that later became the area's first rape crisis centre. She also supported a state law to limit what juries would hear about a rape victim's previous sexual conduct, though the legislation didn't pass.

Despite her reservations about Arkansas, she made close friends in the college town: Ann Henry, a lawyer and wife of a state legislator, and Diane Kincaid, later Diane Blair, a political science professor who became one of her closest confidantes throughout her adult life. Hillary and Bill lived in separate places—the South frowned on unmarried couples (especially politicians) living together—but they still talked a lot, went to movies, and hosted dinners, which were often followed by charades or other games.

At the end of Hillary's first year of teaching, Bill was still talking about marriage, but Hillary wasn't sure whether she should stay or head back East to flex her professional muscle. She took a long trip, visiting friends and former co-workers in Washington, New York, Boston, and Chicago. What was she missing by being in Arkansas?

Bill knew he was asking Hillary to give up a lot. "My political life will be in Arkansas, and this is a woman whose future is limitless," he once told Kincaid. "She could be anything she decides to be. I feel so guilty about bringing her here because then it would be my state, my political life, and my future."

While Hillary was gone, Bill took a more definitive step towards their future. She had commented on a cute house for sale before she left, and he checked it out. It was small, just one bedroom, and it didn't have air-conditioning. But it had a lovely living room and fireplace and was affordable. Bill put down $3,000 and bought it, moving in his furniture and buying new sheets and towels at Wal-Mart.

When he picked her up at the airport, he made his move. "Do you remember that house you liked," he asked her. Actually, she didn't.

He went on, "Well, I bought it, so now you'd better marry me because I can't live in it by myself."

Finally, she said yes.

The news was thrilling to some and crushing to others. Betsey Wright, who had worked with them in Texas and would work with them for years in Arkansas, was terribly disappointed. "I had images in my mind that she could be the first woman president," she said.

They planned a small October wedding in the living room of their new house and recruited the Rodham brothers to help paint and get the house ready. Hillary didn't want an engagement ring, and their wedding rings would be family heirlooms. There were no printed invitations.

The day before the wedding, her mother asked about the wedding gown. There wasn't one. They went to the Dillard's department store, where Hillary bought a Victorian lace dress off the rack.

Bill's mother, Virginia, had done her best to come to terms with her son's girlfriend, even though Hillary still made her grind her teeth. She wished she could plop her down "on the edge of my tub and give her some makeup lessons." Finally, she realized that she was asking Bill to choose between his mother and his love and that she would someday regret it. So as best as she could, she changed her attitude.

But even the day of the wedding, she wasn't exactly ecstatic. She was staying at a local hotel, and Bill came to join them for breakfast—and to tell her something important.

"Well?" she said. "Go ahead."

"Hillary's keeping her own name," he told her.

Virginia had never heard of a woman keeping her maiden name and couldn't imagine it. She burst into tears.

Bill said later that Hillary had decided as a child that she would stay Hillary Rodham when she married because she liked her name and she liked her family. It also helped keep her professional life separate from her politician spouse at a time when two-career marriages were as unusual as choosing not to take your husband's last name.

Wedding day, 11th October 1975.

Somehow, Hillary's new mother-in-law pulled it together. On 11th October 1975, just before Hillary turned twenty-eight, a Methodist minister married the couple in front of close friends and family. Later, Bill would say that he couldn't imagine exactly what he was getting into as a married man. "All I knew then was that I loved Hillary, the life,

Hillary's mother, Dorothy, helped pick out her daughter's wedding dress the day before the big event. She would later plan the trip that became their honeymoon.

work, and friends we now had in common, and the promise of what we could do together," he said. Their relationship, he added, "might not ever be perfect, but would certainly never be boring."

After the ceremony, they went to the Henrys' home for a reception for more than 200 people. A tiered cake was topped with yellow roses, and a bubbly fountain offered endless champagne.

Like many occasions in their future, this one turned into a political event. Bill announced to the crowd, the *Arkansas Gazette* reported, that he would be running for office in 1976, either for the U.S. House seat or for

Arkansas attorney general. Then the newlyweds finished the evening dancing at a disco in the basement of the Downtown Motor Inn.

(They would be awakened at 4:00 a.m. by Hillary's brother Tony, who had been stopped by a state trooper while taking a guest home and ended up in jail for driving under the influence. The rest of Bill's wedding night was spent bailing Tony out.)

Ann Henry had tried to warn Hillary that as a political wife, there would be limits on what she could do personally and in her career. The same Hillary who had commanded respect from other lawyers and worked easily with much-older colleagues thought she could navigate her future differently. She might have been naive—or just stubborn.

"I thought at that point that I had it figured out," she said later. "I knew Bill was interested in politics, so he would go off in the morning and do politics.

"I thought I'd married another professional. You marry a doctor or a lawyer, you go off in the morning, you do your job, and you come home," she said. But the reality wasn't like that—not at all.

"What I didn't realize," she confessed later, "was that when you're in a political life, there are a whole different set of obligations that are imposed upon you from the outside." As smart and educated as she was, she still had plenty to learn.

12

LAWYER

Hillary and Bill never got around to planning a honeymoon. Dorothy Rodham helped them out by finding a great deal on a package to Acapulco, Mexico.

In December, the newlyweds went south, along with Hillary's whole family. It was different, for sure, especially since Bill brought a book about death and human existence and spent some of the time writing thank-you notes to wedding guests. But it was a good break from teaching.

By then, Bill was preparing a run for Arkansas attorney general. He had considered running again for the U.S. House of Representatives, but had come to believe he would have more political opportunities within Arkansas. Governors and senators were far more likely to make the leap to president of the United States than sitting representatives.

Bill took the semester off to campaign from Little Rock headquarters, about 200 miles away. Though he had two opponents in the primary, he had already created a powerful political network of friends and supporters in his first political race, and he won the May election with more than 55 per cent of the vote. Because there wasn't a Republican candidate, he was a shoo-in; he and Hillary would be moving to Little Rock in the autumn.

To Hillary, the "big show" in politics in 1976 was the presidential race, pitting Democrat Jimmy Carter, the former Georgia governor, against Gerald Ford, who had become president after Nixon resigned. Though unseating an incumbent is often difficult, Ford was considered vulnerable for his decision to pardon Nixon after his resignation; that meant Nixon couldn't formally be charged with or convicted of any crimes. Hillary and Bill had

With Hillary at his side, Bill campaigns for Arkansas attorney general in 1976, easily winning his first statewide race.

previously met Carter, and at the Democratic National Convention that summer, they offered to work on his campaign. Then they headed out for a two-week holiday to France and Spain, including a stop in the Basque town of Guernica, the subject of the Picasso painting Hillary had learned about in high school.

Bill was asked to run the Carter campaign in Arkansas. In an appointment typical for women at the time, Hillary was tapped to be the Indiana field coordinator, the number two spot. She took a leave from teaching, and the newlyweds again lived apart for several months.

As with campaigning for George McGovern in Texas, working for Carter in Indiana was a losing proposition. The state usually voted Republican, and Carter was a tough sell. Hillary's job was to find volunteers in every city and county in the state, and to get the right people on the podium during campaign events.

When the campaign couldn't find volunteers to handle the phone banks, she arranged to hire workers at the minimum wage, including senior citizens and some clients of a bail-bond firm that used to occupy the campaign office.

She tried to keep morale up, but she was also straight with people when things weren't going well. And she dug in when she thought she was right. "She could out-argue anybody," one campaign worker remembered. "And the last thing you wanted to do, particularly if it was at the end of the day and you were dead tired, was disagree with her. You always knew she was going to win."

Jimmy Carter won Arkansas easily and the national election. He lost Indiana, though he got a respectable 46 per cent of the vote. Hillary would be rewarded in late 1977 with an appointment to the national board of the Legal Services Corporation, which funds legal aid clinics around the country, including the one she ran in Fayetteville. The non-profit was created in 1974 to help poor, disabled, elderly, or military families with a range of legal problems, such as evictions, debt lawsuits, and divorces or custody battles.

In 1978, thirty-year-old Hillary would become chairman of the board, a position she held for about two years. By the end of her term, Legal Services was disbursing more than $300 million a year to legal aid clinics. (She wasn't reappointed after Republican President Ronald Reagan was elected in 1980.)

Once Bill was elected attorney general, Hillary faced another major decision: What would she do in Little Rock?

Practising criminal law or becoming a public defender would be tricky, since any significant case could end up in conflict with the work of the attorney general's office, which handles criminal appeals for the state. There were few female lawyers to begin with and none at the capital city's major law firms, so she didn't have many role models to follow. She could have pursued her interest in children and practised family law, though it might not have been very lucrative or prestigious.

Instead, she decided to practise corporate law—something she had said she didn't want to do—to gain legal experience and provide income for herself and her husband. (Bill earned about $26,000 a year as attorney general, the equivalent of around $100,000 today.)

A prominent Little Rock firm, the Rose Law Firm, was interested. A partner there, Vince Foster, had met Hillary through the Fayetteville legal aid clinic and was impressed with the smart law professor. He and another partner began to recruit her.

Like many law firms in the 1970s, Rose had never had a woman lawyer, and the other lawyers wrestled with the possible consequences: What would their male clients think about a female lawyer? What if she got pregnant? What if she talked about clients with her attorney general husband?

Despite the reservations, Hillary was brought in to meet each partner and associate one by one. Many were nervous meeting a female lawyer, though one senior partner, who had come in after playing tennis, interviewed her while puffing a cigar, with his sweaty bare feet up on the desk between them.

She managed to charm them all and was hired. As a friendly nod to challenges ahead, Foster and his colleague presented her with a copy of the Charles Dickens novel *Hard Times*.

As the only female lawyer in the office, and an outsider at that, she was constantly in someone's crosshairs. Senior partners complained that her clothing was too informal, or not frilly enough, that her hair wasn't coiffed, that she didn't wear makeup, that her glasses were too big and unflattering. She put up a no-smoking sign in her office, at a time when smokers could smoke anywhere. She spoke too freely in meetings and didn't think twice about going out with a lawyer and his wife when Bill was away, which violated some unwritten Southern rule.

Older partners would approach Foster or another friend of hers, Webb Hubbell, and say, "You've got to say something to Hillary" about whatever fashion offense was bothering them. "No thanks," her friends would respond. "Tell her yourself."

Vince Foster, with wife Lisa, Hillary, and Bill, had ties to both Clintons. He was a childhood friend of Bill's in Hope, Arkansas, and Hillary considered him one of her best friends when they worked together at the Rose Law Firm.

Because they were all in the litigation group, Hillary often went to lunch with Foster and Hubbell. The first time they went out, someone called the wives of both men to report that their husbands were eating lunch with another woman. "In Little Rock at that time," Hillary said later, "women did not usually have meals with men who were not their husbands."

Hubbell and Foster saw Hillary as another lawyer and invited her to come along when they went to a restaurant featuring a lunchtime "lingerie-style show," where models walked from table to table showing off a store's fancy nightgowns and robes. Hillary "would go just to laugh at us and tell us what Neanderthals we were," Hubbell remembered.

In time, the three friends began going to the Villa, an Italian restaurant off the beaten path, where they could talk freely and enjoy wine with their meal. (Later, after Bill was elected governor, it was a place Hillary could eat without being interrupted.)

At the office, she managed to avoid some of the grunt work that other associates were assigned, like handling traffic tickets. In her first trial before a jury, she represented a canning company against a man who bought a can of pork and beans containing the back end of a rodent. The man said that the discovery was so upsetting that he couldn't stop spitting, which interfered with his love life.

The company's position was that rodent parts were actually eaten in some parts of the world and that the man who opened the can hadn't really suffered any loss. Hillary was nervous as she made her case to the jury and was relieved when the jury awarded the man only nominal damages. For some time afterwards, however, Bill teased her about her "rat's ass" case.

She also represented a jewellery-sales company run by women with beehive hairdos. They adored their lawyer, and when she won the case, they all wanted to help Hillary with a makeover. She politely declined.

Still, Hillary struggled to find her place as a corporate lawyer in Little Rock, and before long, she began to "take her show on the road," as Hubbell put it, doing other things to broaden her experience. She handled a few criminal cases. She took on some family law cases pro bono (for no pay) including representing foster parents who wanted to keep a child who had been with them for more than two years. Concerned about state policies affecting children's health and education, she joined with others to start Arkansas Advocates for Children and Families to do research and speak up for families.

She also had the responsibilities that went with being Bill's wife, and he wasn't one to sit still. In 1978, sensing an opportunity, Bill decided to run for governor.

His four little-known primary opponents went after his record and his lawyer wife, questioning her different last name and raising questions about whether her work would pose a conflict of interest for him. "We've had

When Bill ran for governor, Hillary campaigned with him and also on her own, winning praise from the press for her speaking skills and informed answers.

enough lawyers in the Governor's Mansion," one candidate said. "One is enough. Two would be too much."

As Bill travelled from county to county and vigorously defended his wife and her work, Hillary focused on his policy and strategy, and also served as something of a lookout for trouble. "Bill sees the light and sunshine about people, and Hillary sees their darker side," said Rudy Moore, Bill's campaign manager. "She has much more ability than he does to see who's with you, who's against you, and to make sure they don't take advantage of you."

Ahead of the primary election, Hillary often spoke on his behalf. A local newspaper called her an "accomplished speaker," with particularly detailed answers for policy questions. "She intends to be actively involved in policy making if Clinton is governor," it reported.

On the night of 30th May Bill sat at the top of a stairwell in the old house that was his campaign headquarters, "cheering like a kid in the bleachers at a baseball game" as volunteers posted county by county results. Bill won easily and declared victory that night in front of a thousand supporters at Little Rock's Camelot Inn.

He didn't have much of a Republican opponent, and he won the general election that November in a landslide, with more than 60 per cent of the vote. At thirty-two years old, Bill Clinton became the nation's youngest governor in forty years, an accomplishment that would attract national attention for him—and his unusual wife.

13

GOVERNOR

With the youthful Bill Clinton moving into the Governor's Mansion in early 1979, Arkansans got a closer look at the new First Lady. And their response was, well, not unlike that of Bill's mom.

Hillary holds the Bible for Bill's swearing-in as the nation's youngest governor in forty years.

At the least, they were confused. What was with the unstyled hair and those oversized glasses? The First Lady intended to have a career? Didn't she want a family? And what was the deal with her name? That truly seemed to baffle people, even well beyond the Natural State.

The *New York Times* profiled six male political newcomers, and the short item on Bill pointed out that he "is married to an ardent feminist, Hillary Rodham, who will certainly be the first First Lady of Arkansas to keep her maiden name." The Associated Press wire service felt compelled to explain in more detail. An AP story in *Newsday* said that he was married to a former Yale Law classmate and Little Rock lawyer who kept her own name. "She decided to do that when she was nine, long before

For Bill's first inauguration as governor, Hillary *(far right)* commissioned a dress by Little Rock designer Connie Fails *(far left)*.

women's lib came along," Bill said. "People wouldn't mind if they knew how old-fashioned she was in every conceivable way."

A profile in the *Arkansas Democrat* noted, "Despite the fact that she keeps her maiden name, the wife of Arkansas's new governor, Bill Clinton, claims she's really an old-fashioned girl."

How was she old-fashioned? She told the reporter that she believed in the Golden Rule—"Do unto others as you would have them do unto you"—and was a firm believer in a strong work ethic. But she also made clear that she wasn't cut out to be a traditional, full-time First Lady. "I need to maintain my interests and my commitments. I need my own identity, too," she said. Within a few months, in fact, she would be named a partner in the Rose Law Firm after just two years there, though such a promotion often takes much longer.

Her professional accomplishments didn't interest the Style reporter, who also misspelled Hillary's name with one *l* throughout. "Do the Clintons plan a family?" she asked, ignoring the name issue altogether.

"Oh, yes," Hillary responded.

"How many children?"

"Well, one to start with," Hillary said with a smile. Pressed, she added, "I think two or three children make a nice family."

Delving into more personal questions, the reporter asked: Would Hillary keep working after having children?

Hillary was noncommittal. "I couldn't say whether I would continue practising law or not. These things can't be planned, just like my life as the governor's wife," she said.

In the meantime, they had Zeke, a cocker spaniel who would become the First Dog. She and Bill had both had dogs before (and she had a cat as a child), but, she said, this was their first together.

What Hillary didn't say was that she and Bill had been trying to start a family for some time and that it wasn't going well. They made an appointment with a fertility specialist—but first went on a short holiday to Bermuda. Not long after the holiday, Hillary found out she was pregnant.

Bill joined her in birthing classes to prepare for natural childbirth, a relatively new trend that some local officials found bewildering. Hillary went into labour three weeks before her mid-March due date, shortly after Bill had arrived home from a trip. Bill and four state troopers scrambled to pack up the car. Hillary had made a list of the items she would need to take, including a small ice pack. When she got to the car, she saw a well-meaning state trooper lugging a full and heavy rubbish bag.

"What is that?" she asked.

"It's the ice you need," he told her.

Chelsea Victoria Clinton was born 27th February 1980, named after Judy Collins's version of the song "Chelsea Morning." She weighed in at six pounds and one and three-quarter ounces, and Bill carried her all over the hospital to show her off.

Until she moved into the Governor's Mansion, Hillary had been relatively anonymous. But now she and Bill shared space with cooks, housekeepers, state troopers, and a mansion manager, who would know intimate details of their personal business, from their sleeping habits to any angry outbursts. As would be the case whenever her private life was invaded, Hillary grew ever more protective about what the outside world would see of her, and she was especially protective of Chelsea.

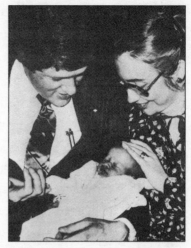

Chelsea's birth in February 1980 was front-page news in the Little Rock newspapers.

The local newspaper reported on 29th February that "Governor Clinton and his wife, Hillary Rodham" had become parents—but it wouldn't have a photo of the new arrival for almost a week.

Though Hillary and Bill wanted to have a bigger family, nature didn't cooperate. Even in the mid-1990s, when she was in her late forties, Hillary said she would love to have more children and mentioned that they had even discussed the possibility of adopting, but hadn't acted on it. "My view is if it happens, it happens," she said of the possibility of a bigger family. But it didn't.

Hillary, as a new mother at thirty-two, was able to take four months off from work because she could afford to as part of a two-earner, professional family. The leaders of the Rose Law Firm questioned whether she should be paid for any time off, though she ultimately received some pay during her leave. Some even thought it was wrong for the new mother to go back to work.

Hillary didn't consider an alternative. She had always worked—and she was also insecure about money. In 1978, when Bill was still attorney general, their combined earnings were $54,593, an income equal to about $200,000 in today's dollars. Around that time, Hillary and Bill also began investing in riskier ventures that they hoped would give them financial security later.

In spring 1978, they ran into an acquaintance, Jim McDougal, at a local restaurant, and he offered them a "sure-thing deal." They would buy a large tract of land in the Ozarks of northwest Arkansas, known for its lakes and outdoor activities. The property would be divided into smaller lots to be sold for holiday and retirement homes. McDougal was something of a wheeler-dealer, and Bill had known him for years, even investing with him previously on a small and reasonably profitable real-estate deal.

Hillary and Bill signed on. The two couples borrowed money for the down payment to buy the land, so they didn't put any cash up front. Over the next couple of years, Hillary and Bill wrote cheques to pay interest on the loans for what became Whitewater Development Company. Their timing was terrible: Beginning in 1978, inflation began to soar and interest rates on real-estate loans skyrocketed, eventually peaking above 18 per cent, far too expensive for most people to borrow for a holiday home. The lots barely sold. In time, the investment would grow even more expensive, both financially and politically, becoming perhaps one of the most costly bad investments any politician has ever made.

Later in 1978, Hillary had better luck with another financial move. Her good friend from Fayetteville, Diane Kincaid, was dating Jim Blair, a smart, personable lawyer who represented the chicken giant Tyson Foods. The couples were close, in touch regularly and often swapping piles of books, such as murder mysteries by Tony Hillerman and Dorothy Sayers, biographies, and contemporary novels by the likes of Joan Didion.

Blair was making a fortune playing commodities, a kind of investing that essentially is a bet on whether the price of goods like corn, coffee, cattle, or pork bellies will rise or fall. Investors can put up very little money and make a lot of money back—but they can also end up losing more than they put in initially, making it a highly risky kind of gamble that isn't for the faint-hearted. Adding to the risk, investors often borrow from a brokerage so they can invest more.

Jim Blair was on such a hot streak and making so much money on these investments that he encouraged his law partners and friends to join him. In October 1978, with Blair's help, Hillary invested $1,000 in the futures market with a northwest Arkansas broker. Though she was a commodities novice, her account mostly went up. Unlike most investors, she was never asked to put up more cash when her account went down.

Between October 1978 and July 1979, following Blair's lead, Hillary rode a strong market in commodity prices and made more than $99,000 in profits on her small investment. Then, pregnant with Chelsea, she said, "I lost my nerve for gambling," and she closed the account.

In September 1979, Bill as governor officiated at the marriage of Diane and Jim, and Hillary stood in as their "best person."

Bill officiates and a pregnant Hillary is "best person" at the September 1979 wedding of Jim Blair and Diane Kincaid, their good friends from Fayetteville.

Later that year, Hillary opened another account in Little Rock, but left commodities trading for good in the spring of 1980, after Chelsea was born. She said she realized the funds could pay for Chelsea's college someday—and more. Those profits would have the buying power of more than $300,000 today, meaning Hillary was a big and unusually lucky winner.

The financial security would give them a cushion that would come in handy, even though they didn't have to worry about a home mortgage or grocery bills while living in the Governor's Mansion. Bill's term was a rocky one. Only a few weeks after their Denim and Diamonds inaugural ball, the *Arkansas Gazette* discovered that the new governor and his wife hadn't properly paid taxes on their cars.

In fact, the paper learned, Bill had been paying taxes in Fayetteville's Washington County, even though he and Hillary had been in Little Rock for two years. And somehow, she had received new license plates even though no one had paid taxes on her 1975 Fiat for two years.

Bill didn't have good answers for the lapse, saying that where he paid taxes was an unsettled legal question and that he would ask his accountant to look into it. It wasn't really a legal question, though; state law clearly said that taxes should be paid in the county where the car is located.

A couple of days later, he paid the taxes on the Fiat. It was a tiny amount, about $79, and the first time he was publicly reprimanded—but it wouldn't be the last time Bill's or Hillary's actions and judgment would be questioned.

The rest of the state felt the pain of car-registration taxes during his term. In an effort to raise money to fix the state's roads, Bill had proposed an increase on taxes for big trucks, while taxing cars based on their value rather than their weight, which was the current method. But the proposal changed as it moved through the state legislature, and the state ended up doubling the taxes on heavy cars, like pickup trucks.

Bill could have vetoed the bill to hold out for a better plan. Instead, he signed it. Residents went to renew their so-called car tags on their birthdays, and the present many of them got from their new governor was a painful tax increase. "It was the single dumbest mistake I ever made in politics," he would later say.

Other challenges followed. There were tornados in the spring and a horrible heat wave in the summer. President Carter decided to house thousands of Cuban refugees at a federal facility in Arkansas, and they rioted, prompting the locals to pull out their rifles and shotguns.

Running for reelection in the May 1980 primary, Bill faced an elderly turkey farmer who had never been a serious candidate. But in a reflection of Arkansans' dissatisfaction, the older man got almost a third of the vote.

Still, polls showed Bill solidly ahead in the general election. Preoccupied with Chelsea, Hillary wasn't as involved in this campaign as she had been in others. But when the Republican opponent began running negative ads about the Cuban riots, she took notice and pushed Bill to respond aggressively. "Hillary keeps telling me I don't understand the modern world," he said, explaining that he wanted to just go out and talk to people.

Her intuition told her to fight back. "I couldn't persuade anyone else to ignore the polls that showed Bill winning," she said later. She also learned a powerful lesson about "the piercing power of negative ads to convert voters through distortion."

Hillary's instincts were right. As Republican Ronald Reagan took the presidency from Jimmy Carter in November 1980, Bill Clinton became the first Arkansas governor to be denied a second term in twenty-six years. The reality of it crushed him. Unable to face his supporters, he sent Hillary out that night to thank them.

Bill spent weeks trying to get his bearings. Hillary began to pick up the pieces, and within days, she was seeking political advisers for a comeback. She also looked inwards. True, car tags, Cubans, and Carter had been problems. But she also blamed herself.

14

COMEBACK

In 1981, Hillary and Bill both replayed the loss over and over.

On reflection, Hillary began to see how she hadn't fit the mould of the governor's wife. Her thick glasses had long been a source of criticism, along with her hair and her fashion style—or rather her lack of it. And her name continued to grate. It had been an issue in both campaigns for governor, and many in Arkansas just couldn't get used to it.

"I think I failed to appreciate how important in political terms an elected person's spouse is to the voters," she said later. "In retrospect, what I didn't appreciate was how personally people viewed those things."

She and Bill moved to a house in a friendly voting district, and Bill took a job at another Little Rock law firm. But he mostly went through the motions of practising law, instead obsessing over what had happened and

Hillary and Bill in the late 1970s.

whether the political future he had planned on for so many years was over. He also began regularly attending a local Baptist church and singing in the choir, something he hadn't done since high school.

Hillary, who was already attending a Methodist Church, continued her work at the Rose firm, without having to worry about any political conflicts. As she pushed her husband to move forward, to lay the groundwork for the next election, she also began a personal makeover. She had tried wearing hard contact lenses before, but couldn't keep them in her eyes. With soft contact lenses now available, she traded her Coke-bottle glasses for new eyewear.

She began to dye her hair and adopted a softer

hairstyle—though she refused to commit to one look. "I like to experiment with my hair," she said later, answering yet another question about it. "I just think you should have some fun with your life and not take yourself real seriously."

She began wearing makeup and hired a fashion consultant. Most personally, she wrestled with whether to keep her name and her individual identity.

Bill told her it was her choice. But her friends, including her law partner Webb Hubbell pointed out the problems it caused. The esteemed lawyer Vernon Jordan came to Little Rock to give a speech, and over a breakfast of instant grits in her kitchen, he told her the right thing to do was to take Bill's name.

The new governor would have to run again in 1982, and with the help of political consultants, Bill was getting revved up to challenge him.

Finally Hillary decided: "It was more important for Bill to be governor again than for me to keep my maiden name."

On Chelsea's second birthday, in 1982, Bill Clinton announced that he was running as a Democratic candidate for governor and was ready for a "good and hot" campaign. Hillary had an announcement of her own: She would now be Mrs. Bill Clinton, and she would take a leave from the law firm to work on the campaign.

While Bill was a natural campaigner, Hillary was a quick learner. With Chelsea on her hip, she knocked on

doors, and she attend-
ed campaign events
with and without Bill.
Sometimes, an aide
remembered, Chelsea
would say, "I want my
mama." And then the
toddler would add,
"Mommy go make
'peech."

Hillary had always
been a good speaker,
but now she got bet-
ter at the politician's
art of pressing the

The Clintons were protective of their only
child, but Chelsea was also a regular on the
campaign trail for much of her childhood.

flesh, connecting with voters at fish fries and Rotary lun-
cheons. Despite her Illinois roots and outspoken nature,
the *Arkansas Gazette* noted, "She has become a good hand-
shaking campaigner in the traditional Arkansas style."

She could also give as good as she got. When the
incumbent governor declined to debate Bill and changed
a schedule so he wouldn't appear at the same place as
Hillary, she had a comeback. He "would probably try to
avoid being in the same room as Chelsea," she told a
reporter. Chelsea—who was two years old—"could debate
him and win."

Hillary was also involved in campaign strategy. This
time, no one backed away from negative campaigning. All

the effort worked. Bill led the pack of Democratic candidates in the primary and won the run-off. In November, he easily reclaimed the governor's office, and the family returned to the Governor's Mansion.

Rejuvenated and humbled, Bill went to work, and he put Hillary to work, too. In his first term, he had named her chair of a rural health committee, where she kept a low profile. This time, one of his key goals was to overhaul the state's lagging education system. He chose Hillary Rodham Clinton to chair a new commission to address school standards.

The Clintons revel in Bill's win in the 1982 Democratic primary runoff, which put him in position to reclaim the governorship he had so painfully lost.

Hillary later wrote in her autobiography that she told Bill putting her in charge would be a bad idea. She turned him down, she said, but he insisted. But Bill told a journalist that after he and Hillary talked about it, she volunteered.

"Maybe I'll do it," she told him, by his account.

He pointed out that she had just finished a long leave for the campaign.

"Yeah," she said, "but this may be the most important thing you ever do, and you have to do it right."

When Bill announced his choice, he made clear that her appointment reflected the significance of the effort. "This guarantees that I will have a person who is closer to me than anyone else overseeing a project that is more important to me than anything else," he said.

It was a risky assignment. Few subjects stir up as much opinion and emotion as schools and teachers,

Hillary wears a dress of lacy taupe silk to Bill's second inauguration in 1983.

and it was especially tricky in a state where each school district had been able to determine its own courses, requirements, and class size. But it also played to Hillary's expertise in children's issues and appealed to her inner policy wonk.

As she began her work, Hillary was surprised by what she found at Arkansas schools. At Maine South in Park Ridge, she had a choice of foreign language, maths, and science courses, as well as Advanced Placement classes. But in Arkansas nearly fifteen years later, many schools—especially small, rural ones—didn't have nearly the same offerings. More than 160 Arkansas high schools failed to offer either art, music, physics, or foreign languages. Dozens of others didn't offer chemistry or advanced maths. It was tough to comprehend that so many of the state's students "would never be exposed to what I was exposed to in the fifties and sixties," she said.

In July 1983, the fifteen-member commission held hearings in each of the state's seventy-five counties, giving thousands of citizens a chance to share their views. At one meeting, a school superintendent bragged that his schools were doing "a fine job" and encouraged a young man in the front row to speak up about the quality of his education. Squirming, the young man responded, "I sure wish I could have taken Spanish."

At the end of the month, Hillary testified before a group of state legislators, giving them a preview of some of her committee's thinking, which included mandatory full-day kindergarten, smaller classes for elementary grades, and more requirements for high school graduation. Students also would be tested at the end of third, sixth, and eighth grades and would have to pass the eighth-grade test to go to high school.

"When you play, you should play hard. And when you work, you should work hard. But you shouldn't confuse the two," she told the legislators, repeating a quote that had been a favourite of her dad's.

She was so articulate and poised that state Representative Lloyd George, a cattle farmer and critic of Bill, could hardly contain his praise. "I think we've elected the wrong Clinton," he said. (Hillary wasn't moved by his compliment, later attributing his enthusiasm to his surprise that a woman could actually talk about the subject in detail.)

In the autumn, Bill called a special session of the state legislature and asked it to pass a one-cent increase in the sales tax to better fund the schools. The state Supreme Court had struck down Arkansas's method of funding schools, and a new plan—with new taxes—was needed. Included in his request were some of Hillary's new standards and raises for teachers, plus a new and highly controversial proposal: requiring teachers to pass a competency test.

Both Bill and Hillary thought the test was needed to raise confidence in the schools and to satisfy people who needed to justify the higher cost of education. But the union representing teachers was furious. It argued that such a test was insulting to teachers and unnecessary, and it accused Bill of racism because it believed the test was aimed at black teachers.

After much wrangling, state lawmakers raised the sales tax to four cents on the dollar from three cents, a hefty increase, and approved both teacher raises and the new test.

The teachers union then tried suing, unsuccessfully. The bitterness toward Hillary and Bill lingered for years. "I spent a lot of time being yelled at and cussed at and snubbed," Hillary said. Teachers hissed at her, and one school librarian called her "lower than a snake's belly." She learned not to take it personally.

In March, the state education board adopted the rest of the recommendations, including a longer school year, more rigorous graduation requirements, and smaller class sizes.

Her committee became known as the "Hillary committee." For all the fuss and furore about her last name, it turned out that it didn't much matter. She was mostly known by her first name anyway.

For her work, Hillary won several honours, including Arkansas Woman of the Year in 1983 and Arkansas Press Broadcasters Newsmaker of the Year in 1984.

The experience whet her appetite for political policy work and tied her to education in the state. In 1985, she read about an Israeli programme to help three- to five-year-olds prepare for school, and asked an assistant to help bring HIPPY—then known as Home Instruction Program for Preschool Youngsters—to Arkansas. The programme, which provides training, support, and materials for parents so they can prepare their young children for reading, reached thousands of families and became a model for other states and communities.

But the thirty-five-year-old Hillary also had to go back to work, for herself and for her family. Bill earned $35,000 a year during his entire time as governor; that was the equivalent of around $82,500 in his second term, but only about $63,000 in 1990, thanks to inflation. (He also got room and board.) With all her other responsibilities, Hillary really hadn't devoted her full energy to legal work. Her not-really-full-time status grated on some of her law partners, and her leaves of absence in 1982 and 1983 were "a financial disadvantage," she said. (Still, their tax returns showed that she had income in 1983 of about $83,000, about $195,000 in today's dollars.)

Her many roles were multiplying: wife, mother, campaign strategist, policy adviser, First Lady, and breadwinner.

15

MOM

Although Hillary was busy, she tried to keep Chelsea the centre of her focus. As often as possible, the family ate dinner together and took turns saying grace. Hillary and Bill also set aside one night just for family activities, whether it was playing games, taking a walk, or playing miniature golf.

Hillary and Bill took turns reading to Chelsea and saying prayers at night. On Saturdays, Hillary took her to ballet class. Afterwards, they had lunch and spent mother-daughter time together.

As an overachiever herself, Hillary had high expectations for her little girl. She insisted that Chelsea learn how to tie her own shoes both to develop hand-eye coordination and to enjoy the rewards of accomplishment. Bill's mom bought Chelsea shoes with Velcro straps, but Hillary wouldn't let her wear them until she mastered bows.

Later, as a pre-teen, Chelsea told her she wanted pierced ears. "Young lady, you are not going to poke holes in your head!" responded a mother who had once written that children should be allowed more decisions. She and Bill told Chelsea she had to wait until she was at least thirteen.

Juggling work, civic activities, and family, Hillary wasn't embarrassed to try to make it all work. She and Bill made it to softball games and ballet recitals. Once she called the chair of the state Board of Education to see if they could move their meeting to a shopping mall so Hillary could see Chelsea sing with her school choir.

Bill easily won reelection in 1984, but in 1986, he faced challenges by two former governors seeking comebacks

Hillary with Chelsea around 1984.

The family at the governor's mansion, 1985.

of their own. With Chelsea now in school, her parents wanted her to begin to understand the dark side of politics.

One night at dinner when Chelsea was about six years old, Hillary explained that Bill was running for another term and that some people may say "terrible things about him." Hillary and Bill tried to turn the lesson into a game. They encouraged Chelsea to pretend to be Bill. Why should people vote for him?

Then Bill pretended to be an opponent who said that Bill Clinton was mean to people. That upset their young daughter. But as they played the game over several evenings, Chelsea made up speeches for her father and even for one of his opponents. Young as she was, she built up a thicker skin about the political process—and also learned how to point out the shortcomings and missteps of political challengers.

Bill was re-elected, and because the governor's term had changed, he wouldn't have to run again until 1990.

Now in his fourth term, he and Hillary were getting national attention. The two of them had been the only Arkansans named on a 1984 *Esquire* magazine list of about 270 "best and brightest" Americans under forty years old. Fewer than a quarter of the honourees were women, and Hillary, at thirty-seven years old, joined a list with celebrities like Meryl Streep and Glenn Close, astronaut Sally Ride, and cookie-maker Debbi Fields.

She already was on the Yale Law School Executive Committee and was board chair of Marian Wright Edelman's Children's Defense Fund, and companies,

The Clinton family at the 1987 inaugural ball, beginning Bill's fourth term as governor.

looking for more women on their boards of directors, came calling. In 1986, she was elected to the board of fast-growing Wal-Mart Stores Inc., based in Bentonville, just north of Fayetteville.

The appointment raised some eyebrows. Wal-Mart was one of the state's largest companies, and Bill had worked closely with it. Hillary was the first woman on the board, and some sniped that founder Sam Walton had chosen the governor's wife for political reasons—especially since Hillary didn't have much corporate experience.

At the time, Wal-Mart was a fast-growing regional retailer that was expanding nationally. Walton had been reluctant to name women as store managers and executives. Hillary pushed him to promote more women, but change was slow. By 1989, the company had two female vice presidents out of sixty-eight top executives.

Hillary also led an environmental advisory committee for the company, which encouraged Wal-Mart to push suppliers to use less packaging, to let customers bring in car batteries for recycling, and to add skylights in stores to reduce energy costs. Walton, like many business executives, was also vehemently opposed to his workers' organizing into labour unions. Given Democratic support for labour unions, Hillary was criticized later for failing to press Walton on the issue. The position also was lucrative, initially paying $12,000 a year and increasing to $18,000.

While serving on other corporate and non-profit boards, she continued to have myriad First Lady duties, from hosting dinners to speaking to women's clubs, Girl Scouts, and business groups. A high school yearbook in Augusta, Arkansas, asked her to select the year's Annual King by picking out a photo from the twenty-five senior boys. In a handwritten note to her assistant, she declined, saying, "cannot do this—I'd probably think they all should win."

All those demands cut into the time she spent on legal work. She helped build the firm's business defending clients' patents but didn't have a large client base, and she appeared publicly in just seven cases between 1978 and 1987, according to *American Lawyer* magazine. There were many other clients, the Rose Law Firm said, but it declined to identify them.

"We're very proud of Hillary, and if she had ever quit having two lives and concentrated on the law practice, she'd have been a superb lawyer," the firm's chief operating officer told the magazine.

Still, when the firm changed its method of calculating pay, it rewarded her for "enhancing the firm's reputation" with her non-profit work and First Lady status.

Trying to keep so many balls in the air also had a personal cost. "What I have given up in trying to balance my life," she told an interviewer, "is primarily time with friends. If I had one less role, that's what I'd add back in: the spur-of-the-moment decision to go see a movie, the weekend with friends in Hot Springs, just getting together with people for dinner. But there really is no way."

A family crisis also demanded her attention. In 1984, Bill's brother, Roger, was arrested and charged with selling cocaine to support his drug addiction. The experience was shocking and deeply painful, as well as publicly embarrassing, rocking the family. Bill had to sit on his hands even though he knew his brother was being investigated and then watch as Roger pleaded guilty and was sentenced to prison, where he would serve fourteen months. Even after other setbacks, Hillary would say Roger's ordeal remained among the most wrenching.

By 1987, Bill's energy and effectiveness had caught the eye of Democratic movers and shakers. Now forty years old, he was starting to get restless. President Reagan was ending his second term, and Bill thought voters might be ready for a Democrat to return to the White House.

Though voters had just re-elected him governor, he started to explore the possibility of running for the highest office of all: president of the United States.

Hillary began to contact their extensive network of friends, and her long list included her old boyfriend Geoffrey Shields and her Watergate friend Bernard Nussbaum. She measured the support Bill might get and started to raise the much-needed money to get a campaign off the ground. Bill travelled the country, scouting out Iowa and New Hampshire, important early primary states, and making speeches and appearances at key political events.

The door opened a bit for him in March, when a potential Arkansas candidate, Senator Dale Bumpers, said he would not run. It seemed to open further after a leading candidate, the dashing former Colorado Senator Gary Hart, dropped out of the race.

In early July, both the *New York Times* and *Washington Post* reported that Bill was close to deciding to run. Some campaign staff had been hired, and he had lined up more than $1 million in commitments. "I would say that he has been running for the office for many weeks, many months," said Kip Blakely, executive director of the Arkansas Democratic Party. "He is obviously doing the things that presidential candidates do."

Bill set a deadline of 14th July to make up his mind and reserved a hotel ballroom. Many of his longtime friends travelled to Little Rock as the date approached. He was still terribly torn, and in typical form, he quizzed them all about what he should do.

One old friend had chilling advice. Chelsea was just seven years old, and he told Bill that after a campaign, "your relationship with her will never be the same."

While he visited with another friend, Chelsea wandered into the conversation and asked her father about their upcoming holiday. Bill told her that if he ran for president, he wouldn't be able to go.

"Well," Chelsea responded, "then Mom and I will go without you."

The day before the big scheduled press conference, Bill surprised his supporters, politicos, and the media. He wouldn't run after all.

In a statement and at a press conference the next day, he said he needed personal time and family time, especially for young Chelsea. As he spoke, Hillary wiped away tears.

"My head has told me to enter this race, but my heart says no," he said. For a man who never got to know his biological father, one reason stood out, he said: "A long, long time ago I made a promise to myself that if I was ever lucky enough to have a child, she would never grow up wondering who her father was."

Hillary, too, said she wanted more family time after five gubernatorial campaigns in less than a decade. "I want to go to supper with my husband," she said. "I want to go on holiday with my family. I want my husband back."

Still, they didn't close the door all the way. "For what it's worth," Bill said, "I'd like to be president. Perhaps there will be another day."

Perhaps. But what was unsaid, and what wouldn't become public until much later, was a much darker side to his decision, reflecting a powerful and painful shift in American politics. The reason why Gary Hart, a successful politician and the man who had led the

```
                    HILLARY RODHAM CLINTON

                              1985
                    SPEAKING ENGAGEMENTS

                    xxxxxxxxxxxxxxxxxxxxxx


     MARCH

     MARCH 23, 1985..........ARKANSAS WOMEN'S HISTORY INSTITUTE
                             STATE CAPITOL

     MARCH 25, 1985..........B'NAI BRITH BANQUET
                             LITTLE ROCK, AR

     MARCH 26, 1985..........FEDERATION OF WOMEN'S CLUB
                             ANNUAL CONVENTION
                             WOMEN'S CITY CLUB, LITTLE ROCK, AR

     MARCH 26, 1985..........LEVI HOSPITAL TESTIMONIAL HONORING
                             GOVERNOR
                             HOT SPRINGS, AR

     MARCH 27, 1985..........FORT SMITH JR. LEAGUE
                             FORT SMITH, AR

     MARCH 28, 1985..........TOUR TO MARKED TREE AND W. MEMPHIS
```

Hillary kept up a busy speaking schedule as Arkansas's First Lady while also working and serving on nonprofit boards.

McGovern campaign years back, had dropped out was that a newspaper had exposed an extramarital affair.

The *Miami Herald*, following up on a tip, had staked out Hart's Washington home and caught him with a young model he had met on an overnight yacht cruise to Bimini. The story caught fire in part because of a profile on Hart in the *New York Times Magazine*, which ran at almost the same time. In that piece, a reporter pestered the candidate about rumours of his womanizing. Exasperated, Hart had said, "Follow me around. I don't care."

Though Hart had dropped out of the race—his political career ruined—that story was still smoldering as Bill was making his decision. And truth be told, Bill Clinton had a similar problem.

Rumours about his extramarital relationships had been persistent since his first term as governor, when, according to a friend, "Bill was like a kid with a new toy," enjoying his new influence, meeting powerful people and beautiful women. Betsey Wright, who helped with his political comeback and became his chief of staff, had heard him make dates with women and had seen him slip out of the office to meet them.

In the days before he was to announce his candidacy, she had confronted him in a guts-on-the-table meeting, asking him about the women she had heard about and what had happened. But then he offered up more names. "I thought I knew everybody," Wright said. "And he came up with these people I didn't know about."

Hillary endured the painful reality of Bill's behaviour in private. She didn't moan about it to her friends or seek their comfort, and she remained deeply committed to the marriage.

Up until that point, a politician's sexual activities had been considered mostly a private matter, unless they somehow were very public. Numerous presidents are said to have engaged in extramarital affairs, including Warren Harding, Dwight Eisenhower, John Kennedy, Lyndon Johnson, and Franklin Roosevelt. Their behaviour may have been wrong, but it had never been front-page news.

Now that was changing. Nixon's involvement in Watergate had made a candidate's character and morals a bigger issue in political races. "Hart's undoing marked the moment when political reporters ceased to care about almost anything else," said Matt Bai, who wrote a book on the Hart story. In the coming years, political reporting would focus more and more on character issues rather than stances on education, budgets, or taxes. For much of the political press, Bai said, "there was no greater calling than to expose the lies of a politician, no matter how inconsequential those lies might turn out to be or in how dark a place they might be lurking."

Had Bill run, Hillary's private suffering would have become very public in that new environment—and it would have become Chelsea's pain as well. No one was ready for that.

Despite his decision, Bill was devastated by the idea that he had missed his one big chance to run for president. But rather than straighten up, he slid back into bad habits. He engaged in a long relationship with a divorced marketing executive, and at one point, according to biographers, he considered divorcing Hillary.

She refused. Hillary's mother had suffered because of her own parents' divorce, and Hillary knew it would be bad for Chelsea. Plus, she didn't believe in it. "It absolutely was not an alternative that she gave him," Betsey Wright said.

Now in her early forties, Hillary did start to exert more independence, however. She told a friend that she worried about finances and about potentially becoming a single mother, especially since they didn't own a home. She joined more company boards and billed more at work, bringing her total income to almost $120,000 in 1989, about $230,000 in today's dollars.

She was asked to be the first chair of the American Bar Association's Commission on Women in the Profession, and in 1988, the *National Law Journal* named her among the 100 most powerful lawyers in the country, one of just four women on the list.

More significantly, she considered running for governor herself. Bill was up for re-election in 1990 and was starting to wear out his welcome with Arkansans. Bill recommitted himself to trying to mend their marriage, and he weighed taking some time off to prepare for a presidential run. Hillary, however, hadn't developed her own stature with the state's voters. Her election would have been a long shot—and Bill decided to run anyway.

Publicly, Hillary never stopped standing up for him. During the 1990 campaign for governor, Hillary appeared at the state capitol to listen to

Bill gives Hillary a hug and a kiss after announcing that he will run again for governor in 1990.

Bill's top Democratic opponent, Tom McRae, hold a news conference while Bill was out of town. When the candidate displayed an unflattering caricature of her husband and questioned why Bill wasn't there, Hillary spoke up from the crowd.

"I went through all your reports because I've really been disappointed in you as a candidate, and I've really been disappointed in you as a person, Tom," she said, challenging the challenger.

As television cameras swung between the two, Hillary cited quotes from a foundation McRae used to lead that praised Bill's previous work. Before she was done, McRae was complimenting Bill's record.

Some saw the daring confrontation as unfair and unprofessional; others admired her toughness and determination. She was also highly effective. Bill won again.

Bill and Hillary had conquered Arkansas. The toughest challenges of their lives, however, were still to come.

16

CAMPAIGN

In the summer of 1991, Bill and Hillary gathered a few aides and close friends in the Governor's Mansion to discuss a run for the presidency. Could they raise the millions of dollars needed? Could Bill finish ahead of a long list of potential Democratic candidates? And could he possibly beat an incumbent, President George H. W. Bush, who had followed Ronald Reagan?

It seemed daunting, and the group debated the options for a while, including the possibility that a race might just be practice for another campaign in 1996.

Finally, one of Bill's friends raised a challenging question: "But, governor," he said, "what if we win?"

Hillary had the answer. "Well, we just serve," she said. "We do the job."

Bill would have an uphill climb. Arkansas was a small state, and he was hardly known nationally. He had led the National Governors Association and the centrist

Democratic Leadership Council, but if the average citizen knew him at all, it was for something less-than-impressive: At the 1988 Democratic National Convention, he had droned on for so long in nominating Michael Dukakis that the audience cheered when he said, "In closing . . ."

Bill later won back some respect by making fun of himself on Johnny Carson's *Tonight Show*. He wanted to make Dukakis look good, he told Carson, and "I succeeded beyond my wildest imagination."

By late summer, Hillary and Bill had put their marital problems behind them and laid the brickwork for a campaign. An exploratory committee was formed, which allowed Bill to start taking donations, and an initial team of advisers was in place. In September, Hillary and Bill attended a breakfast in Washington, D.C., for political journalists, hoping to dispense with some of the more delicate questions about Bill's background.

The reporters and columnists asked about political issues, such as foreign affairs and taxes. Then someone asked for his response to the rumours about his "personal past."

With Hillary by his side, Bill was ready with a response. "Like nearly anybody that's been together twenty years, our relationship has not been perfect or free of difficulties," he said.

He told the reporters that he and Hillary were committed to their marriage of nearly sixteen years, to Chelsea, and to each other. "We love each other very much," he said, adding, "and we intend to be together thirty or forty years from now, regardless of whether I run for president or not." They hoped that would be enough to settle any further questions.

On 3rd October 1991, Bill Clinton became the fifth Democrat to formally enter the race for president, throwing his hat in the ring from the Old State House in Little Rock. The local *Arkansas Gazette* wrote a long profile of him, accompanied by a shorter story on Hillary, calling her intelligent, persuasive, and his "most influential adviser." It also noted that she could be demanding and impatient and that critics called her "pushy, cold, and

Bill embraces Hillary and Chelsea in October 1991 after announcing that he will run for the Democratic nomination for president.

domineering," adjectives that would be used again and again (and that are often used to describe assertive and successful women).

The next few months would be focused on refining his political message, filling out the campaign team, and raising funds—more than $3 million by early 1992. Bill would skip the Iowa caucuses, the launch of most presidential campaigns, because an Iowa senator was running and surely would win. (He would also pass on several other caucuses, reasoning that they attracted a lower turnout and more left-leaning voters.) So his first primary test would be in New Hampshire in mid-February. That would set the stage for him to focus on primary elections in five states and the caucus in Maine, followed by Super Tuesday, a day of primaries and caucuses in eleven additional, mostly Southern, states.

Typically, the candidate's wife is merely an extension of the candidate's team. But Hillary began to assemble her own small staff to manage her schedule and travel. (A campaign aide later nicknamed her section of the office "Hillaryland.") She was impressive on the campaign trail, so much so that Bill often quipped that voting for him was "like a buy one, get one free deal."

Despite spending much of their adult life in politics, she said later, "we were unprepared" for the hardball politics and relentless scrutiny they would face and the way political opponents and journalists would sift through the details of their lives "as if we were some sort of archaeological dig."

The diggers hit pay dirt in January, just a few weeks before the New Hampshire primary. On 23rd January, the *Star*, a supermarket tabloid, broke a major story: A former Little Rock singer, Gennifer Flowers, said that she had a twelve-year affair with Bill and that she had audio recordings in which he urged her to deny a relationship.

The Clinton campaign said the story wasn't true. But the tabloid allegations soon were in every major newspaper and on national newscasts. Bill had been the frontrunner in New Hampshire, but now his campaign could end before it had really begun.

To address the charges, Bill and Hillary agreed to appear on *60 Minutes*, which would air that week directly after the Super Bowl on CBS. His pollsters believed voters would judge his behaviour less harshly if his wife knew about it and still accepted him.

Preparation for the interview was emotional. Hillary told aides how important her family was to her, and before she was done, they were all in tears. She shared that she was afraid she would cry on television.

Later that day, Hillary and Bill met with the crew, and she fussed over chair heights and camera angles. "My sense of it was that she was in control," *60 Minutes* correspondent Steve Kroft told *Vanity Fair*'s Gail Sheehy.

In the taped television interview, Kroft asked about politics and the campaign as well. But because Washington's Super Bowl victory over Buffalo had run long, the segment was only about ten minutes long, leaving everything on the cutting room floor except for the questions about the Clinton marriage.

Hillary was so composed and came across so strong that her quotes were trimmed down "to keep her from becoming the dominant force in the interview," Kroft said.

For most Americans, this was their first good look at Bill Clinton's wife. What they saw was a serious-looking and articulate speaker with a Southern twang who didn't hesitate to jump in. What wasn't seen: During the taping, a heavy light fell, nearly hitting Hillary. But Bill had quickly pulled her out of the way, and she wasn't hurt.

Also unseen: Twice during the taping, *60 Minutes* producer Don Hewitt urged Bill from off-camera to admit that he had committed adultery. Bill refused, saying that it was only the business of a married couple and not anyone else.

But he did say in the interview, "I have acknowledged wrongdoing. I have acknowledged causing pain in my marriage. I have said things to you tonight and to the American people from the beginning that no politician ever has."

With Bill facing charges of infidelity just before the New Hampshire primary, he and Hillary answer questions about their marriage on *60 Minutes*.

He argued that they had worked at their marriage and at keeping it together.

When Kroft said that was admirable, that they obviously had reached "some sort of an understanding or an arrangement," Bill interrupted him.

"Wait a minute, wait a minute," he said. "You're looking at two people who love each other. This is not an arrangement or an understanding. This is a marriage. That's a very different thing."

Hillary said that she believed everyone was entitled to "have some zone of privacy" and added her own defense. "I'm not sitting here, some little woman standing by my man, like Tammy Wynette," she said, citing the singer of the country song "Stand by Your Man."

"I'm sitting here because I love him, and I respect him, and I honour what he's been through and what we've been through together," she said. "And, you know, if that's not enough for people, then heck, don't vote for him."

An estimated 40 million people watched the show. That included Tammy Wynette, who was furious that Hillary had dragged her into the conversation. Hillary apologized to her privately and in a television interview.

In an interview with *People* magazine soon after, she elaborated on her marriage, saying she never considered walking away. "You've got to be willing to stay committed to someone over the long run, and sometimes it doesn't work out," she said. "But often if you become real honest with yourself and honest with each other, and put aside whatever personal hurt and disappointment you have to really understand yourself and your spouse, it can be the most wonderful experience you'll ever have."

In early February, former President Richard Nixon weighed in with his own view, implying that the Clinton campaign should rein in Hillary. "If the wife comes through as being too strong and too intelligent, it makes the husband look like a wimp," he said.

More bad news hit when the *Wall Street Journal* ran a story indicating that Bill had avoided the Vietnam draft by agreeing to join the Reserve Officers' Training Corps (ROTC) and then backed out on his promise.

With the one-two punch of Flowers and the draft, Bill was sinking in the polls, from a first or second place finish in New Hampshire to a possible distant third or fourth. If that happened, donations would dry up quickly and his presidential race would screech to a halt.

The staff was demoralized. But Hillary was more determined than ever. At one point, she joined a conference call, rallying the whole team. "Let me tell you something. We are going to fight this thing, because this campaign is about something bigger than us," she said. "We're going to fight it to the end."

Bill continued to speak and shake hands, and he spoke at a televised town hall meeting. Dozens of Arkansans travelled to New Hampshire to knock on doors and pass out about 20,000 videotapes about Bill.

Later, Mickey Kantor, the campaign chair, called it "the most incredible week I've ever seen in my twenty years in American politics." He saw Hillary and Bill "grab a state by the shoulders and say, 'You will not ignore us, and you won't write us off.'"

When the votes were tallied, Bill had returned from the dead to run a strong second to Paul Tsongas, who was from nearby Massachusetts. Bill dubbed himself the "Comeback Kid" and began to gain momentum.

He won convincingly in Georgia and South Carolina, and then was the clear winner on Super Tuesday. As he became the front-runner, he and Hillary were increasingly under scrutiny, especially as part of the first generation of political couples where wives worked outside the home in professional jobs.

Just before the Illinois primary, another opponent, Jerry Brown, then a former California governor, accused Bill of sending state business to the Rose Law Firm to pad Hillary's pay and giving special treatment to Rose clients. Bill responded angrily that the charges weren't true, that her share of the firm's income didn't include legal fees paid by the state. (According to *American Lawyer,* she was one of the firm's lower-paid partners, and the firm didn't have a very big piece of state business.)

The next morning, at a campaign stop at a Chicago coffee shop, reporters quizzed Hillary about the charges. She responded that they were "the sort of thing that happens to women who have their own careers."

Could she have avoided a conflict of interest? they asked.

"I suppose I could have stayed home and baked cookies and had teas, but what I decided to do was to fulfill my profession, which I entered before my husband was in public life," she said.

Almost immediately, campaign aides knew she had fumbled the response. True, as a First Lady, she could easily have spent her time as a hostess—but her comments appeared to criticize women who stayed home and who no doubt did a lot more than bake cookies and have teas. The campaign aides arranged an impromptu press conference, and Hillary tried to explain that much of her life's work had been aimed at giving women choices.

But the damage was done. Even more than the allegations of conflicts of interest, the cookies-and-teas comment would follow her. The heat was intense enough that Barbara Bush, the immensely popular U.S. First Lady, said that she thought the criticism was unfair and that a First Lady should be allowed to have an independent career.

The First Lady may have regretted her statement when it became clear that Hillary could throw her own punches. In a lengthy *Vanity Fair* interview, Hillary, thinking she was off-the-record and wouldn't be quoted, shared a rumour that President Bush, too, had carried on an affair—with a woman who was also named Jennifer.

When the quote appeared in print that April, she had to apologize again. "Nobody knows better than I the pain that can be caused by even discussing rumours in private conversations, and I did not mean to be hurtful to anyone," she said.

By late spring, Hillary's series of tart responses and political gaffes were distressing both voters and campaign managers. Though she was "HRC" in campaign memos, they sometimes called her "H-bomb" behind her back.

Once again, it was time for a makeover.

Friends encouraged Hillary to ditch the dowdy headbands that were a quick and easy style in favour of more fashionable haircuts. They helped her improve and soften her wardrobe. Bill dropped references to "buy one, get one free" and to the idea that he might give her a job in his administration. Hillary avoided discussing political topics or a future policy role, saying, "I want to be a voice for children in the White House."

Behind the scenes, campaign leaders began to carefully recraft Hillary's image. Before, Hillary had, for the most part, said what she wanted to. But beginning with the 1992 campaign, her persona would increasingly be more carefully sculpted and tailored for the public eye, making the real Hillary harder and harder to see.

In a 27th April memo, Clinton's top campaign strategists recommended Hillary disappear into the background for a while as they repositioned Bill as the Democratic nominee. Then, when she returned, she should talk more about her family and emphasize another side of herself: her laugh and her humour, as well as her work on behalf of children.

When polls showed that people didn't even know she was a mother, she agreed to let *People* magazine write a feature story on their family life, including Bill's habit of embarrassing his daughter by waving at her during dance recitals. By then, Chelsea, who had skipped third grade, was twelve years old and in eighth grade; in addition to her parents, she was under the watchful eye of her grandparents. The Rodhams had moved to Little Rock in 1987 and Bill's mother and her fourth husband were just an hour away.

Being away from Chelsea, Hillary told the magazine, "has been the hardest part of the campaign."

Despite her campaign schedule, Hillary made sure to come home at least every weekend during the primary season. But Bill had won the primaries and soon would be anointed the Democratic candidate at the July Democratic convention. Campaigning six days a week after that, Hillary didn't always get home on weekends, so she sometimes came home for a day or two during the week.

"She had to come home to see Chelsea, she just had to," said Patti Solis, later Patti Solis Doyle, her scheduler. "And of course, when Chelsea had school plays or ballet or [parent-teacher] conferences, she had to be home for that—and so did he, for that matter." For select events, like trips to New York and, later, the debates, Hillary took Chelsea along.

"Wherever they were" during the campaign, Chelsea remembered as an adult, "at least one of them would fly home to be with me while I was doing my homework and to tuck me in at night."

Despite her public image, Hillary brought both intelligence and laughter to the campaign. Her team nicknamed themselves Herc and the Girls, a play on her initials, and had a good time joking around. One night, on a plane to Detroit, someone put Motown music in a tape player, and they convinced Hillary to dance in the aisles.

On Bill's trips, "every time she came on the road, things were better," said Paul Begala, who helped direct campaign strategy. "The governor's spirits were so much better when she's around," he said. Her campaign staff were fun, and there was more laugher when they were all together.

Beginning with the Republican convention in August, Hillary again became a target. Political historians called the criticism an unprecedented assault on a potential First Lady. The Republican national chairman attacked her writings about children, saying she supported children suing their parents. She was tagged as a "radical feminist," or worse, "a feminazi." Conservative writers labeled her a Lady Macbeth in a headband, a the scheming Shakespearean wife who persuades her husband to kill the king so he can become the ruler.

And onetime candidate Pat Buchanan said that as part of a "Clinton and Clinton" administration, she would push for "homosexual rights, discrimination against religious schools, women in combat units."

Mary Matalin, Bush's deputy campaign manager, had a photo of Hillary Clinton on her wall, with the caption: "I will get you, my pretty, and your little dog, too," a reference to the Wicked Witch in *The Wizard of Oz.*

Hillary held her tongue. As she joined Bill and vice presidential candidate Al Gore and his wife, Tipper, on bus tours and other campaign trips, she engaged in nothing more controversial than a chocolate chip cookie bake-off against Barbara Bush, sponsored by *Family Circle* magazine. Hillary's recipe, using vegetable shortening instead of butter and adding oatmeal, won the contest.

It was a good omen.

THE WHITE HOUSE

Hillary Clinton's Chocolate Chip Cookies

1 1/2 cup unsifted all-purpose flour	1/2 cup granulated sugar
1 teaspoon salt	1 teaspoon vanilla
1 teaspoon baking soda	2 eggs
1 cup solid vegetable shortening	2 cups old-fashioned rolled oats
1 cup firmly packed light brown sugar	1 (12-ounce) package semi-sweet chocolate chips

Preheat oven to 350 degrees. Grease baking sheets. Combine flour, salt and baking soda. Beat together shortening, sugars and vanilla in a large bowl until creamy. Add eggs, beating until light and fluffy. Gradually beat in flour mixture and rolled oats. Stir in chocolate chips. Drop batter by well-rounded teaspoonsful on to greased baking sheets. Bake 8 to 10 minutes or until golden. Cool cookies on sheets on wire rack for 2 minutes. Remove cookies to wire rack to cool completely.

Hillary Rodham Clinton

The recipe that won the bake-off between First Lady contenders.

17

PRESIDENT

Unseating an incumbent president is difficult. But the Clinton campaign honed in on three key themes and posted them on a sign in the campaign headquarters:

Change vs. More of the Same
The Economy, stupid
Don't forget health care

The economy had turned sour. People were losing their jobs and voters were angry with Bush for raising taxes when he said he wouldn't. Health-care costs were soaring, and an increasing number of Americans lacked decent health insurance. Moreover, a third candidate, Texas billionaire H. Ross Perot, was running as an independent determined to fix the federal budget, and he was taking votes from both candidates.

On 2nd November 1992, the day before the election,

Bill and Hillary started their day at a Philadelphia diner. Then they flew to Cleveland, Ohio; Detroit, Michigan; St. Louis, Missouri; and Paducah, Kentucky, holding short campaign rallies at each place. The day ended with a quick visit to South Texas, and Election Day began with an after-midnight stop in Fort Worth.

The three planes carrying the Clintons, their staff, and journalists spent a short night in Albuquerque, New Mexico, where Bill finished off a plate of Mexican food after a middle-of-the-night gathering. From there, they headed to Denver, where they saw the sun come up for their last campaign event. More than 5,000 people greeted them at a maintenance hangar at 5:00 a.m. With Bill's voice down to a whisper from all the speaking, Hillary delivered his speech.

Then, after travelling 4,000 miles through eight states to urge supporters to cast their votes for Clinton-Gore, they flew home to Little Rock, where friends and family were gathering. They arrived mid-morning, and after greeting family and headquarters' staff, Hillary and Bill headed straight to their local community centre to cast their own votes with Chelsea.

The voting booth was old-fashioned, with mechanical levers and a handle for pulling a curtain closed for privacy. Bill took Chelsea with him and shut the curtain. The twelve-year-old got the privilege of pulling the lever next to her father's name and then gave him a hug.

The afternoon was spent at the Governor's Mansion,

watching a John Wayne movie and grabbing a nap. Bill went for a jog, and Hillary made another round of calls to supporters, including her Fayetteville friend Diane Blair. The political science professor had been weepy all day, "having completely emotional feelings about democracy and the power of the people." But Hillary first wanted to know how Diane was and how her children were doing.

By early evening, the results were coming in. Perot turned out to be a bigger factor than expected. He captured nearly 20 per cent of the vote, the most won by a third-party candidate since Teddy Roosevelt ran as a Progressive in 1912. But Perot didn't win any states.

Bill won just 43 per cent of the popular vote—the smallest percentage for a winner since Richard Nixon won in 1968, beating Democrat Hubert Humphrey and George Wallace, the American Independent Party candidate. But Bill also won thirty-two states and more than two-thirds of the electoral votes. He and Hillary were headed to the White House.

George H. W. Bush called to concede and congratulate the president-elect that night. Afterwards, Hillary and Bill went to their bedroom and prayed, thanking God for their blessings and asking for guidance with the task ahead. Then they drove to the Old State House, where Bill had declared his candidacy.

Many of their closest friends had made the trek to Little Rock to celebrate this historic day. Hillary's best buddies from Park Ridge were there, as well as Reverend Don Jones. Her Wellesley pals and their Yale friends came in, too, many of them partying with Bill's mother, Virginia, at the Camelot Inn.

Thousands of people filled the streets, watching on large television screens as states' votes were recorded. When Bill finally had enough electoral votes to win, the crowd erupted in that Arkansas cheer Hillary had heard when she first arrived in Fayetteville nearly two decades earlier: "Woooooo, pig, sooie!"

Bill and Hillary and Al and Tipper Gore showed up around 11:30 p.m. to shake hands and declare victory. Though he didn't have a clear majority, Bill called on

Hillary cheers as Bill greets supporters at Little Rock's Old State House after election returns showed he had won the presidency in November 1992.

Americans to work together, "to be interested not just in getting but in giving, not just in placing blame but in assuming responsibility, not just in looking out for yourselves but in looking out for others, too."

After the exhilarating night, the hard work of preparing to take on the biggest job in the country started the next day. Bill had to be briefed on national security issues, meet foreign leaders, and start appointing a cabinet and filling thousands of other government jobs. Hillary was offering her advice, but also working to pack up the Governor's Mansion, pick a school for Chelsea, and prepare for the inauguration and all its events.

Among her worries: Where would she put the family's extensive library? Bill and Hillary had "hundreds and hundreds of books, and they've read these books," not just collected them, a friend told a reporter. When Barbara Bush gave the next First Lady a tour of the White House, an aide said, Hillary was mostly concerned with where all their books would go. The Clintons would add bookshelves wherever they could in the White House, including a storage room that became an overflow space for their library.

Zeke the dog had passed away in 1990, but the black-and-white family cat, named Socks, would be moving to Washington. Because Socks could just slip through the wrought iron White House fence, he would have to be on a leash when he went outdoors. One animal wouldn't go: Just before they headed to their new home, Bill followed

The family cat, Socks, moved from Little Rock to Washington but was required to stay on a leash when he went outside to keep him on the White House grounds.

Chelsea's wishes and released her pet frog into the Arkansas River.

As Bill worked on the transition, Hillary decided to maintain a social secretary's office and a visitors' office in the East Wing, where most First Ladies of the twentieth century did their work, sometimes from bedrooms or dressing rooms. But Hillary also made groundbreaking plans to set up an office in the West Wing, the nerve centre of the White House. As in the campaign, her domain would become known as Hillaryland.

In early January 1993, the books and personal items in the Arkansas Governor's Mansion were packed up and shipped off to the White House, and on 16th January, Hillary, Bill, and Chelsea waved good-bye to Arkansas and 2,500 friends and well-wishers who had gathered to send them off. Once in Washington, they stayed at Blair House, where visiting heads of state stay, until the swearing in. The next few days were a blur of concerts, a prayer service, receptions, and speeches.

On 20th January 1993, Hillary held the Bible as Bill took the oath of office. Bill was noted for his inaugural

Hillary, in her "flying saucer" hat, and Bill in the inaugural parade on 20th January 1993.

address, including the memorable line: "There is nothing wrong with America that cannot be cured by what is right with America." Hillary was noted for her bright blue coat and round hat, which later would be compared to a flying saucer. Because they couldn't move in until just after noon, the Clintons checked out their new home only briefly. They spent the evening hugging supporters and dancing at eleven inaugural balls before returning to their new home after 2:00 a.m.

Chelsea and some Little Rock friends went home earlier, and the staff treated them to a scavenger hunt around the White House.

Beyond their new jobs, the family had to adjust to their new living quarters. More than a hundred people worked in the White House, from cooks and carpenters to butlers and florists. Hillary and Bill were reminded of that on their first morning in the White House, when they were awakened at 5:30 a.m. by knocking on their bedroom door. A butler, unaccustomed to their late-night habits and not-too-early mornings, marched in with a breakfast tray, as the

The Clintons dance at one of eleven inaugural balls on 20th January 1993.

staff had done for the Bushes. It would take some effort to convert both the White House staff and the Secret Service to this younger couple and their less-predictable lifestyle.

First Lady Jacqueline Kennedy had added a dining room to the upstairs family area so that her children could eat in the private quarters; before, families ate in the more formal Family Dining Room downstairs.

Hillary went further, converting a small butler's pantry, or prep area, into a family kitchen where they could eat breakfast and dinner together and raid the refrigerator for late-night snacks.

At Hillary's request, a butler's pantry in the family area was converted into a small kitchen where the family could eat dinner together. Here, they celebrate Chelsea's fifteenth birthday in 1995.

Even so, the chefs in the White House were protective. One evening, when Chelsea wasn't feeling well, Hillary went to the kitchen to make scrambled eggs for her. When she called downstairs for a utensil, she said, the professionals were "completely undone at the thought of a First Lady wielding a frying pan with no supervision." She and Chelsea also went to a grocery store to buy boxed macaroni and cheese to show them what kind Chelsea preferred.

The Secret Service was a constant presence; Bill had the code name "Eagle," Hillary "Evergreen," and Chelsea "Energy." One agent was typically posted right outside the president's bedroom door, but Hillary finally convinced him to relocate farther away.

Early on, she sought advice from Jacqueline Kennedy Onassis about raising a child in the public glare. Onassis urged her to keep Chelsea's life as normal as possible without spoiling her or allowing her to feel entitled. She encouraged Hillary to teach her daughter to respect the Secret Service and staff, and to do her best to keep her away from the press.

Hillary and Bill decided to send Chelsea to Sidwell Friends, a Quaker school, primarily to protect her privacy. Over the next eight years, Hillary would have a hard time keeping much of her own life private. But for the most part, she and Bill would successfully keep their only child off-limits from prying reporters and photographers so she could be a normal teenager—at least as much as anyone could be normal living in the White House.

Drawn and Quartered

Editorial cartoons offer sometimes biting commentary on current events. As a couple in politics for decades, Hillary and Bill were often featured in such cartoons.

'OH, WHAT A FEELING!'

Good!

"I need a jacket for the office. Nothing too Hillary."

PART THREE

FIRST LADY

"Always aim high, work hard, and care deeply about what you believe in. And when you stumble, keep faith. And when you're knocked down, get right back up, and never listen to anyone who says you can't or shouldn't go on."

18

FIRSTS

As the First Lady of Arkansas, Hillary had gone off to her own paid job. But no president's wife has ever done that. Instead of continuing with her career, Hillary hoped to put her years of experience to work with a substantive role in developing policy, along with advising her husband and supervising state dinners.

The Washington gossip machine churned with possibilities. Asked *People* magazine: "Will she be a kind of Joan of Arkansas, fighting for her own agendas in the White House?" She couldn't actually have a paid position, or a cabinet spot, because of nepotism rules dating back to President Kennedy's term, when he named his brother Robert as attorney general.

On the first Monday of his presidency—also twelve-year-old Chelsea's first day at her new school—Bill settled the issue when he formally gave Hillary her assignment. She would lead one of the toughest and most important efforts of his administration: chairing a task force charged with overhauling an increasingly expensive health-care system.

It was a daring and risky move. Hillary would take on the most powerful post ever held by a First Lady, whose role was often undefined and misunderstood.

In 1932, just before Eleanor Roosevelt became First Lady, the *New York Times* wrote that the president's wife "must be a silent partner. The unwritten law is that the First Lady gives no interviews, makes no public utterances." She was to greet guests, smile effortlessly, and essentially play the role of most gracious First Hostess.

In reality, the wives of the presidents did much more—and much more was unofficially expected of them. In 1845, Sarah Polk was an unpaid assistant to her husband James K. Polk, working right outside his door. Just after Woodrow Wilson's inauguration in 1913, his first wife, Ellen, began a push to replace ramshackle shacks and shanties in Washington with new homes for those with low incomes. Congress finally passed housing legislation on the day she died in August 1914. Wilson's second wife, Edith, stepped in for him for several months after he suffered a debilitating stroke in October 1919.

Eleanor Roosevelt was far from silent, opposing racial segregation, speaking up for the underdog, and becoming her husband's eyes and ears on many issues. She held press conferences, lectured widely, wrote a popular newspaper column, and was the first First Lady to testify before

Eleanor Roosevelt, the first First Lady to appear before a congressional committee, testifies in 1942 about the tough conditions facing migrant workers.

Congress. She was also widely criticized for her opinions and her more public role.

More recently, Rosalynn Carter, wife of Jimmy Carter, sat in on cabinet meetings and became the honourary chair of her husband's Commission on Mental Health, where she helped oversee a number of task forces. She lobbied for more funding for mental health services and research and testified before a Senate subcommittee. As a result, Congress passed new mental health legislation in 1980.

Hillary's new job was as challenging as they come. Though she had successfully overhauled education in Arkansas, she wasn't a health-care expert. She would have to win over group after group: Congress with its complex politics, skeptical employers that foot much of the health-care bill, hospitals, insurers, and people who wanted access to great medical care but weren't sure who should pay for it. If she failed, so would a major promise of Bill's presidency.

If Hillary succeeded, overhauling the health-care system would be the biggest shift in domestic policy in nearly sixty years, since Social Security was created under Franklin Roosevelt. The goal was to ensure that all Americans had access to health care. At the time, an estimated 37 million Americans were uninsured and often turned away by hospitals and clinics because they couldn't afford to pay the bill.

An additional 70 million or more of the nation's 258 million residents didn't have insurance to pay for prescriptions. Many health plans wouldn't cover pre-existing conditions, like cancer, diabetes, or asthma, so people with a chronic illness risked losing insurance coverage for their condition if they changed or lost their jobs. Meanwhile, health-care costs were soaring.

Leading the change was tricky in other ways. Would advisers and legislators be frank with the First Lady? Or would they sugarcoat their responses to avoid tangling with the person closest to the president? Given the complexity of their relationship, would Bill challenge or question her as he would another top official? Or would he back off in the interest of marital harmony?

Even more daunting, Bill wanted his administration to hit the ground running. He announced that he expected the task force to have a plan ready for Congress within a hundred days, or by early May.

"It is hard to imagine a more difficult assignment," the *Washington Post* noted.

Hillary didn't speak at the announcement or give interviews. But within hours, she was on the phone, calling top senators and representatives to introduce herself.

Despite the big job, she still had her family and First Lady duties. The day after the health-care announcement, Hillary was on a plane to New York to get an award for her work on behalf of children. She visited a school and joined in a game of multiplication bingo with fourth and fifth graders, after telling them how her father used to drill her on multiplication before breakfast.

Within the first two weeks, she also hosted the first big dinner, for the National Governors Association, a group that Bill once led. In her first White House interview, she talked only of her First Lady duties—and how she was banning smoking in the White House, which previously had been forbidden only in certain areas.

The White House would now feature American food, rather than French, and try to buy local and organic ingredients. President Bush had hated broccoli, but she would be bringing it back. "We are big broccoli eaters," she said. Though her husband was known for his love of

The day after Bill put her in charge of reforming health care, Hillary stops in at a New York elementary school.

fast food, she said that in reality, "we do a lot of vegetables and a lot of fibre and a lot of fruit."

Behind the scenes, she tried to be in the residential quarters in the late afternoon when Chelsea got home from school and to have an 8:00 PM dinner with Chelsea, who would turn thirteen in late February and who was adjusting to the move and a new school.

Still, Hillary wasn't always available. Once during Chelsea's first few months, a school nurse needed to reach a parent to see if she could have some medication. "Don't call my mom," Chelsea told the nurse. "She's too busy. Call my dad."

With so much to juggle, Hillary admitted to exhaustion.

One congressman recalled her yawning repeatedly between meetings. "There has been so much to do initially," she said. "Sleep has taken a backseat."

She had encouraged people to share their health-care stories, and ultimately received 800,000 letters. By March, she was becoming a familiar fixture in the halls of Congress, meeting with legislators and aides to listen and talk about health-care solutions. She had travelled to several states to promote the changes the task force hoped to make. Serious and close-lipped as she went about her business, a news account described her as "joyless, unsmiling," and "mechanical."

Already, some groups were angry with her. She and health-care policy chief Ira Magaziner had created dozens of task forces to look at the many parts of an overhaul plan, but they had not disclosed the names of the more than 600 people who were working on various pieces. The hope was that they could gather data and make recommendations without the interference of powerful lobbyists for doctors, hospitals, and insurers. But the lack of transparency made the work look suspect and secretive, leading to worries and rampant rumours about what was really going on behind closed doors. A doctors' group sued the White House to insist that the participants be disclosed.

Hillary had also got off to a terrible start with the powerful Washington press. Journalists complained that it was easier to snag an interview with the president than with the First Lady. During the brutal press coverage of the

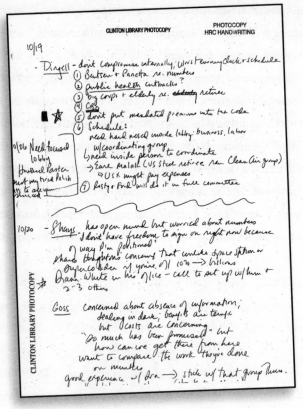

Hillary's handwritten notes about congressmen helped
her prepare for her meetings on Capitol Hill.

campaign, she had mostly given interviews to local media,
figuring that they reached more voters than the national
media and that they might be friendlier. In Washington,
however, ignoring big media outlets was risky. The combination of seemingly secretive work and a poor rapport
with the press encouraged hard-charging reporters to
seek out other sources of information, including those who

would share criticism and rumours about half-baked ideas or plans that weren't seriously under discussion.

Usually a new president and First Lady enjoy a bit of a honeymoon in their first months, where they are cut a little slack and given the benefit of the doubt as they adapt to their new jobs. But there was no welcome mat laid out for the Clintons from either Congress or the press. Whether she was arrogant or just naive, Hillary was already feeling the relentless sting of constantly being in the public eye. That turned out to be a modest introduction to the personal tragedies and public attacks ahead.

19

SAINT HILLARY

Hillary was midway through lunch with her staff in March 1993 when an aide came in to whisper some devastating news: Her father had suffered a serious stroke back in Little Rock just before his eighty-second birthday.

Hillary and Chelsea hurried to Little Rock. Hugh was unconscious, in a deep coma. They both talked to him, hoping he would respond. Trying to get a reaction out of him, Hillary's brothers sang the theme song to *The Flintstones*, a cartoon they loved as children and their dad hated. No luck.

Bill came in twice, but had to return quickly to Washington.

Overwhelmed by the family crisis, Hillary couldn't focus on her other duties. She did manage to quiz doctors, nurses, and other patients' family members about their thoughts on health care. But despite the tight deadline for a health-care plan, she just couldn't do more. Vice

President Al Gore and his wife, Tipper, stepped in to handle some of her health-care speeches and appearances.

In late March, Hillary and her family made the difficult decision to take Hugh off life support, including a respirator that was helping him breathe. Doctors expected he would die soon without the machine. Everyone said good-bye.

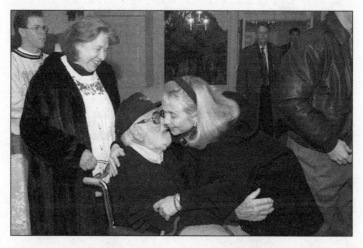

Hillary hugs her dad, Hugh, during her first month in the White House. He would pass away in April.

But when the respirator was removed, Hugh held on, continuing to breathe on his own for several days.

Chelsea had stayed through her spring break, but by early April, she needed to get back to school. Despite her best efforts, Hillary wasn't able to cancel a speech at the University of Texas in Austin. So she took Chelsea back to Washington, and two days later, headed to Texas.

Grieving for her father, she struggled with what to

say. Her heart and her mind were full with spiritual teachings and the Big Questions that go with watching someone you love die: What gives life meaning? What is our mission here? How do we die with dignity?

Hillary had wrestled with those questions much of her life—but never publicly. She had shared her thoughts with Reverend Don Jones in letters and phone calls, and she had talked about them with close friends. Friends knew she always carried a small Bible with her and she took her faith seriously. But the Arkansas First Lady, the civic leader, and the candidate's wife had kept that mostly private.

She wrote the speech on the way to Austin, drawing on a collection of inspiring quotes she carried with her, and thinking in the moment, much as she had when she rebutted a senator way back at her Wellesley graduation. Moved by the last days of her father's life, she shared her spiritual quest in an Austin basketball stadium filled with 14,000 people.

"We need a new politics of meaning. We need a new ethos of individual responsibility and caring," she told the crowd. "We need a new definition of civil society which answers the unanswerable questions posed by both the market forces and the governmental ones, as to how we can have a society that fills us up again and makes us feel that we are part of something bigger than ourselves."

Referring to the challenges of providing affordable health care, she noted that the modern world poses complex new questions: "When does life start; when does life end? Who makes those decisions?" While people struggle with those questions every day, she said, "these are not issues that we have guidebooks about. They are issues that we have to summon up what we believe is morally and ethically and spiritually correct and do the best we can with God's guidance."

This was no typical political speech, and her comments caught reporters and columnists off guard. They weren't accustomed to hearing about God from Democrats. In the following weeks, several took aim at her public musings about faith and politics. "The Politics of What?" said a *Time* magazine headline. The conservative columnist Charles Krauthammer compared it to "adolescent self-discovery." A *New York Times Magazine* article

The First Lady and her challenges and travails were headline news in the early months of the Clinton administration.

followed up with an interview and then questioned what she really meant, dubbing her "Saint Hillary." The skewering gave her more reason to hide her personal side.

The day after the Austin speech, 7th April 1993, Hugh Rodham passed away.

Bill eulogized his father-in-law at a memorial service in Little Rock and again at the funeral in Scranton, Pennsylvania, Hugh's hometown.

The family then headed to Camp David, the president's country getaway, for an Easter retreat. Hillary had little time to grieve. The Monday after Easter, she had to be at the annual Easter Egg Roll on the White House lawn. And after nearly a month away, she needed to give health-care reform her full attention.

Because of other political issues, including Bill's efforts to balance the budget, she was not going to make her 100-day deadline. Work was still underway, and there were legislators, doctors, hospital executives, and many others to speak with before a plan could be finalized.

Before the spring ended, she had travelled to Florida and Montana to hear about health-care concerns and promote reform. She had also become a target for criticism, gossip, and pointed jokes. *Time* magazine reported that Republican operatives sent anti-Hillary talking points to talk shows daily, and stories alleged that her face had been lifted and that she had thrown a lamp in the private quarters (which she said didn't happen). In Chicago and Washington, radio stations played a parody of Helen Reddy's "I Am

Woman": "I am Hillary, hear me roar. I'm more important than Al Gore." The right-wing radio broadcaster Rush Limbaugh played a bit of the presidential "Hail to the Chief" whenever he mentioned Hillary's name.

Bill was still struggling to sell his budget. Then, in mid-May, the White House abruptly fired several long-time members of the White House travel office, which chartered planes and arranged hotel rooms for reporters who travelled with the president and First Lady. Staff members were accused of mishandling money and were replaced with Clinton associates, creating a firestorm.

The firings put a spotlight on a White House staff that included friends and colleagues from Arkansas—among them, Hillary's Rose Law Firm friend Vince Foster, who was deputy White House counsel. Foster had struggled to adjust to the Washington culture. Though his and Hillary's offices were fairly close in the White House, he had little direct contact with his old work pal. He had helped defend Hillary's health-care task force and felt responsible for some of the travel-office brouhaha, which had resulted in a friend and colleague being reprimanded. He grew increasingly depressed.

In mid-June, as part of a series of biting critiques of the Clinton administration, the *Wall Street Journal* ran an editorial titled, "Who Is Vincent Foster?" The paper chastised the White House for "carelessness" in following the law and specifically scolded Foster for failing to give the paper his photo when the paper requested it. Though others might have shrugged off the attack as petty, it hurt him; he knew his friends back in Little Rock read the paper religiously.

There were also some wins. Foster had successfully helped vet a Supreme Court nominee and a new Federal Bureau of Investigation director, but he took little joy in that accomplishment. In mid-July, he went to a local park, removed his jacket and tie, and shot himself. He left behind a wife and three children and a shocked administration.

Hillary was in Little Rock when she got the call, having just returned from a combined business and pleasure trip to Asia. The news unravelled her, and she spent the long night crying and trying to understand what had happened.

Bill once again delivered a eulogy in Little Rock, this time for a boyhood friend who had been a neighbour in Hope and had become a close family friend years later.

Foster's boss, Bernard Nussbaum, searched Foster's office for a suicide note. All that was eventually found, however, was a torn-up note at the bottom of his briefcase that was later pieced together. Foster had written that *Wall Street Journal* editors "lie without consequence" and offered a chilling conclusion about the nation's capital: "I was not meant for the job or the spotlight of public life in Washington," he wrote. "Here ruining people is considered sport."

Hillary, as the First Lady, was in the audience as just another observer. But within a week, she would be the person on the hot seat, testifying before five congressional committees over three days, another first for a First Lady. She started with the House Ways and Means Committee, answering questions for two hours, without help from aides. She was calm and well informed, and the usually grumpy committee applauded as she left, "a virtually unheard-of tribute," said the *New York Times*.

She finished up at the end of September with the Senate Finance Committee. It, too, applauded her. The *New York Times* reported that she "dazzled" each committee. In truth, the committees may have just been kowtowing to the president's wife. Hillary had been around long enough to see the applause as just another version of the response she got in Arkansas years before—that is, genuine surprise that the First Lady might know her stuff.

After the public appearances, the real work began. Hillary and her team had originally expected Congress to craft a bill, but instead, her group was encouraged to write one. With so many special interests, the draft began to bulge. Pediatricians wanted vaccinations to be covered along with regular checkups; dentists wanted fillings to be insured; and dermatologists wanted acne treatments covered.

Amid the work, her staff secretly planned a forty-sixth birthday party for her. On 26th October she arrived home from a meeting and was told to don a black wig and hoop

In Washington circles, the tragic death became a source of speculation and conspiracy theories, including unfounded rumours that he had been murdered because he knew too much about the Clintons. Five separate inquiries over several years, however, concluded that Foster committed suicide.

The loss of her father and Foster within a few months left Hillary hurting. At the same time, Bill's mother, Virginia, was battling breast cancer and didn't have long to live. Unsure what else to do, Hillary returned to a wall-to-wall work schedule of meetings and speeches, but her emotions remained close to the surface. "This was one of the times when I kept going on sheer willpower," she said later.

She also found strength in a prayer group made up of women from both parties. They sent her notes and devotionals, visited her, and prayed with her and for her. As someone who prayed daily and looked to prayer for strength and comfort, "I was very touched by their desire to choose me to pray for," Hillary said.

Bill's budget finally passed in August, after Vice President Gore cast the tie-breaking vote in the Senate. After an end-of-summer holiday, Bill and Hillary returned to Washington, ready to finally get going on health-care reform. He scheduled an evening speech to Congress for 22nd September to reach prime-time television viewers. Already, an insurance industry group was running catchy television ads opposing any government meddling in health plans, featuring characters named Harry and Louise. Bill's speech would set the tone for the work the White House and Congress still had to do.

Two days before the big event, a draft of the speech was flat and uninspiring. At Bill's request, Hillary took a look and called in reinforcements. The next day, new speechwriters started over. Just four hours before the speech, Bill finally had a version to try out.

He used the family theatre in the East Wing to run through the speech and make final changes. Hillary, wearing a sweatsuit, was there to listen, as were other advisers. They tinkered with sentences and added in new anecdotes. As aides went off to enter the changes in the computer and to prepare for the event, Bill continued to practise until it was time to leave. He was ready.

As members of Congress took their seats and television cameras began to roll, Bill looked up to see the wrong speech loaded in the teleprompter. In the rush to finish, he was given only a regular paper copy rather than one with extra-large type, and he didn't have his reading glasses. For the first seven minutes, he had to rely on memory and a few glances at the paper. Knowing what was on the line, he did his best to follow what had been written, saying, "The health-care system of ours is badly broken, and it is time to fix it."

He singled out Hillary, saying he needed a "talented navigator—someone with a rigorous mind, a steady compass, a caring heart. Luckily for me and our nation, I

With Hillary watching, Bill makes last-minute changes to his health-care speech on 22nd September 1993, in a limousine on the way to Capitol Hill.

didn't have to look very far." Lawmakers gave him—and her—a standing ovation.

To make the complex process of overhauling health-care understandable, he held up a prop, a red and blue "health care security card," which would guarantee coverage. Bill was short on details. But he envisioned a future when people will "find it unthinkable that there was a time in this country when hard-working families lost their homes, their savings, their businesses—lost everything—simply because their children got sick or because they had to change jobs."

It was the smooth-talking Bill Clinton at his very best, and Congress gave him another standing ovation. The effort was off to a strong start.

Hillary as Dolley Madison and Bill as James Madison at her 1993 birthday celebration.

skirt. Then she was escorted to a costume party with more than a hundred guests. Several staffers put on blond wigs, playing headband Hillary, health-care Hillary, and so on. Bill, wearing a white wig and tights, was James Madison to her Dolley. It was a fun and well-timed break, though Hillary noted later that Bill "looks better in a suit."

The next day, her health-care bill was delivered to Congress. With all the details and requests, it had bloated to 1,342 pages and weighed more than five pounds—and many interest groups still weren't satisfied. The size and complexity of the bill, Hillary said later, was "a tactical mistake for us." Given all the controversy over the original task forces, it wasn't the first one—and it wouldn't be the last.

20

WHITEWATER

The health-care bill was formally introduced in Congress near the end of the 1993 legislative session and wouldn't be considered until 1994. Hillary and Bill were hopeful that negotiations would produce a workable plan.

Despite a rough start, Bill had already notched a number of successes. In addition to hammering out a federal budget, Congress had passed some significant legislation: the North American Free Trade Agreement, easing the red tape in trading with Canada and Mexico; the Brady Act, which required licensed gun dealers to check the backgrounds of handgun buyers; and the Family and Medical Leave Act, which allowed workers to take up to twelve weeks off, without losing their jobs, for the birth of a child or to care for a sick family member.

Revamping how health care would be paid for, however, would require new taxes and a new way of thinking about one of the biggest industries in America. For many, it would be a bitter pill to swallow.

The battle became even tougher when details from the Clintons' past bubbled back to the surface and onto the front pages again. On Halloween 1993, the *Washington Post* revisited the Clintons' investment in Whitewater, the Arkansas holiday-land deal, reporting that a federal agency was investigating whether the Clintons' former real-estate partner, James McDougal, had used a financial institution to illegally channel money to Arkansas political campaigns—including Bill Clinton's.

Through November, the newspaper and other major media outlets would start digging deeper and deeper into the relationship between the Clintons and McDougal and his failed savings and loan. The *Post* sent questions to the White House, but it wasn't getting any answers. It sent a letter to one of Bill's advisers. Still no answers. By December, the paper's reporters and top editors were running out of patience and appealing to others in the White House for assistance.

Some top aides, including communications experts David Gergen and George Stephanopoulos, argued strongly that cooperating with the paper would help Bill, rather than hurt him, and might keep the story from exploding into something bigger. Bill was open to the idea. But not Hillary.

She felt the press had burned her and her husband over and over, and she had never become comfortable working with reporters. Thinking more like a lawyer than a politician, she didn't see the value in starting now, and neither did the Clintons' attorneys.

Gergen and Stephanopoulos tried to appeal directly to Hillary, but couldn't get a face-to-face meeting.

The *Post* got less—a paragraph explaining that it wouldn't be getting any answers. Hillary would cooperate with government investigators, but not the media.

It was another serious tactical mistake. The press redoubled efforts to see what Hillary might be hiding. Its cause was stoked later in December, when news broke that White House aides had removed Clinton files related to Whitewater from Vince Foster's office just after his death. Whether anything important was in those files wasn't at all clear, but just the idea of taking files out seemed highly suspicious.

The same month, another story broke: The conservative *American Spectator* and then the *Los Angeles Times* published extensive interviews with some Arkansas state troopers who alleged that they had helped Bill conduct illicit affairs with women and deliver gifts to them while he was governor; they also helped him hide his activities from Hillary. The troopers, who were represented by a longtime critic of Bill's, implied that the president had offered them government jobs to keep quiet. None of the women who were supposedly involved confirmed the stories.

The *Spectator*'s sensational story went further, portraying Hillary as a foul-mouthed political animal. It suggested that Hillary and Vince Foster once had an affair; it didn't offer any proof, nor has there ever been any evidence to support the rumour. Foster had told his boss Nussbaum the previous spring that the most scandalous thing someone might say about him was that he had an affair with Hillary—and, he added, it wasn't true.

The combination of all the coverage was a reporter's Holy Trinity: sex, money, and power. And without straight answers from the White House, the stories would grow and multiply like a highly contagious virus. What had been a failed effort to sell land for holiday homes became story after story about the smallest details of the Clintons' relationship with McDougal, McDougal's improper business and financial dealings, the Clintons' personal investments, their tax returns, Hillary's legal work, and internal discussions at the White House. Because Hillary had handled the family's finances, she would be investigated as much as Bill, perhaps more so.

Within the White House, the outbreak of aggressive news coverage also highlighted the complexity of Hillary and Bill's relationship. When David Gergen joined the staff as counsellor to the president in the middle of 1993, Chief of Staff Mack McLarty drew an organization chart for him. In the top box, McLarty explained, was not just the president, but also the vice president and Hillary. "All three of them sign off on big decisions. You'll just have to get used to it," McLarty told him.

Gergen had previously served in three Republican White Houses, but this was a first for him. He never really got used to it.

For a time, Hillary and the vice president competed for Bill's attention, but Gore began to find his own focus in trying to pare down the government. They both remained important advisers. Though Hillary and Bill may have had marital issues, Hillary was also his most ardent guardian, watching his schedule and questioning aides in an effort to protect him.

"The Bill Clinton I saw needed the emotional approval of his wife on a daily basis," Gergen said later. "He depended on her, spoke of her, and acted as if she were his Rock of Gibraltar." He assumed that she "drew heavily from him, too."

In many ways, they complemented each other. "He was the dreamer, she the realist. She was the strategist, he the tactician. He was outer-directed, she turned inward. She helped him gain office, he helped her gain power," Gergen said.

They were a combustible pair. Hillary and Bill "don't do anything with each other without tremendous emotion behind it," one friend told journalist Elizabeth Drew. They were passionate about political strategy and policy, but they also got into "tough arguments about a book they've read, or what Chelsea should wear to school."

Beyond that, "Bill Clinton knew how to charm people; Hillary Rodham Clinton knew how to get things done," wrote longtime Washington journalists Haynes Johnson and David Broder, who chronicled the health-care battle.

When it came to handling conflict, they differed. He was willing to compromise to make things happen. Confident in her judgment, she often took a harder line, wanting to fight for what she thought was best or right. Even Bill sometimes struggled with her determination. "Once in a while," he told reporter Connie Bruck, "she'll come in and say, 'I want to talk about such-and-such.' And, you know, I might as well try to lift that desk up and throw it through the window as to change her mind."

Both of them could be tough to work for. Bill could explode in temper if things didn't go right, yelling and turning red in the face. But when the anger passed, it was usually forgotten. Hillary might be less volcanic, but she remembered. She could be cutting with Bill's aides, especially when she didn't think they backed him enough. She was distrustful of political opponents and outraged at press coverage. Her anger might take form as sharp disapproval of someone's work, and reminders about those errors or slights might resurface time and again.

The two also fought in front of staff, disagreeing with pointed words. It took guts for his aides to challenge her directives. Few were willing to do it, or to appeal to the president to overrule her.

The troopers' allegations in mid-December added a new level of tension to this complex relationship. It was tricky enough that the president of the United States

The Clintons' cat, Socks, checks out the 1993 Christmas gingerbread house named the House of Socks in his honour.

was relying on his wife to guide a major piece of legislation. Now, as the troopers made the rounds of television news shows, the new accusations hurt and humiliated Hillary. Bill was in the doghouse once again and was increasingly reluctant to ignore her wishes.

At the same time, Christmas was approaching, and the Clintons had big plans for sharing the season. An estimated 150,000 people visited the White House to see more than twenty well-decorated Christmas trees, and there was a reception or party nearly every day for a range of people, from kids to dignitaries. Hillary, of course, was the very public hostess at these gatherings.

Before one party for their family and friends, she collapsed into a chair, feeling frustrated and dejected. So much was falling on her, when her husband was the one who had been elected. But a friend reminded her that she had to hang tough, for her family and the country. She knew he was right. But she also felt exhausted and "very much alone."

By the new year, Republicans were calling for a special counsel—an independent investigator—to look into whether the Clintons had engaged in any improper activity related to Whitewater.

The Clintons were considering what to do when Bill and Hillary got the call they dreaded. In early January, Virginia Kelley, Bill's outgoing and endlessly optimistic mother, passed away from breast cancer at the age of seventy.

As with the loss of Hillary's dad and their friend Vince Foster, they had little time to grieve. After a quick trip to Hot Springs and Hope, Arkansas, for Virginia's funeral,

Bill celebrates Christmas in 1993 with his mom, Virginia, and brother, Roger. Virginia passed away from cancer just a few weeks later.

they returned to a Washington abuzz over failed land development in the middle of the Ozarks. Bill dropped off Hillary and Chelsea at the White House and then headed overseas for a series of visits.

Hillary and some of the lawyers opposed a special counsel, worried that they would be opening up the administration to all kinds of unforeseen investigations. Bill was torn. He was still mourning his mother, and he believed he and Hillary had done nothing wrong—but he also felt political pressure. In one of the very few times that he didn't side with Hillary, he ultimately gave in to his political advisers. He would ask the attorney general to name someone.

On 20th January the first anniversary of Bill's inauguration, a special counsel was appointed to investigate whether the Clintons had engaged in wrongdoing. Later, Bill would write, "It was the worst presidential decision I ever made, wrong on the facts, wrong on the law, wrong on the politics, wrong for the presidency, and the Constitution." In retrospect, he should have released records and tried to line up support from congressional Democrats. But there was no going back.

Five days later, Bill delivered his State of the Union address, touting the accomplishments of his first year and reminding Congress and the American people that health-care reform was still ahead. He added a dramatic touch: Holding up a pen, he threatened to veto any bill that didn't provide health coverage for everyone.

It was meant as a promise that all Americans would benefit from his health plan, and Hillary had encouraged it. But others, especially his political opponents, interpreted it as a threat, an arrogant challenge that made them want to short-circuit the effort. In time, it would make Hillary and Bill's work more difficult.

21

PINK

Throughout the spring of 1994, efforts to keep a health-care bill moving through Congress kept being stalled. Several congressional committees had to sign off, each with its own politics, and many Republicans were determined to kill the idea. Health-care industry groups were spending tens of millions of dollars to fight the undefined plan. Meanwhile, the endless appetite for Whitewater details put Hillary's credibility on the line.

As reporters dug deeper into Whitewater and the Clintons' finances, they stumbled across another surprise: Hillary's huge profit from commodities trading back in the late 1970s. In mid-March 1994, the *New York Times* reported that with the help of her good friend Jim Blair, Hillary had made $100,000 trading mostly in cattle futures on a $1,000 investment.

There was nothing improper about earning a profit, even a very large one. But it *was* unusual and surprising,

	HILARY RODHAM			DATE 10/31/78		ACCOUNT NO. 28349	
	720 N 3RD ST						
	LITTLE ROCK ARK 72201						
	REGULATED ACCOUNT			SALESMAN 18601		PAGE 1 I.L.O.I.	

TRANS.	DESCRIPTION	DATE	DEBIT	CREDIT	LEDGER BALANCE	
					DEBIT	CREDIT
CASH		10/11/78		1,000.00		1,000.00
P & S	FOR TODAY	10/12/78		5,300.00		6,300.00
CASH		10/23/78	5,000.00			1,300.00
P & S	FOR TODAY	10/23/78		7,850.00		9,150.00
P & S	FOR TODAY	10/30/78		7,277.00		16,427.00
ENDING	LEDGER BALANCE	10/31/78				16,427.00
	CASH TRANSACTION		5,000.00			
	PURCH. & SALE,			20,427.00		

A brokerage statement shows how Hillary made a quick profit in just a month of trading commodities.

and the way the information dribbled out was troublesome. Initially, Hillary's people said that she did her own research and made the trades. A few days later, they acknowledged that she had worked with Blair. Then in April, the White House said that Blair had actually placed the trades.

The White House initially said that Hillary had stopped trading in 1979; in fact, she traded in some accounts in 1980.

Around the same time, the Clintons released their tax returns from their Arkansas years and admitted that they lost only $46,635 from their Whitewater investment, rather than the $68,800 they had claimed previously. A little later, they said a review found that Hillary had made an unreported profit of about $6,500 in commodities trading in 1980, and the Clintons were paying back taxes, with interest and penalties.

The individual revelations didn't point to any specific misdeeds or even unethical behaviour. But the changing stories were head-spinning. The responses raised serious questions about whether the Clintons and their advisers—and Hillary in particular—could tell a straight story. The White House blamed faulty memories and incomplete documents, but could they be that naive? Were the Clintons listening too closely to their lawyers, who liked to play their cards close to the vest, and not enough to their political and media experts? What else were they hiding?

Revealing tidbit after tidbit certainly kept the press busy. In the month of March alone, ninety-two Whitewater stories appeared in the nation's seven largest newspapers, and 126 aired on the three major networks, ABC, NBC, and CBS. All that coverage dwarfed everything else the White House had done: In the first three months of the year, only forty-two health-care debate stories appeared on television network news.

The right-wing radio broadcaster Rush Limbaugh latched on to the media parade. He embellished a newsletter report in a broadcast, saying that Vince Foster had been murdered in an apartment that Hillary owned—though she didn't have an apartment and there was no basis for such an outrageous rumour. It was so shocking that U.S. stock and bond markets fell that day.

He also linked Whitewater to the health-care debate, saying people were taking Bill's word on what would be in the plan. Given that, he said, "I think it's fair to examine whether or not he keeps his word."

Having grown up with an alcoholic, Bill said he was used to "leading parallel lives" and putting aside ugly experiences to focus on his real work. But the unending drumbeat was hard on Hillary, who was less comfortable being the centre of attention and whose natural instinct was to resist pressure and fight back. "Remind me," she said to an aide at one point, "have I ever done anything right in my life?"

Finally, in April, Hillary realized that she needed to stop fighting the media. She called her first press conference. For more than an hour, reporters pelted her with questions about Whitewater, her commodities trading, her lack of openness, and to a lesser degree, health care.

Impulsively, she had picked a pink sweater set for the occasion—some thought so she could soften her image. But she was straightforward in her responses in what became known as the "pink press conference." She apologized for confusion about her commodities trading, saying they were her trades, made on the advice of Blair, and often placed by Blair. The 1980 trading had been done by a Little Rock broker, not by her, and she had forgotten that he invested in commodities as well as stocks and bonds. "The confusion was our responsibility," she said, and statements weren't as precise as they should have

Amid controversy over her 1979 commodities trading and the Whitewater investment, Hillary takes questions at her first—and only—press conference as First Lady.

been because "I probably did not spend enough time" on them.

She attributed some of the problems to "our inexperience in Washington" and to not really understanding what the press needed.

Revealing one reason for her ongoing conflict with the press, she shared that her parents taught her, "Don't listen to what other people say; don't be guided by other people's opinions." Rather, she said, "what was important was what you thought about yourself and how you measured up to the standards you set for yourself."

She admitted that she had tried hard to keep "a zone of privacy" for her family, to keep some part of their lives to themselves. But, she said, "I've been rezoned."

She told reporters that she was still hopeful there would be a health-care resolution and said she was open to any compromise that still provided coverage to everyone.

She indicated she would meet again with reporters—but this one turned out to be the only true open-ended press conference during her time in the White House. It helped reduce some of the antagonism, at least temporarily. But it didn't do a thing for health-care reform. Bill was trying to negotiate with Congress, but one by one, supporters disappeared.

In July, hoping to jolt the process forward with grassroots support, health-reform supporters planned a national bus tour. Speakers would be "Reform Riders," people who hadn't been able to get appropriate medical care for themselves or their families because of the failures of the current system. The name was a throwback to the Freedom Riders of the 1960s; they called the tour the "Health Security Express."

But the opponents were one step ahead. Conservative groups and business trade groups had rallied their own troops, especially conservatives who were angry at the Clinton administration for new gun laws and now, in their view, government efforts to control their health care. The groups sent out mail and faxes and scripts to hundreds of local radio stations calling on listeners to greet the buses with loud opposition.

The kickoff in Portland, Oregon, got off to a terrible start. As Hillary and a sixteen-year-old cancer patient

Hillary stumps for health-care reform at the University of Colorado–Boulder in March 1994.

spoke, a plane flew overhead with a banner reading, "Beware the Phony Express." The number of signs protesting reform almost equaled the number supporting it. On the highway out of town, the Reform Riders passed a broken-down bus wrapped in red tape with a sign, "This is Clinton Health Care."

The crowd in Seattle was so hostile that Hillary agreed to wear a bulletproof vest under her clothes.

As the buses moved across the country, protesters were always there to greet them, and they became the bigger story, drowning out the reform message. Some stops had to be canceled. In time, the media lost interest in the battle.

Ultimately, Congress did, too. Hillary had started on the wrong foot, with too many closed-door meetings and too much silence about their plans. She and Bill had never won over any Republicans to their effort, and they held on to their own plan for too long, missing opportunities to compromise and negotiate and win more supporters. Other pressing matters and distractions, like war in the former Yugoslavia and Whitewater, killed any momentum they had. And they didn't effectively counter exaggerated statements made by opponents, like the Harry and Louise ads, losing their chance to frame how average citizens saw the plan.

The proposal never made it out of House committees. By August, it was clear that neither the House nor the Senate would vote on it in that session. After so much effort, so many meetings and speeches, the promise to change America's health system simply passed away.

The failure of health-care reform would be considered one of the greatest political disasters of the Clinton presidency. As the person most responsible, Hillary Rodham Clinton would have to find something else to do.

22

ELEANOR ROOSEVELT

In public, Hillary was composed and sharp. She smiled, but projected a serious demeanour. She could move a crowd to tears talking about sick children who were turned away from emergency rooms and an uninsured person's inability to get treatment for cancer.

Despite all the criticism about her, when the Gallup Poll was taken in 1993 and 1994, Hillary was America's most admired woman.

In private, the health-care fight and the never-ending public attacks on her financial decisions and her judgment ate at her, though she was too proud to let outsiders see it.

In mid-1994, she was angry. Behind the scenes, she unloaded on aides and sometimes reporters, railing against the seemingly endless attacks from political opponents and the press. Once, when White House staffers gathered for a meeting, she launched into a tirade about Whitewater coverage that was so intense no one could sit down for twenty minutes. Despite her years in politics, she was personally offended when the *New York Times* went with a story that she had said wasn't true.

"I've always had a reputation for honesty; I'm forty-six years old; I'm the wife of the president," she told her friend Diane Blair. What else could she do?

Hillary often confided in her close friend, Diane Blair, and Blair was a frequent visitor at the White House.

Her defensiveness wasn't just paranoia: Longtime Clinton political opponents had helped the Arkansas troopers tell their story to reporters. Later, it would be disclosed that the conservative philanthropist Richard Mellon Scaife had spent more than $2 million to fund investigations to find dirt on Bill and to try to tie Vince Foster's death to the Clintons. Newt Gingrich, an ambitious Republican in the House of Representatives, boasted that uniting the Republicans to vote together against health-care reform would be a spring-board for Republican victories in the midterm elections.

Hillary didn't keep a diary because she didn't think it could truly be kept private. But in response to the intense battle, she urged her friend Blair to start taking notes and to interview Hillary's deeply loyal staff about what really had happened.

"What for?" Blair asked her.

"Revenge," Hillary responded.

(That was a Hillary characteristic, Blair would note later, in response to another issue: "As always," she wrote, Hillary "thinks the only answer to anything is to go on the offensive.")

Later, Hillary was more tactful. She wanted to be able to record her side of the debate, her experiences, and to have a record—maybe a feminist perspective, since her staff was nearly all women. Blair wasn't so sure she was the one to do this. But she typed up single-spaced notes of discussions for several years, at least some of which are now among Blair's papers at the University of Arkansas in Fayetteville.

The failure and fallout of the health-care effort turned Hillary's mood darker. As Gingrich had hoped, Republicans dominated the 1994 elections. In an historic defeat, Democrats lost more than fifty seats in the House and eight in the Senate. Republicans won control of both houses of Congress for the first time since 1954, when Eisenhower was president. The health-care debacle and higher taxes were the main culprits, though two major gun laws—the Brady Act and a ban on assault weapons—also fired up conservative voters.

Pursuing Bill's legislative goals would now be even harder—and the hardball politics would continue.

Hillary and Bill both felt responsible, and both went into a funk. Bill felt like voters had sent them a personal message, trouncing everything they had worked for during the first two years. Hillary had become divisive, admired as a role model for young women, but despised by those who saw her as a symbol of the rebellious 1960s and the women's rights movement. "She reminds most men of their first wife—or mother-in-law," a Republican pollster said.

Hillary said she was "deflated and disappointed" by the election results, and "Bill was miserable," hurting even more than when he lost the governor's election in 1980.

To get Bill back on track, Hillary helped bring in friends and advisers. To get Hillary back on track, her own staff and advisers rallied to her side. They knew a different Hillary—a woman who always asked about their families and encouraged them to be home with new babies and sick children. They knew her wicked sense of humour and her hokey, old-fashioned style. She might welcome someone with, "What's up, buttercup?" or end a conversation with "okeydokey, artichokey."

In late November, ten of those women—a mix of White House staffers and longtime advisers—pulled her into one of their regular strategy meetings. Hillary fought back tears as she told them she was sorry if she had let them down. She told them she was thinking about pulling back from public view.

One by one, the women explained how much she was needed, how many women looked up to her and depended on her. She couldn't give up, they told her.

They lifted her spirits.

So did the spirit of another who wasn't present. Since the 1992 election, Hillary had looked to the experience of Eleanor Roosevelt to guide her. When Hillary was under fire, she told *People* magazine, "I've had conversations with her in my head and would ask, 'How did you put up with this?'" Her imagined response: "You're just going to

Hillary's large, loyal, and mostly female staff in the White House, known as Hillaryland (dressed here for a party), watched out for her—and kept a stash of cookies for visiting kids.

have to get out there and do it, and don't make any excuses."

She was fond of Roosevelt's quotes, like "the thing always to remember is to do the thing you think you cannot do." Hillary especially took to heart her advice: "Every woman in public life needs to develop skin as tough as rhinoceros hide."

Roosevelt had also had some very Hillary Rodham Clinton–like experiences. Congress had demanded to see her personal tax returns—a first. When legislators saw that she earned income from her radio show and lectures, they accused her of using her First Lady position to make money, even though she donated it to charity.

At one point Franklin named Eleanor deputy director of civilian defense, an unpaid position. But she tangled with the director over the agency's focus, and she was criticized for how she did her job. She ended up resigning after five months. Afterwards, she was despondent, taken over by "Griselda moods," where she just wanted to avoid everyone. Eventually, she came to another conclusion, which Hillary adopted: "If I feel depressed, I go to work."

Hillary began to regain her confidence, in part thanks to a tiff with the new Speaker of the House, Newt Gingrich. As part of a plan to overhaul assistance to poor families, Gingrich proposed denying federal welfare payments to young unmarried mothers and using the savings to build orphanages that would take children whose mothers couldn't afford to raise them. He and other supporters said the move would help reduce the number of children born to single moms.

Hillary said his proposal was "unbelievable and absurd." She followed that with a long column for *Newsweek* magazine, saying, "This is big government interference into the lives of private citizens at its worst." Children are nearly always better off with their own families, she said, and being poor shouldn't keep anyone from being a parent.

It didn't help that Gingrich's sixty-eight-year-old mother told a television interviewer in early January 1995 that she couldn't repeat what her son said about Hillary. The interviewer urged her to whisper it, and Kathleen Gingrich shared a word that rhymes with witch. "About the only thing he ever said about her," she said.

Hillary happened to be speaking at a school that day. "The best way to handle criticism," she told sixth graders, "is to remember the Golden Rule."

At a White House lunch with advice and gossip columnists and food and style writers, she blamed herself for the failure of the health-care effort and her own harsh image, saying, "I think I was naive and dumb" in handling national politics. When she read articles about herself, she cringed at how she appeared. "I am surprised at the way people seem to perceive me," she said, "and sometimes I read stories and hear things about me and go 'ugh.' I wouldn't like her, either. It's so unlike what I think I am or what my friends think I am."

She asked for help in softening her image—but also said she would continue to speak her mind.

Inspired to write about women and children, Hillary soon began working on a book about the role of communities in helping to raise healthy children. She was still sharing her advice with Bill, but less often, and she had stopped attending weekly White House strategy meetings. She didn't have a formal role, and he had a new, strong chief of staff, Leon Panetta. She also embarked on her first First Lady trip, to five South Asian countries, a goodwill visit to speak up for women's and children's rights. There, she met with top officials, and she and Chelsea, now fifteen, visited schools and clinics and cultural sites and even rode an elephant.

Between speeches and formal appearances in India, Hillary and Chelsea visit with a group that helps women run their own businesses.

In India, she found special inspiration in a poem written by a senior at a local school, given to her with a note that read, "More power to you." Touched by the words, she included the poem in a planned speech for the Rajiv Gandhi Foundation, which serves some of India's most disadvantaged people. The words of Anasuya Sengupta began:

Too many women
In too many countries
Speak the same language.
Of silence. . . .

The poem resonated with the audience and with the travelling press corps, who saw a new way for Hillary to speak out. The *New York Times* reported that Hillary was finding a new voice herself, speaking up for women and children around the world.

It wasn't the voice she initially envisioned for herself, but it was a good fit. Health care had failed, and she had suffered other setbacks. The three lawyers who had come to Washington from her Little Rock firm were all gone. One, William Kennedy, had been reassigned and then resigned. Vince Foster was dead. Almost as shocking, her old friend Webb Hubbell had returned to Little Rock to answer questions about overbilling the Rose Law Firm and some clients. In late 1994, he admitted to cheating the law firm and his clients out of about $400,000, and he would soon be sent to prison. Outside of her staff, she didn't have many compatriots left.

In April, she helped Bill comfort victims of the bombing of the Oklahoma City federal office building, which killed 168 people, including nineteen children. In July, following in Eleanor Roosevelt's footsteps, she began writing a regular syndicated newspaper column. She encouraged older women to be screened for breast cancer and spoke up for Gulf War veterans who had returned from the 1991 war with undiagnosed illnesses.

She hadn't lost her feistiness or her fight. In September, George Stephanopoulos was arrested on charges involving an auto accident and an expired driving licence; in a conversation later that month, she congratulated him on leaving the police station with a smile on his face.

"That's what I've learned how to do," she told him. "I have just learned to smile and take it. I go out there and say, 'Please, please, kick me again, insult me some more.' You have to be much craftier behind the scenes, but just smile." She would have many more chances to do just that.

23

SUBPOENA

On the heels of her successful South Asia trip, Hillary spent part of the summer of 1995 preparing for a higher-profile appearance, the United Nations Fourth World Conference on Women, to be held in Beijing, China, in September. She was to chair the U.S. delegation and deliver a major address.

It was a tricky assignment. Relations between the United States and China were tense, and there were concerns about China's record on human rights. Complicating matters was the imprisonment of Harry Wu, a Chinese-American human rights activist. Wu had been detained when he tried to enter China with a valid visa that June and charged later with spying and stealing state secrets. Shortly before the U.N. conference, China announced that Wu had been found guilty and would be deported as punishment.

Hillary and her advisers decided she should go to Beijing despite the concerns, and she set out to "push the envelope as far as I can on behalf of women and girls." When the time came for her speech on 5th September, she was nervous. A lot was at stake, both for women around the world and for the United States and its global relationships. More than 180 countries were represented.

Harking back to the theme she had touched on earlier in the year, she said, "It is time to break our silence. It is time for us to say here in Beijing, and the world to hear, that it is no longer acceptable to discuss women's rights as separate from human rights."

Then, in her twenty-minute speech, she offered an unnerving litany of ways women and girls are abused around the world:

> *It is a violation of human rights when babies are denied food, or drowned, or suffocated, or their spines broken, simply because they are born girls.*
>
> *It is a violation of human rights when women and girls are sold into the slavery of prostitution.*
>
> *It is a violation of human rights when women are doused with gasoline, set on fire, and burned to death because their marriage dowries are deemed too small.*
>
> *It is a violation of human rights when individual women are raped in their own communities and when thousands of women are subjected to rape as a tactic or prize of war.*
>
> *It is a violation of human rights when a leading cause of death worldwide among women ages fourteen*

to forty-four is the violence they are subjected to in their own homes by their own relatives. . . .

If there is one message that echoes forth from this conference, let it be that human rights are women's rights—and women's rights are human rights, once and for all.

Hillary's address in China was considered the best of her time as First Lady and helped chart a path for her as an advocate for women around the world.

As she spoke, delegates cheered and applauded and pounded on tables. When she was done, she received a standing ovation, and delegates rushed to thank her and touch her.

Unfortunately, the Chinese people did not see it. Officials there didn't air the speech on radio or television, or include it in official news accounts.

Outside of China, however, it was a true home run. In an editorial, the *New York Times* called it "an unflinching speech that may have been her finest moment in public life."

When Hillary returned home, her staff tried to build on her momentum. In internal memos, two top aides drew up long proposals calling for media interviews, speeches, and listening sessions with women. To promote and polish her image, they suggested scheduling regular meetings with editors of women's magazines, appearances on women's radio and daytime television—and even a cameo on the popular sitcom *Home Improvement*.

Then there was another possibility: "Hillary could speak to young women through Internet," wrote Lisa Caputo, Hillary's press secretary, in the early days of the World Wide Web. "*People* magazine is tinkering with the possibility of using Internet" and Hillary might be able to chat with parents about children and families across the country that way.

That Internet was about to take off, changing not only the way Americans communicated, but also how quickly both real news and concocted rumours travelled. The Clinton administration had launched the White House website in 1994, and many companies and news organizations were trying to launch their own. The *Wall Street Journal* launched its news website in 1995, and the *New York Times* followed in January 1996.

In those years, getting online meant tying up a telephone line; loading a page was agonizingly slow. By 1996, however, more than one in five Americans had Internet access, and the percentage would soon skyrocket.

With Internet access, more and more people were getting their news online, and within a year, another shift would change the reporting of political news. Taking a page from conservative talk radio, Fox News, a news and political commentary cable channel with a conservative bent, would be launched in 1996, promising a new mix of opinions and criticism of a Democratic administration.

Keeping the glow from China alive, however, turned out to be difficult. Hillary had a Thanksgiving book deadline and she was writing it in longhand, without even the help of a personal computer. She buckled down to work on it after reconnecting with Chelsea, who was now a high school junior taking ballet every day after school and pushing for more independence.

An avid ballet dancer, Chelsea took classes every day after school. Here, she dances in a dress rehearsal of a Washington Ballet performance of *The Nutcracker*.

Much to Hillary's frustration, the Whitewater investigation was still chugging along.

Ken Starr, a former judge who had worked in the Bush administration, had replaced Robert Fiske as independent counsel in 1994 and was leading a more aggressive investigation. With broad powers, he pursued every possible avenue, expanding a satellite office in Little Rock and inter-viewing anyone who had a connection to the Clintons.

Just after the Oklahoma City bombing, Starr had come to the White House to interview Bill and Hillary, one at a time, under oath. Bill was able to roll with the punches, but Hillary had trouble containing her irritation. "The idea of hard-core Republican partisans rummaging through our lives, looking at every cheque we had written in twenty years, and harassing our friends on the flimsiest of excuses infuriated me," she said later.

The following month, the Senate jumped in as well, launching hearings into Vince Foster's death and Whitewater.

Between Starr and the Senate, many of the Clintons' friends and aides were called to testify or had agreed to sworn interviews, requiring them to hire lawyers at their own expense. Hillary couldn't do anything to help them. Anything she might say or write in a memo could become part of the legal case or appear to be part of a conspiracy; she was forced to bite her tongue, except when she was with Bill or their personal lawyer.

The end of 1995 was relatively uneventful for her, though chaotic for Bill. He was unable to get a new budget passed in the Republican-controlled Congress, and the government had shut down for six days in mid-November.

A temporary budget was passed, but it expired, too, requiring a partial government shutdown from 16th December to 6th January. During these shutdowns, when paid "non-essential" staff had to stay at home, interns helped pick up the slack. And during these two shutdowns—unknown to almost anyone else—a twenty-two-year-old White House intern named Monica Lewinsky had a chance to meet and get to know the president. This, too, would become part of the Whitewater investigation.

As 1995 came to a close and 1996 began, Hillary was preparing for the big launch of her first book, *It Takes a Village: And Other Lessons Children Teach Us*—and once again, she found herself in the centre of a new round of White House storms. In late December, White House lawyers responding to a congressional investigation of the travel-office fiasco ran across a troublesome memo that had been written in 1993. David Watkins, a White House assistant to the president, had written that Hillary had insisted he act swiftly in removing the travel-office employees. The memo, released to the media in early January, contradicted what Hillary had said many times—that she had no real role in the travel-office mess.

Just as the travel memo was making headlines, a personal aide to the Clintons found a thick file of Hillary's billing records that showed how much work she had done in Little Rock for Jim McDougal's failed savings and loan. The independent counsel had subpoenaed, or formally demanded, the files more than a year before, but the

Clintons hadn't been able to find the records. The aide said she had unintentionally put them in a box months before, not knowing what they were; the box ended up crammed behind a table in her office.

She alerted Clinton and White House lawyers, who told Hillary the documents had been found. Both the memo and the billing records were turned over—but the back-to-back disclosures left observers stunned. Could the White House possibly be that messy and inept? To many people, it appeared that Hillary, in particular, had to be hiding something.

The next issue of *Time* featured a ghostly looking Hillary on the cover; *Newsweek* ran the headline "Saint or Sinner?" William Safire, a conservative *New York Times* columnist, used the strongest of words. "Americans of all political persuasions are coming to the sad realization," he wrote, "that our First Lady . . . is a congenital liar." In an angry screed, he accused her of lying about her commodities trading, about the files taken from Vince Foster's office, and about her legal work.

Incensed by Safire's attack, Bill said that if he weren't president, he would deliver "a more forceful response to the bridge of Mr. Safire's nose."

For Hillary, the timing of all the disclosures and revelations couldn't be worse. She was just about to set out on her book tour, giving a television interview to Barbara Walters, appearing on Diane Rehm's radio show, and talking with national and local journalists as she visited

As Starr moved to compel her to testify before a grand jury, major news magazines questioned Hillary's credibility.

eleven cities. She wanted to talk about families and kids, about committed parents and communities. She would later win a Grammy award for the audio version of the book, becoming the first First Lady to win that award. But in interview after interview on her tour, she had to answer questions about Whitewater, missing documents, and the travel office.

In the middle of the book tour, she made a comment to a reporter that had to be corrected. In a conversation with a White House lawyer, she nearly broke down from stress and frustration. "I can't take this anymore," she said. "How can I go on?"

She would have to pull it together. A few days later, she learned she would have to answer more questions: Starr issued a subpoena requiring her to testify before a federal grand jury, a group of citizens who hear testimony and decide whether criminal charges should be filed. If she had hidden the billing records or deliberately delayed their release, then she might have interfered with an investigation, a potential crime known as obstruction of justice.

It was another first for the First Lady, an embarrassing and humiliating one. No First Lady had ever been called to testify before a grand jury. Hillary's lawyers tried to negotiate videotaped testimony or another interview at the White House, but Starr wouldn't hear of it. She would have to go to the courthouse and face the photographers and TV cameras as well as the justice system.

She was questioned for four hours about the billing records and how they had gone missing. Afterwards, in the early evening, she addressed the waiting press. How was she? they asked.

"It's been a long day," she said.

"Would you rather have been somewhere else today?"

"Oh, about a million other places," she responded.

In the spring, the Senate hearings led by New York Senator Alfonse D'Amato fizzled out. More than 200 people were interviewed, and more than 10,000 pages of testimony had been compiled over a year's time, without any meaningful revelations. In the final report, Republicans would accuse the Clintons of stonewalling and being less than transparent. Democrats would accuse

Questions about Hillary's role in travel-office firings and the discovery of Whitewater billing records took attention away from the launch of her first book.

Republicans of a "modern-day witch hunt" that focused mostly on Hillary.

"The venom with which the majority focuses its attack on Hillary Rodham Clinton is surprising, even in the context of the investigation," the Democrats' minority report said.

As the Senate poured energy and resources into investigating Hillary, polls showed that most Americans saw Whitewater as a minor scandal that wouldn't affect whether they voted for Bill—even if Bill and Hillary weren't telling the whole story. But Hillary's reputation suffered, and those who already found her too aggressive or self-righteous had even more reasons to dislike her. Wrote Henry Louis Gates in the *New Yorker*: "Like horse-racing, Hillary-hating has become one of those national pastimes" shared by people from all walks of life.

Bill said later that Starr, Safire, and Senator D'Amato seemed to enjoy "beating up on Hillary." But after twenty-five years together, he knew "that she was a lot tougher than they would ever be."

"Some guys don't like that in a woman," he wrote in his autobiography, "but it was one of the reasons I loved her."

24

RE-ELECTION

Bill was up for re-election in 1996 and would face an established Republican challenger in longtime Kansas Senator Bob Dole, who had opposed health-care reform.

This time, Hillary had a low-key role. Some aides saw her as "damaged goods" because of the failure of the health-care effort and the endless Whitewater questions, but at the same time, Bill didn't need as much help. He didn't have competitors in the primaries, and in the autumn campaign he could boast of a stronger economy, a drop in crime, and the beginning of a technology boom.

Hillary spent part of the summer taking Chelsea to visit six colleges in the Northeast—Amherst, Brown, Harvard, Princeton, Wellesley, and Yale—ahead of her senior year. At Chelsea's insistence, they also travelled to California to check out Stanford University in Palo Alto. That would become her first choice, despite her mother's reservations that it was a long way from Washington.

Politically, Hillary remained divisive. Dole singled her out during his speech at the Republican National Convention by taking a swipe at her book. "We are told that it takes a village . . . and thus the state, to raise a child," he said. "The state is now more involved than it ever has been in the raising of children."

"With all due respect," he continued to cheering Republicans, "I am here to tell you it does not take a village to raise a child. It takes a family to raise a child."

Hillary would get the last word. Eleanor Roosevelt had spoken at a convention in 1940, but since then, only a few

In a televised, prime-time address, Hillary speaks in support of Bill's re-election at the Democratic National Convention in 1996.

First Ladies—all Republicans—had spoken at a national convention. In 1996, Hillary would make her own speech, pointing out that her village wasn't the government; it was teachers, clergy, businesspeople, and community leaders.

"It takes all of us," she said. "Yes, it takes a village. And it takes a president." The Democrats cheered.

Ross Perot would run again as an independent, grabbing 8 per cent of the votes cast. This time, Bill would get more than 49 per cent of the vote—still not a majority—and win thirty-one states, handily beating Dole and getting four more years to pursue his agenda.

In Bill's second term, Hillary's role would be completely different. Four years before, she had taken charge of one of Bill's most important projects. When that failed, she had worked behind the scenes to lobby for smaller steps: medical insurance for children, more breast-cancer screening, and the availability of low-cost vaccinations. She had advised Bill on reforming the welfare system and fought for the arts and education. She had travelled the world and spoken to and on behalf of women, winning fans around the globe.

Now, she said, she would concentrate on speaking about policies affecting women, children, and families.

Despite the pressures of living in the White House fishbowl, where every comment or outburst could become a rumour or a news story, Hillary and Bill both felt like their marriage was still intact. "I still lit up when he entered a room, and I still found myself admiring his handsome face," Hillary said later. They'd had problems, but "we still made each other laugh."

Bill told his friend Taylor Branch that "I think we are closer today than we were the day we showed up." Branch, who had known the couple for more than two decades, regularly interviewed Bill during the White House years with the intention of recording presidential history. There, he still saw a warm and loving relationship.

All the stress and criticism "either breaks you down or builds you up," Bill told him in mid-1996, "and I think it has built us up."

After the election, Hillary and Bill headed to Australia, the Philippines, and Thailand for meetings and speeches, as well as some snorkeling and golf. They should have been riding high as they prepared to start a second term. But as seemed to happen every so often with Hillary, she stuck her foot in her mouth—twice—causing another political kerfuffle. Perhaps it was just human nature that honest but off-putting comments slipped out from time to time, like "stay home and bake cookies" during the first campaign. Or maybe when she was off script, she was simply tone deaf, unable to anticipate how her words sounded to others.

After Hillary gave a speech at the Sydney Opera house, a woman asked her if she felt stereotyped. Hillary responded with quips about the problems Martha Washington and Dolley Madison faced, as well as her own experiences. The only way to really escape politics, she said, is "to just totally withdraw, perhaps—I don't know—have a bag over your head when you come out in public or in some way to make it clear you have no opinions and no ideas about anything and will never express them publicly or privately."

She had intended to be ironic and funny. But in print, the comments instead came across as defensive and thin-skinned.

More criticism followed when she told a reporter on the trip that she was interested in a "formal role" in implementing changes to the welfare system. Aides quickly clarified that she meant that she would be supportive and serve in an advisory role, not in a direct policy role as she had with health care. But her comments still prompted Wisconsin's Republican Governor Tommy Thompson to say, "We really don't need the tender loving care of Hillary Clinton to mess" up welfare reform.

The quick response to any misstep just compounded Hillary's irritation at the way the press worked and the constant sniping at her perceived role, her comments, and her appearance, especially her hairstyle.

Chatting with her friend Diane Blair during Thanksgiving, after she and Bill had returned from their trip, the conversation turned to the role of First Ladies. Blair told Hillary that she believed Hillary was a "pioneer" in a role that no longer fit the times.

Speaking friend to friend, Hillary let her frustrations pour out.

In Manila, 15,000 people had come to hear her speak, she told Blair. Overseas, she was a genuine celebrity, a woman who represented hope and opportunity for women who had little of either. But at home, she was still divisive, a lightning rod for relentless criticism.

Blair suggested she could be friendlier with the press, even if the friendliness was fake. As others had told Hillary again and again, reporters had to generate stories

A personal note to Diane Blair about their shared love of reading.

day after day—that's what they did for a living—and she could help them do their jobs or make it hard for them.

But Hillary wasn't having it. "She has about come to the conclusion that no matter what she does [she] is going to piss off some people, so will just continue to be herself and let everybody else make whatever adjustments they have to," Blair wrote in her notes.

Hillary told Blair that she knew she should be nicer to the press, that she shouldn't change her hair so much, and that "I know I should pretend not to have any opinions—but I'm just not going to."

She *had* compromised over the years, giving up her name and trying to be what others expected. "But I'm

Sixteen-year-old Chelsea joins her parents in the 1997 inaugural parade. Hillary wasn't happy about her daughter's short skirt—but Hillary didn't see it until it was time to leave the White House.

not going to try to pretend to be somebody that I'm not. I'm a complex person, and they're just going to have to live with that," she told her friend. "Why can't they just relax about it?"

She also felt unfairly characterized. Bill was outgoing and drew strength from being around others. He relaxed by schmoozing, shaking hands, and talking to people. She preferred quiet time—reading, hanging out, or watching movies—which sometimes was described as "brooding" or hiding out to nurse her wounds.

Blair suggested she focus on a couple of key areas where she could make a difference. But Hillary told her the First Lady role meant she could only be an advocate or a cheerleader or a nag—but she didn't have any real power to bring about change.

"What I really love is policy," she confessed, not cheerleading or advocacy. "I'd be happy in a little office somewhere thinking up policies,

For the second inauguration, Hillary chose a coral suit and a gold tulle gown by designer Oscar de la Renta.

making things happen." But that wasn't part of her job description.

Despite her friend's well-meaning advice, Hillary made clear that she wasn't willing to bend just to please others. "On her death bed," Blair wrote, she "wants to be able to say she was true to herself." The events of the second term would make that wish more challenging than ever.

25

LEWINSKY

Just a few months into Bill's second term, a long-festering issue began to turn into a serious problem.

In May 1997, the U.S. Supreme Court ruled that a lawsuit charging Bill with sexual harassment could move forward while he was still in office.

A former Arkansas state employee named Paula Corbin Jones had filed the lawsuit three years earlier, charging that when Bill Clinton was governor, he made unwanted advances and sexually harassed her in a hotel room in 1991. Bill flatly denied her account.

The lawsuit raised a host of legal issues. Could you sue a sitting president? Was the president guilty of hitting on a state employee—and was it harassment if it didn't affect her job or job security? Sexual harassment occurs when a supervisor or coworker makes unwanted sexual advances or engages in verbal or physical abuse related to sex or gender. Schools, individual companies, and other workplaces may have their own standards and consequences, but generally, the harassed have standing to file a lawsuit if they have been threatened with dismissal or a demotion for rejecting an overture or if the workplace is so hostile that they can't effectively do their work.

The Supreme Court ruling, following years of rulings and appeals, meant Bill would have to answer specific questions about his alleged meeting with Jones and perhaps with women other than Hillary.

Within a few weeks, the Jones case intersected in an unusual way with the long-running Whitewater investigation. Over three years, special counsel Ken Starr hadn't been able to link Bill or Hillary to any illegal behaviour involving the Whitewater real-estate project, billing records, Vince Foster's death, or any transactions with James McDougal's failed savings and loan, despite spending millions of dollars and interviewing dozens of people. Now his prosecutors were asking about Bill's extramarital affairs, supposedly to see if he might have shared information about his financial dealings—but more likely, looking for other misdeeds.

As Starr continued to pry, Hillary and Bill faced one of the greatest challenges of their adult lives: Chelsea went to college.

In the spring, as Chelsea prepared to graduate from the Sidwell Friends School, Hillary had joined in the annual mother-daughter skits intended to lampoon their teens. For her part, she had donned a pink tutu and black

Chelsea's graduation from Sidwell Friends School.

leotard and pulled her hair into a ponytail to do a pirouette or two in imitation of her dancing daughter. Hillary's best line: "Your mother embarrasses you in front of maybe a couple hundred people," she told another mom dressed as a daughter. "My mother embarrasses me in front of millions."

Hillary's father had put limits on where she could apply to college, but she and Bill had done no such thing. Chelsea chose Stanford, all the way across the country. Hillary and Bill worked to arrange an easy transition that would allow youthful-looking Secret Service agents to protect Chelsea without interfering too much with her college experience. But the transition for them was much harder. Hillary had tried to have dinner with Chelsea nearly every night, and the two were close.

Between attending the funerals of Princess Diana in England and Mother Teresa in India, Hillary had shopped for dorm supplies with Chelsea. When the move-in date came in mid-September, she buzzed about trying to cram everything into the tiny dorm room. She even lined dresser drawers with paper, something only a parent would do. The time to say good-bye came just as she was about to drive Chelsea crazy with suggestions.

Hillary thought she was steeled for Chelsea's departure. But, said a friend, "it left an emptiness that I don't think even Hillary expected." Hillary had a full travel schedule, and she celebrated her fiftieth birth-

Hillary and Bill help Chelsea move into her Stanford dorm.

day a month later with a party in Washington, followed by a day of events in Chicago, featuring old teachers and friends from grade school, high school, and church. Still, she missed seeing Chelsea twirl down the hallway. "I was surprised by how barren the White House seemed without the sound of Chelsea's music coming from her bedroom or the giggles of her friends," she said later.

The Clintons tried to fill the gaping hole with a Labrador puppy that Hillary gave Bill as an early Christmas present. They named him Buddy.

As Chelsea adjusted to school and Hillary adjusted to life without her, Bill continued to wrestle with his legal troubles. Over the summer and in the autumn, his lawyers worked to settle the Jones lawsuit and put an end to the distraction. At one point, Jones refused a deal. Hillary and Bill had been reluctant to pay her because they believed that the suit was purely political and that no harassment had occurred. Bill worried that more women might try to get money out of him. Hillary believed "it would set a terrible precedent for a president to pay money to rid himself of a nuisance suit."

As the case inched towards a trial, Bill was called to give a deposition, to be interviewed under oath to provide evidence that might be used in court. In mid-January 1998, Jones's lawyers had their chance to ask questions, but they spent just ten or fifteen minutes asking about what happened with Paula Jones. They spent far more time asking unexpected questions about a new woman: Monica Lewinsky, the White House intern whom Bill had gotten to know during the government shutdowns in late 1995 and early 1996. Bill tried to answer them, without admitting to anything inappropriate.

In early January 1998, Lewinsky had given a sworn statement to Paula Jones's lawyers, denying she had a sexual relationship with the president.

Shortly after, a little known political-gossip website ran a scandalous story. BLOCKBUSTER REPORT, read the headline, 23-YEAR OLD, FORMER WHITE HOUSE INTERN, SEX RELATIONSHIP WITH PRESIDENT. The Drudge Report, a relatively new kind of site that pulled together and pumped up headlines from lots of sources, had learned that *Newsweek* had pulled a story at the last minute "that was destined to shake official Washington to its foundation."

The killed story was to detail a relationship between the intern and the president—and, the website promised, "tapes of intimate phone conversations exist."

That wasn't true. There were tapes, but not of intimate conversa-

Former White House intern Monica Lewinsky after allegations that she had a relationship with the president.

tions, and the story had been killed in part because it wasn't clear that the tapes were legal. Regardless, Drudge's error-riddled disclosure marked the beginning of a new kind of immediate, around-the-clock news cycle. The rapid growth of the World Wide Web and its quick adoption meant news and rumours that used to be reported in print and during radio and television newscasts would now travel faster and further than ever. Political maneuvering and gossip mongering would escalate well beyond what anyone had ever seen before.

The Drudge Report would make its name and build a following starting with this enormous scoop. In the immediate aftermath, rumours flew through Washington as reporters scrambled to find out what was going on.

Three days later, on Wednesday, 21st January, Bill woke up Hillary early to warn her about a story in the morning paper. The *Washington Post* had its own explosive exclusive: Special counsel Starr was investigating whether Bill had asked Lewinsky to lie under oath to Jones's lawyers about their relationship. And there was more: The story said Lewinsky, now twenty-four years old, had confided in a work friend, Linda Tripp, and Tripp had secretly taped conversations in which the former intern described her relationship with Bill in great detail.

Bill assured Hillary, repeatedly, that there was no improper behaviour between him and Lewinsky. He told White House staff and friends the same thing over and over.

Suddenly the questioning in the deposition made sense: The Jones lawyers had hoped to catch Bill lying under oath, a crime called perjury, or to argue that he had obstructed justice by failing to be forthright.

Though the problem was Bill's, Hillary would once again be back in the spotlight. People would try to read her for clues about what was true and what wasn't. She would have to answer questions—and her answers would be carefully dissected. She was rattled by the news. It hurt just to hear the allegations, but she couldn't show it or share her feelings. "It was, for me, an isolating and lonely experience," she said.

Between reporters and round-the-clock politics, Washington is always in a whirl of its own, but the shocking charges sent everything into overdrive. Not only was the president accused of having a relationship with an intern just six years older than Chelsea, but it was also alleged that Lewinsky had kept a Gap dress that might be stained with his semen. As bits and pieces emerged, people on both sides of the political aisle began to believe the president might have to resign.

The scandal-seasoned White House, however, wasn't going to give in easily. It chose the tactic that Hillary nearly always advocated: It went on the offensive.

The following Monday, Bill unexpectedly joined Hillary at a ceremony to highlight an after-school programme. Before the cameras, with Hillary standing nearby, he pointed his index finger defiantly. "I did not have sexual relations with that woman . . . Miss Lewinsky," he said, momentarily forgetting her name. "I never told anybody to lie, not a single time, never," he added. "These allegations are false."

The next day, almost exactly six years after Hillary defended Bill on *60 Minutes*, she kept a long-standing date to appear on the *Today* show. She would have rather been just about anywhere else, but her appearance was crucial to how Bill would defend himself and how the public would see the situation. "At that moment," wrote political and legal reporter Jeffrey Toobin, "no one was more important to Bill Clinton's political future than his wife."

At the end of a White House press event, Bill jabs his finger as he insists that he didn't have a sexual relationship with Lewinsky.

Host Matt Lauer peppered Hillary with questions about what Bill had told her, whether her husband had apologized to her ("Absolutely not, and he shouldn't"), and finally about the investigation. Somehow, she explained to him, an inquiry into a failed land deal had turned into a four-year investigation costing more than $30 million that had now become a sex scandal. The other side of that sensational story was also a great story worth pursuing, she said, of "this vast right-wing conspiracy that has been conspiring against my husband since the day he announced for president."

Was there actually a conspiracy—which would imply illegal behaviour? That was far from certain, and her comments later would be seen as somewhat paranoid and self-serving. But at that very moment, her retort was a well-timed brushback aimed at the special counsel and a challenge to the media to consider another side of the story.

The *New York Times* called her comments "a blistering White House counterattack," and the *Washington Post* said Hillary's determined performance "dramatically reshaped the debate over the sex scandal" and "boosted morale at the White House" and among Democrats. It was followed by Bill's strong and confident State of the Union address, which didn't include any mention of the scandal. For a time, the furore cooled a bit.

The Lewinsky case wasn't going to fade away—but the Paula Jones case did. The lawyers in the case, who were supported by conservative organizations, had spent a lot of time prying into Bill's sex life, but they had not built a great case for their own client. In April 1998, a judge ruled in Bill's favour, finding that the Jones case didn't need to go to trial because neither Jones nor her job suffered as a result of whatever happened in the hotel room.

Jones appealed, and later in 1998, Bill finally settled the suit. To make the lawsuit go away forever, he agreed to pay Jones $850,000, more than she initially sought. An insurance policy covered about $475,000 of the cost, and the remaining amount came from personal investments. It was a big chunk of the family's savings—much of which had come from Hillary's earnings during her years as a breadwinner.

Back in Washington, Starr's investigation revved back up. The special counsel aggressively pursued his belief that Bill had lied about his relationship with Lewinsky, a path that would lead to some of the most difficult days Hillary would ever face.

26

IMPEACHMENT

Starr had a deadline.

He wanted to recommend that Bill Clinton be impeached for lying under oath. But to do that, he needed to get his evidence to Congress in the summer of 1998. If he waited until the autumn, he would be accused of political motivations, of trying to sway the midterm elections.

In late July, after months of negotiations, the special counsel finally granted immunity to Monica Lewinsky. In January, she had said in a sworn statement that she hadn't had a sexual relationship with the president. Immunity meant she could change her story and testify about what happened without facing charges for lying. It also meant she would turn over her Gap dress to Starr's team for testing.

Starr subpoenaed Bill to testify before the grand jury. After some back and forth, Bill agreed to testify via video from the White House on Monday 17th August, for no more than four hours. He would be asked the most personal questions, the most embarrassing details about what happened, and his testimony would be compared with hers. Bill was also required to provide a blood sample so that his DNA could be compared with the stain on her dress. His months-long story was crumbling.

On the Friday night before the testimony, Bob Barnett, Bill and Hillary's lawyer, tried to warn Hillary about what was ahead.

"What if there's more than you know?" he asked her.

"I don't believe there is," she told him. "I've asked Bill over and over again."

Barnett pushed the issue. "But you have to face the fact that something about this might be true."

She wasn't buying it. "Look, Bob," she said. "My husband may have his faults, but he has never lied to me."

Early the next morning, Bill shook her awake. He had been up all night, agonizing. Now, unable to stay still or to lie any longer, he began to confess, his words hitting Hillary like punches to the gut, making it hard for her to breathe.

He did have an inappropriate and physically intimate relationship with the young woman, he told her.

He had been too ashamed to admit it. He knew how angry Hillary would be and how painful the truth would be for her and Chelsea.

As Bill talked, Hillary's tears mixed with rage. She roared back at her husband: "What do you mean? What are you saying? Why did you lie to me?"

All Bill could do was pace and apologize. "I'm sorry. I'm so sorry," he told her. "I was trying to protect you and Chelsea."

She was stunned. One emotion tumbled over another. Her heart was broken. And she was "outraged that I'd believed him at all."

It was, she said later, "the most devastating, shocking,

News coverage of Bill's confession focused on Hillary as well.

and hurtful experience of my life." Everything she had believed about their long and intense relationship was in question. "I didn't know whether our marriage could—or should—survive such a stinging betrayal," she said.

They were supposed to have started their summer holiday that weekend, so she didn't have to appear in public for a couple of days. Just dealing with Monday was difficult enough. Bill was to testify and then make a speech to the nation, where he would have to tell Americans and the world that he had lied to them as well. When adviser James Carville saw Hillary that afternoon, her hair was pulled back into a ponytail and her eyes were puffy. "She'd obviously been crying," Carville remembered.

Though Bill was far from the first cheating husband in the White House, no president had ever had to make such an intimate confession on national television. Nor had a First Lady ever had to suffer through such personal disclosure about her marriage or endure such public humiliation.

Initially, Hillary stayed away as Bill's

Bill waits to go on television to tell the nation that he had lied and that he did have an inappropriate relationship with Lewinsky.

lawyers and White House aides wrestled with what he should say. He needed to apologize to the nation, but he didn't want to appear too weak or vulnerable. He was also seething at Starr and the investigation and wanted to say so, though some advisers thought that was a bad idea.

Finally, Hillary went up to the meeting room and listened to the discussion. Though she was livid, she still found it painful to see how upset her husband was at the day's events. This time, she wasn't offering guidance. "Well, Bill, this is your speech," she told him. "You're the one who got yourself into this mess, and only you can decide what to say about it." Then she left the room.

Bill made the four-minute speech alone, without a wife by his side. He confessed that he had, in fact, had a relationship with Lewinsky that "was not appropriate; in fact, it was wrong." He admitted to a lapse in judgment and personal failure, but also insisted that he never asked anyone to lie.

He had, however, not been truthful himself. "I misled people, including even my wife," he said. "I deeply regret that."

Then, unable to contain his anger, he took a shot at Starr and the seemingly endless investigation. "This has gone on too long, cost too much, and hurt too many innocent people," he said. "Now, this matter is between me, the two people I love most—my wife and our daughter—and our God. I must put it right, and I am prepared to do whatever it takes to do so."

His aides, and many in Washington, felt like he wasn't nearly remorseful enough. But in polls, public opinion of him remained positive. The many months between the first disclosure and his confession, noted journalist Peter Baker, had given people time to come to terms with and accept the possibility that the president had stupidly fooled around outside of his marriage.

The next day, Hillary, Bill, and Chelsea left for their scheduled holiday to Martha's Vineyard. As she headed to the helicopter, Hillary stared straight ahead, sunglasses covering her eyes. Chelsea, walking between her parents, reached out and took each of their hands, a poignant move for an only child caught in the middle.

In a poignant move, Chelsea holds hands with both parents as they leave for holiday following Bill's painful confession.

Buddy, the Labrador puppy, came along, too, "to keep Bill company," Hillary said, adding wryly, "He was the only member of our family who was still willing to."

Before she left, Hillary's press secretary issued a supportive statement, keeping the First Lady's anger in check: "Clearly, this is not the best day in Mrs. Clinton's life," it read. "This is a time that she relies on her strong religious faith. She's committed to her marriage and loves her husband and daughter very much and believes in the president, and her love for him is compassionate and steadfast. She clearly is uncomfortable with her personal life being made so public, but is looking forward to going on holiday with her family and having some family time together."

In reality, she was hurt and furious, and not at all looking forward to that holiday. She didn't want to be with Bill or hear his apologies, and the next few days were excruciating, so much so that she could hardly share what she was feeling with anyone. Her friend Diane Blair tried to reach her a couple of times, but couldn't. The pain was just too intense, too raw to share.

Immediately after the holiday, Hillary and Bill took off for Russia for a state visit, and then Ireland for meetings, before returning to Washington just before Labor Day. That week, Hillary returned to her usual schedule, visiting an elementary school, supporting a colon-cancer prevention event, and attending a Democratic Business Council dinner.

Blair finally caught up with Hillary in September, and they exchanged small talk about upcoming White House events and books they had read. Finally, Hillary told her friend that she was very sorry for her silence. She was still trying to work through what to do. Bill had been her best friend for twenty-five years, Hillary told her, and they were "connected in every way imaginable." He had made a huge mistake—but, she added, maybe she hadn't been smart or sensitive enough to see the pressure he was under.

Calling Lewinsky a "narcissistic loony toon," Hillary called Bill's behaviour grossly inappropriate, but said it was also consensual.

In an echo of her support during the 1992 campaign, she also told Blair that she believed Bill had done "brilliant things as president" and that she was committed to the issues and causes for which they had worked so hard.

So, Blair wrote in her notes, "she's in it for the long haul. Partly because she's stubborn; partly her upbringing; partly her pride—but, mostly because she knows who she is and what her values and priorities are."

Friends believed it was important to Hillary to keep the marriage together. "I don't think she ever stopped loving him," said Susan Thomases, a longtime friend and adviser. "She would have hit him with a frying pan if one had been handed to her, but I don't think she ever in her mind imagined leaving him or divorcing him."

With a little time and distance from Bill's shocking confession, Hillary later expressed a similar sentiment.

"As his wife, I wanted to wring Bill's neck," she said. She loved him, just as she had when she gave up a promising East Coast career to move to Arkansas. And while she wasn't sure the marriage would make it, she decided he certainly shouldn't lose his job for what he had done. She would fight for him.

In mid-September, Starr sent a thick report and three dozen boxes of supporting documents to the House Judiciary Committee, listing eleven potential counts for impeachment, including lying under oath, witness tampering, obstruction of justice, and abuse of power. The report was most striking for its embarrassingly graphic detail, including more than 500 references to sex.

A few days later, the House made the report public. Millions of people rushed to read the titillating specifics about their commander in chief, jamming websites. It was another round of humiliation for both Clintons. That would be compounded a week later, when House Republicans made public Bill's videotaped grand jury testimony, even though grand jury testimony is supposed to be secret.

In between the two disclosures, while the news and the Internet overflowed with stories, analysis, and opinions about the scandal, a group of Democratic congresswomen visited Hillary at the White House. Rather than offering comfort or consolation to the First Lady, they had an urgent request. They needed Hillary to fight for something more than Bill. They needed her to work for them, on behalf of Democrats seeking office or re-election.

The two dozen elected women who came to the White House were concerned that Democratic Party issues were being drowned out in the uproar over the Starr report and pending impeachment proceedings. Though the public still supported Bill as president, his tattered reputation wasn't going to help them on the campaign trail. But Hillary's star was soaring as she again showed strength and resilience in coping with a crisis. Polls showed her popularity reaching new highs.

"We honest-to-goodness need her," said Lynn Woolsey, a House member from California. "We don't want the issues in this country to be buried."

With their urging, Hillary hit the road with less than two months to go before the election. She made six appearances in California on behalf of Senator Barbara Boxer, who also happened to be the mother-in-law of Tony Rodham, Hillary's brother. She supported Senator Patty Murray of Washington state, campaigned for candidates in Illinois, Florida, and Georgia, and hit stops in Ohio, Nevada, and Wisconsin.

She recorded more than a hundred radio spots and telephone messages and spoke at fifty fund-raisers. Women, in particular, came out to see her at coffees, lunches, and rallies.

She spent so many hours on aeroplanes that she developed a dangerous blood clot behind her knee, causing her leg to swell. Rather than cancel appearances, she took a nurse on the road to help her with medication and monitor her condition.

Hillary campaigned especially hard for Representative Charles Schumer's effort to unseat New York Senator Alfonse D'Amato, who had led the Whitewater hearings that took aim at her. She travelled to New York several times to stump for Schumer, giving him a much-needed lift and winning friends in the powerful state.

Representative Charles Schumer of New York gives Hillary a Yankees cap at a fund-raiser supporting his campaign for the U.S. Senate.

When the votes were tallied in November, Schumer won, a particularly sweet victory. Boxer won, too. Even the unsuccessful races were closer than expected. The political columnist Mary McGrory called Hillary a "political force," and "a one-woman rescue squad for her party."

Some had predicted Republicans would gain seats, but voters sent a different message about their view of Washington politics. While Republicans still controlled Congress, Democrats picked up five seats in the House, and their numbers held steady in the Senate.

"We all thought a woman who has loved Bill Clinton would dramatically influence the midterms," said a *Time* magazine pundit. "And we were right. It just wasn't Monica."

In mid-December, the House Judiciary Committee recommended that the full House consider four articles of impeachment. In deciding what constituted "high crimes and misdemeanors," the committee had studied the work of the Nixon Judiciary Committee lawyers, the very report that Hillary had worked on just out of law school. Debate in the House started a week later, and just before the formal vote, Hillary agreed to speak to a meeting of House Democrats.

She still wasn't talking much with Bill, and the long-term fate of their marriage remained unresolved. But on Capitol Hill the morning of the scheduled vote, she rallied the troops for her husband as never before. "Certainly, I'm not happy about what my husband did," she told them. "But impeachment is not the answer."

She told the group that she cared deeply for her husband and that he would not resign. She thanked them for supporting the Constitution and "the commander in chief, the president, the man I love." She received several standing ovations.

That afternoon, the House narrowly voted to impeach Bill Clinton on two counts, perjury and obstruction of justice, making him the first elected president to be impeached, or charged with wrongdoing that could cost him his job. (The only previous president to be impeached was Andrew Johnson, who took office after Abraham Lincoln was assassinated in 1865.) Soon, Bill would be tried in the Senate, which would need a two-thirds majority to remove him from office.

Later that day, two busloads of Democratic members of Congress converged on the White House to show support for their president. To the surprise of Bill's aides, Hillary showed up as well. She put her arm in Bill's and walked with him to the Rose Garden, where he gave a short speech. No one had expected her to be there—but once again, she would stand by her man.

As personal as that choice was, her decision to stand with him had much larger consequences. Had she left Bill, he might well have lost the presidency. "All she had to do was just push, and Clinton would have been out of there," ABC News White House correspondent Sam

Donaldson told *People* magazine, echoing the view of other Washington insiders. Once again, she had saved Bill.

But she wasn't done. Out of that wretched and wrenching experience, she would also forge a new path for herself.

27

NEW YORK

The rumblings started just a few days after the November 1998 elections. Longtime New York Senator Daniel Patrick Moynihan told a reporter that he wouldn't run for reelection in 2000, after more than two decades in office. For the first time in years, a Senate seat in one of the nation's largest and most powerful states was totally up for grabs.

For New York Democratic power brokers, it was hard to imagine a better potential candidate than Hillary Rodham Clinton—except that it was also hard to imagine a more unlikely candidate.

Hillary didn't live in New York, and never had. She and Bill didn't even have a home outside of the White House. Her political résumé consisted mostly of being First Partner. She had no real ties to the Empire State, short of campaigning there. But New York had a history of adopting powerful carpetbaggers. And its loose residency requirements opened the door for outsiders to come in.

Robert Kennedy, President Kennedy's brother, had been elected to the U.S. Senate from New York in 1964 though he had no ties there, either. And more than fifty years before, Harold Ickes, a member of President Roosevelt's cabinet, had tried to convince New York's former First Lady Eleanor Roosevelt to run herself. She had turned him down, writing, "I feel very strongly that running for office is not the way in which I can be most useful."

The state's Democrats believed Hillary could be very useful and began to push the idea. The likely Republican candidate was New York City Mayor Rudy Giuliani, a blunt-talking politician who could raise big money and who had unusual support from the city's liberals. Hillary would be a formidable competitor to Giuliani and could bring in the boatloads of donations needed to mount a challenge.

She was riding a crest of popularity for standing up for Bill, as painful as that had been. An experienced campaigner, she was smart and hardworking, and she now knew intimately how Washington worked—though perhaps a little too well.

As early as Christmas 1997, a friend who chaired New York's Democratic Party told Hillary that she should run for the seat if Moynihan stepped down. In the autumn of 1998, as Bill was under fire, Charles Rangel, a Democrat who represented Harlem in the House, had told Hillary that if she was considering seeking public office, she should do so from New York. She already had support, he told her, from the state's eighteen Democratic House members, labor leaders, and the state's Democratic party.

In late 1998, the idea picked up steam. Her friend Diane Blair found Hillary to be "almost jolly" over the 1998 holidays. Hillary had loved the movies *Shakespeare in Love* and *Life Is Beautiful* and was reading a biography of Catherine the Great. Everywhere the family had gone—to church, theatres, restaurants—they had been warmly received. Though she and Bill were still at odds, Hillary seemed almost proud that they hadn't folded and instead had almost flourished, much to their critics' dismay. "Most people in this town have no pain threshold," she told Blair.

In early January 1999, the idea of Hillary as a legitimate candidate became more public: On the long-running Sunday morning public affairs show *Meet the Press*, commentators discussed her potential future Senate run.

Publicly, Hillary responded that she had no plans to run and that she was busy. Bill's impeachment trial was about to begin, and she was just recovering from terrible back pain, which was partly caused by greeting lines of holiday visitors while wearing high heels. She got better with physical therapy and medicine, prompting her to ask her therapist, "Can I wear high heels again?"

"With all due respect, ma'am," he told her, "why would you want to?"

While the Senate prepared to put her husband on trial, Hillary began to think about joining that elite group. Many times she had said publicly that she wasn't interested in running for office—except that she had seriously considered it back in Arkansas, when Bill was in a funk. Though clearly ambitious from the time she was young, she had never been forthright about those ambitions. It was Bill who was direct about returning to Arkansas and seeking public office. Hillary had always kept her own plans close to the vest, often working behind the scenes and telling people that she had no specific long-term career goals. Confident in her abilities, she admitted to wanting to influence policy but never said outright that she aspired to power.

The idea of serving in the Senate got her thinking: Where could she be most effective? She had been approached about a range of options, such as running a foundation or serving as a college president, where she could have had influence without living under a microscope. But then she probably couldn't work on all the issues that meant the most to her, like women's rights, health care, children, and families. Could she be a candidate herself—and could she win?

On 12th February 1999, the very day the Senate was voting on whether to remove Bill, Hillary sat down to discuss a potential Senate campaign with Bill's former aide, Harold Ickes, an astute political operative, who was also the son of the man who had tried to recruit Eleanor

Roosevelt. Together, they studied a map of the state and its diverse personalities: conservative voters upstate and in the suburbs and the more liberal-leaning New York City and its five boroughs. She would have to campaign across the state. She would also have to tangle daily with reporters who would chronicle her every move.

And there was another little detail: No woman had been elected to statewide office in New York since the early 1940s.

The Senate that day acquitted Bill of the impeachment charges, voting 45 for, 55 against on one count and 50-50 on the other, far short of the two-thirds majority needed. Just a few days later, Hillary publicly confirmed she was considering a candidacy.

At Ickes's suggestion, she began making phone calls to test the waters. She talked to Moynihan, state party leaders, and former New York City mayors. But she also called small-town mayors and Democrats in rural counties to learn the issues and voter concerns, seeking insight from more than 200 people.

In late March, Ickes shared his thoughts in a memo about the challenges of a race. "Voters have a very favourable attitude about you personally," he said. But he warned, "This does not, however, necessarily carry over to you as a candidate for Senate."

People who favoured Giuliani had real reservations about her, he wrote. They also wanted to know whether she intended to promote her own interests or "to represent and promote the interests of New Yorkers and NY." She would need to address that.

Most importantly, he noted that a race between her and Giuliani was a 50-50 proposition "at best. No coronation here."

Her aides worried that she might not be able to win—and fretted over whether they could keep the president of the United States on the sidelines and out of the way.

Just the prospect of Hillary running got the wise-crackers cracking. "I hear 'Run, Hillary, Run' bumper stickers are popular in N.Y.," went one joke that made the rounds by email. "Democrats have them on their back bumpers, and Republicans have them on the front."

Taking the plunge was a big move. Later, she would say it was one of the most difficult decisions she had ever made, right up there with deciding to stay with Bill. The two had been in marital counselling and were trying to rebuild their relationship based on "our faith, love, and shared past." (Bill would later say that he "had always loved her very much, but not always very well. I was grateful that she was brave enough to participate in the counselling.")

Ironically, a potential campaign got the two of them talking to each other again, rekindling their passion for strategy and campaign ideas.

In late May, Hillary called Ickes with an answer. She would run.

Moynihan generously allowed her to use his farm in Pindars Corners, New York, in early July to announce that she was forming an exploratory campaign committee. The notion that a sitting First Lady—especially a controversial one—would run for the Senate was so unprecedented that more than 200 reporters and photographers followed her to the one-stoplight town west of Albany.

Hillary and Senator Patrick Moynihan at his farm, as she prepares to announce her plans to seek his U.S. Senate seat.

Off the bat, she tried to address "the questions on everyone's mind: Why the Senate? Why New York? Why me?"

Her answer: New Yorkers shared her concerns about such issues as health care, education, and jobs. She told them she would devote the rest of the summer to a "listening tour," travelling all over the state to meet voters and hear their concerns.

Though she had campaigned for Bill and others for years, she was still a rookie candidate, and she made her share of rookie mistakes, beginning at this first event. When it was time for questions, she started to call on a familiar Washington reporter, when by tradition, a New

York City television reporter always asked the first question; Moynihan gave her a nudge to straighten her out.

She got in hot water later that summer when she donned a New York Yankees cap, a sign to many of fake fandom from the Chicago native. In fact, Hillary had been a Yankees fan as a kid, and there were news stories from the early 1990s confirming that; her campaign neglected to share them.

The Clintons bought a New York place in the autumn, a $1.7 million, five-bedroom home in Chappaqua, a wealthy, white, and Democratic town about thirty-five miles from New York City. Because the couple had millions of dollars in legal debts from the long investigations, a Democratic friend and fund-raiser put up $1.35 million in cash to help them buy it—causing another outcry about ethics. (They replaced the loan with a regular mortgage a couple of months later.)

As she began visiting each of the state's sixty-two counties, Hillary also had an image problem. "Despite everything people know about you personally," her longtime consultant Mandy Grunwald wrote to her, "they actually know very little." They didn't know who Hillary was, why she was really running, or what she stood for as a candidate.

Then there was the Bill problem. During one campaign meeting at the White House, Bill looked over the polling data and saw a pattern: "Women want to know why you stayed with me," he told Hillary.

The Clintons' house in Chappaqua, New York.

"Yes, I've been wondering that myself," she answered with a wry smile.

"Because you're a sticker," Bill told her, someone who keeps her commitments. "You stick at the things you care about."

Usually, philandering men have to do all the explaining. But as First Lady, Hillary somehow was also expected to justify why she stayed married. Perhaps hoping to put the matter to rest, she offered a long explanation in an interview for a new publication, *Talk* magazine—though she also questioned why she was supposed to share so much. "Why do I have to talk about things no one else in politics does?" she asked.

Never actually discussing Bill's actions, Hillary said that her husband needed to be more disciplined and more

~ed his turbulent childhood
. She called his behaviour
r than a "sin of malice." But
that he was, at heart, "a very

ill loved him. "You don't just walk
meone—you help the person," she said.
continued to share a sincere passion
politics, and when they were talking, they
tant conversation, she said. She even shared a
nal detail: "We like to lie in bed and watch old

ne media critics felt that she was making excuses
Bill's behaviour and that she should have expressed
ore anger, her own and on behalf of the nation he lied to. Her comments didn't end the questions. But she wouldn't say much more publicly—and that was another Hillary problem. As journalist Michael Tomasky wrote, "There was something about the way she answered questions that only raised other questions." Some politicians can put a question to rest with a vague answer; Hillary seemed to leave the impression, especially with reporters, that she was giving only part of the story.

Before the year was out, she had made another major gaffe. On a First Lady trip to Israel, she went to Ramallah, in the Palestinian territories, to announce U.S. funding of a maternal-care program. The event quickly turned political when Suha Arafat, the wife of the Palestinian

leader, accused Israelis of using cancer-causin[g]
against Palestinians. Hillary "sat mute" during th[e]
attack on Israel, according to the *New York Times*, [as]
inflammatory charges quickly caused an uproar a[mong]
Israeli leaders. At the end of the event, Hillary gave A[rafat]
traditional kisses on the cheek.

The warm embrace and the lack of a swift response [to]
the false allegations made big headlines in New York a[nd]
angered many Jews, a key Democratic constituenc[y.]
Hillary later said that the translation she heard of Arafat's
comments was less offensive than a more accurate version
she got after the event and that she didn't think the
remarks required an immediate rebuttal.

The blunder would take some time to blow over.

As 1999 came to a close, Hillary was still playing like
a rookie candidate. She was trailing Giuliani in the polls
and didn't seem to have a strategy for beating him.
Longtime political reporters were beginning to wonder if
the First Lady's ambition was exceeding her ability.

28

WINNER

After months of campaigning, Hillary Rodham Clinton officially entered the race for senator from New York in February 2000. Bill; her mother, Dorothy Rodham; and Chelsea sat on the podium to cheer her on. Bill was there as the supportive spouse, nothing more.

The sign behind her said only "Hillary," vaulting her into the ranks of one-name superstars like Oprah, Madonna, and Bono.

Dressed in a black trouser suit, she was well spoken and well coiffed. "I may be new to the neighbourhood," she said, "but I'm not new to your concerns." She promised she would stand for better education, better child care, a balanced budget, "more police on the beat, and fewer guns on the street."

To those in the political press who had covered many candidates before, she was a little dull, a little wooden, and too rehearsed. Mario Cuomo, once the governor of

The formal launch of Hillary's U.S. Senate campaign, February 2000.

New York, used to say, "You campaign in poetry. You govern in prose." Hillary had the prose part—but despite her rhyme, she had not mastered the poetry.

Still, reporters had never covered a candidate quite like her. Because of her celebrity, perhaps twenty reporters followed her on a typical day, with up to a hundred showing up for a big event—the kind of coverage presidential candidates get. Journalists from around the world made their way to upstate New York to write about one of the most famous women in the world.

As if to emphasize what a tradition-breaker she was, fashion writer Robin Givhan wrote an entire story in the *New York Times* on Hillary's trouser suit progression. Professional women adopted trousers as far back as the 1970s, but the women in Bill's cabinet and the relatively few women serving in Congress wore skirts and jackets as "their uniform," she wrote. Hillary, too, had started out in skirts and then transitioned to trousers in neutral or ladylike pastel colours. But as she became a candidate, Givhan noted, she had adopted clothes that were "more authoritative, stronger, and sharper."

In other words, she wore more black—apparently "the uniform of power" and a sign of her growing independence.

Her fashion didn't make her more accessible, however. Reporters were used to being able to approach a candidate between stops or over meals for questions and general schmoozing. But Hillary always had Secret Service around her, and getting near enough to chat or interview her was nearly impossible. And almost everywhere she showed up, crowds gathered, jamming the streets.

When reporters did get interviews, they often left frustrated by the experience. When she was off-the-record and knew she wouldn't be quoted, she could be blunt and insightful. She was intelligent on policy issues, although also a bit wonkish. But "when the topic was personal," wrote Elizabeth Kolbert of the *New Yorker*, "it was like talking to someone through several layers of Plexiglas."

In the spring, the story began to shift to Giuliani. He and Hillary were a perfect pair of bookend opponents— two tough, strong-willed, and well-known candidates duking it out. But while Hillary had been stumping throughout the state, Giuliani had been reluctant to leave New York City. He was at odds with the city's black voters, while Hillary had their support. Some pundits questioned whether he really wanted to run.

The issue was unexpectedly forced on him in late April, when he disclosed he had been diagnosed with prostate cancer and would need treatment. Then, just two weeks later, he said that he and his wife, Donna Hanover, were separating and that he would be spending more time with a woman he called "a very good friend." Hanover, who hadn't expected the disclosure, accused him of carrying on a long relationship with a staffer the year before. Hillary wasn't the only candidate with marital issues.

Shortly after, Giuliani dropped out of the race.

Almost immediately, Rick Lazio, a Long Island congressman, stepped in. He was a completely different kind of competitor, low-key, suburban, and far less divisive than Giuliani. Hillary's campaign would have to rethink its game plan.

At the same time, Hillary was quietly grappling with another tragedy. Her best friend, Diane Blair, had been diagnosed with lung cancer in March, and it had spread. The two had been as close as sisters, and Hillary often confided in her and sought her advice. Bill appointed her to the board of the Corporation for Public Broadcasting in Washington, and Blair had often stayed at the White House, sometimes helping out with Chelsea. Just the year before, Hillary had hosted an elaborate baby shower for Blair's son and daughter-in-law.

Hillary tried to make time to call her every day, and she and Bill jetted down to Fayetteville to see her. In their last visit, Blair urged her to win the election for her.

Blair passed away in late June, at the age of sixty-one, leaving a painful void in Hillary's life. "I never had a

The Blairs and the Clintons in 2000, in front of a plaque at the University of Arkansas law school recognizing that both Clintons once taught there.

better friend," Hillary wrote in 2003, "and I miss her every day."

Hillary had to return to the campaign trail. She had become much better at glad-handing, and now instead of leaving events quickly, she would spend hours shaking hands and listening to the concerns of potential voters who came out to see her.

She still continued to struggle to win over women voters. Some were angry and disappointed at Bill's misbehaviour and took it out on her; others remembered the lost billing records and commodities trading profits and simply didn't trust her. Suburban women, especially, saw her intelligence and her resilience as controlling and ambitious, her confidence as arrogance. In their view, she wasn't like them.

To make inroads, her campaign encouraged women supporters to host small gatherings in their homes, inviting two dozen or so other women. There Hillary could chat with them about marriage and child-care or other topics on their mind without the public watching. She also hit the luncheon circuit, reaching another broad female audience. After they saw her, women who had been undecided would think differently, said Beth Harpaz, who covered the campaign for the Associated Press. "She's so much prettier in person than she is on TV," they would tell her. She's much nicer and warmer, too. And, they would add, "she's so brilliant." Little by little, she won over women.

Her willingness to be a bit more open helped her relationship with the press. Reporters had more chances to ask questions and were surprised to find she had a sense of humour. They also learned some basic facts, such as her favourite colour (yellow) and her favourite snacks (chocolate and fruit).

She was also able to close some of the most difficult chapters of the White House years. In June, Ken Starr's successor as special counsel, Robert Ray, issued a final report, saying that Hillary had more influence in the 1993 travel-office firings than she had disclosed in sworn testimony. But he said there wasn't enough evidence to prove in court that her testimony was "knowingly false."

In September, he reached a similar conclusion about the long-running investigation into the Whitewater deal, saying there wasn't enough evidence to prove that either Bill or Hillary had committed crimes related to the real-estate venture or kept information from investigators. Specifically, Ray said, the circumstances around the lost billing records were inconclusive, and there wasn't enough information to show Hillary obstructed justice or knowingly gave false answers.

Reached on the campaign trail, Hillary told reporters, "I'm just glad this is finally over."

The news didn't seem to have much influence on the race. Her Republican opponent was raising money by the armful, largely by tapping into Hillary-haters in his party.

But Lazio was also having a hard time defining himself, and he lacked the stature of the First Lady.

In their first debate in mid-September, he made a tactical error. The two had been arguing about each other's use of "soft money," donations that are supposed to support the party or issues rather than a specific candidate. Lazio pulled out an agreement from his pocket and demanded that Hillary sign it, walking over to her, putting it in front of her, and jabbing his finger emphatically that she should do it right now. "Why don't you show some leadership, because it goes to trust and character," he said.

Hillary, keeping her composure, reached out and shook his hand, almost as a way to push him away.

Lazio's aggressive move toward Hillary backfired. Women in particular felt like he had bullied her—and they had seen enough of that. Lazio never did catch up.

The biggest news of 2000, however, was the presidential election. Vice President Al Gore, the Democratic candidate, faced off against Texas's Republican Governor George W. Bush, son of Bill's predecessor, George H. W. Bush. Though the economy had improved and the nation was in the midst of a technology boom, Gore distanced himself from Bill and especially Bill's behaviour.

In a stunningly close race, a winner couldn't be determined on Election Day. Ultimately, Gore won over 500,000 more votes than Bush did, but fell short by five electoral votes. The race came down to Florida, where Bush led by roughly 500 votes out of almost 6 million cast. The unusually slender margin led to a recount and a legal battle, which dragged on for weeks. Finally, on 12th December the U.S. Supreme Court, in a five-to-four decision, ordered an end to the recount, effectively declaring Bush the winner.

Hillary's race, by contrast, was a landslide. On Election Day, she won 55 per cent of the state's vote, compared with 43 per cent for Lazio, a much larger victory than anyone had expected. And she was especially successful with women, winning 60 per cent of women's votes. In New York City, three-quarters of the women voted for her, while she won 55 per cent upstate. She had finally been elected to public office.

She got a laugh in her acceptance speech when she declared, "sixty-two counties, sixteen months, three debates, two opponents, and six black trouser suits later, because of you, we are here."

Hillary had always been her own woman, but for two decades it had been hard to see the growth of the one-time rising star outside of her role as the wife of Bill Clinton. Now, at fifty-three years old, she was a prominent politician in her own right. Suddenly, the possibilities seemed endless.

Hillary celebrates her win in the 2000 Senate race.

At a press conference the day after the election, she was asked if she would run in the next presidential election. No, she answered quickly: "I'm going to serve my six years as junior senator from New York."

It was an answer that left plenty of room for speculation.

Drawn and Quartered

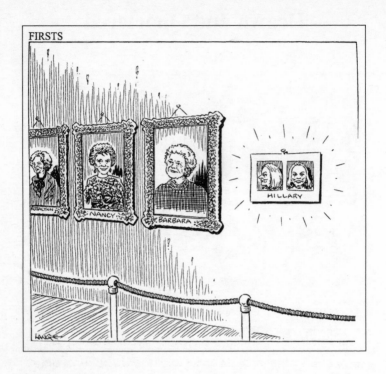

PART FOUR

HILLARY

"I've had every opportunity and blessing in my own life, and I want the same for all Americans. And until that day comes, you'll always find me on the front lines of democracy, fighting for the future."

29

SENATOR

On 3rd January 2001, Hillary Clinton again made history.

At midday, she was sworn in as a United States senator by Vice President Al Gore, who was coming to terms with his painful loss.

Meanwhile, the sitting president of the United States, just like every other family member, was in the Senate chamber's visitors' gallery, along with Chelsea and Dorothy Rodham. Bill held Chelsea's hand and beamed as Hillary became one of thirteen women in the hundred-member Senate—and the only one who would continue to serve as First Lady until the new president was inaugurated in three weeks.

"Words cannot describe how thrilled I was for her," Bill later told Taylor Branch. He called it the happiest day of his life, after the day Chelsea was born.

It was a day filled with historic irony. The senior New York senator, Charles Schumer, looked at Hillary on the floor and the president in the audience and wondered to himself what George Washington and Thomas Jefferson would have thought.

After eight years of White House scandals, the swearing-in should have marked a fresh start for the freshman senator, a clean slate for a new career. But nothing in Washington—or with the Clintons—is quite that simple.

Al Gore reenacts Hillary's swearing-in as a U.S. Senator for the cameras.

Between Election Day and Hillary's first day on the job, the publisher Simon & Schuster had agreed to pay her $8 million for a memoir, the biggest book advance since an $8.5 million deal with Pope John Paul II in 1994. During the transition, she and Bill also sent gifts that they had received as president and First Lady to their new home in Chappaqua. The gifts, valued at nearly $200,000, included furniture, silverware, fine china, and other items.

Famous people often receive big book advances, and hers

would have been allowed under Senate rules. Previous presidents had also taken thousands of dollars in gifts with them after their terms ended. But the size of the book advance prompted another outcry about her ethics from government watchdog groups and the shipping of gifts appeared as if she was arrogantly sidestepping proper procedures.

Had she already started her $145,000-a-year job, she couldn't have accepted any gift with a value of more than $50. In addition, some donors said their gifts were intended for the White House, not its inhabitants.

Amid the furore over tables and place settings, the Clintons reconsidered. They returned at least $28,500 in gifts to the White House and paid $86,000 to essentially buy other gifts.

Then, at the end of his term, Bill issued dozens of pardons, forgiving those who had been convicted of crimes—

Hillary and Bill and Laura and George W. Bush leave the Capitol on Bush's inauguration day.

which brought yet another round of outrage and charges of political dealing. Among those pardoned were Bill's brother, Roger, and a fugitive billionaire named Marc Rich, whose ex-wife, Denise Rich, had donated to Hillary's campaign. A bit later, it was disclosed that Hillary's brother Hugh had been paid $400,000 to lobby on behalf of two clients with criminal records.

Hillary said she had nothing to do with any of the pardons and didn't know about her brother's role. She said she was "extremely disappointed in this terrible misjudgment that he made," and she called on him to return the payment. He did.

Despite the new controversies dogging her, Hillary dove into her new job. When she was elected, then-Senate Majority Leader Trent Lott said pointedly that "she will be one of a hundred, and we won't let her forget it." But it was impossible to forget who she was. She was the only senator with Secret Service protection, and she was such an international celebrity that tourists stopped to gawk. Just the simple act of getting coffee might set off a blinding round off press photos.

Even her hair was still in the news. In February, Lloyd Grove, a *Washington Post* columnist, commented that now she was out of the White House, she was sporting "a rough-and-ready do" more appropriate for a soccer mom. He didn't mince his assessment of her styling skills: "The dry-and-go bangs hang limply down her forehead like rain-battered weeds, and she doesn't appear to be using much in the way of hair spray, mousse, or even makeup."

Responded her press secretary: "We're here to talk about what's on her mind. Not what's on her head."

Hillary had hoped to get a spot on the Appropriations Committee, which doles out a big chunk of the federal budget. But Republicans on the committee felt she was too biased for that assignment; instead, she was assigned to the less powerful Budget Committee, as well as the Committee on Health, Education, Labor, and Pensions, and the Senate Environment and Public Works Committee.

By April, she had delved deeply into the details of her job. One press release touted a measure she pushed to help communities upgrade their water-treatment systems. She was trying to get help for the upstate New York economy while working to rename a New York City courthouse and win historic-preservation funding for Ellis Island. She hadn't missed a single vote or a committee meeting. Colleagues called her hardworking, methodical, and collegial.

A headline in the *New Republic* summed up her first few months in office: "Dull and Duller."

Quietly, she also joined a Wednesday morning Christian prayer group that included several conservative senators. Early on, one of those, Sam Brownback from Kansas, told Hillary that he had said terrible things about her and her character. He asked her for her forgiveness, which she gave him. "I think that a prayer network often can move us to do things we might not otherwise do," she said later.

Though she kept a low profile as a freshman senator,

she was continuing to build her base in the Democratic Party. Using part of her book advance, she and Bill bought a $2.85 million home near Embassy Row in Washington, which would be a venue for fund-raisers and also Dorothy Rodham's full-time home. Bill was living in Chappaqua, and the two tried to be together a few nights a week, with Bill in Washington one weeknight and Hillary in New York on weekends.

But they weren't together nearly that often. Bill was on the speaking circuit, making up to $250,000 a day for appearances and speeches as part of his mission to repay an estimated $14 million in legal debts that he and his aides owed. He was also working on his presidential library and foundation.

Hillary started a political action committee called HillPac to raise money for Democratic candidates for federal office and to pay for political travel. Her ability to raise millions of dollars would also extend her political influence beyond her elected role.

By summer she was settling in, holding regular fund-raisers at the home they called Whitehaven, for its street name, and pushing for legislation to aid New York. Most days, her security team of Secret Service and Capitol Police drove her to work around 8:30 a.m. while she conferred with staff on the phone. Between meetings, hearings, and appearances, she often left the office between 8:00 p.m. and 10:00 p.m.

And then everything changed.

nguage for the attackers: "Our country not only
taliate directly against those who perpetrated this
ut we have to make it very clear that we cannot
any state, any government, any institution, or
al to pursue terrorist aims that are directed at
ed States or any country," she said.

said she expected many countries to unite behind
on. "It's not just an attack on the United States,"
. "It's an attack on everyone who cares about free-
l dignity and justice and humanity."

r spending much of the long night on the phone,
ed the Senate the next morning to approve a reso-
condemning the attack. That afternoon, she and
r flew from Washington to New York on a special
Emergency Management Agency plane. All other
had been grounded the day before, after it was
at four planes had been hijacked. (In addition to
hat crashed into the World Trade Centre and
on, a fourth plane came down in a Pennsylvania
ter passengers fought back against the hijackers.)
h September theirs was the only plane in the air,
of Air Force fighters. At New York's LaGuardia
t, they boarded a helicopter to tour the damage.

site of the World Trade Centre was still smolder-
l smoky as they flew over. As rescuers desperately
ed for survivors below, Hillary could see the twisted
s and shattered beams where two stunning and
ous buildings had once stood.

11th September 2001, was to be another historic day:
First Lady Laura Bush was to testify about early childhood education before one of Hillary's committees. It
would be an unusual First Lady meeting. Hillary put on a
bright yellow suit for the event.

She was on the phone with Ann O'Leary, her legislative director, when the first plane hit the World Trade
Centre. Initially, they thought it was an accident—until
the second plane hit. At that point, O'Leary said, Hillary
was sure it was a terrorist attack.

By the time Hillary arrived at work near the Capitol, a
third plane had crashed into the Pentagon, and police were
evacuating her office building. She met some of her nervous
staff outside, where she tried to assure them that they would
be okay and dispatched them to a staffer's nearby home.

By then, police were trying to clear traffic, and Hillary
got back in the car. One of Bill's former advisers, Gene
Sperling, happened to be nearby, and she offered him a ride.
While the radio reported the grim news, Hillary frantically
dialled her cell phone. First she tried to reach Chelsea. Now
twenty-one and a Stanford graduate, Chelsea was staying
with a friend near Union Square in Manhattan before she
was to go to England for graduate school. Her mom knew
she often went for a jog at that hour of the morning.

Hillary couldn't get through. Next, the senator from
New York dialled officials at the Federal Emergency
Management Agency to ask about their response to the
crisis.

"It was like watching her move back and forth from each role in her life minute by minute," Sperling said. "Then suddenly, the radio announcer starts screaming, 'Oh my God, the World Trade Tower has collapsed; oh my God, the World Trade Tower has collapsed,' and suddenly the whole world came to a stop."

The images of planes crashing into the towers had been horrible beyond words. But then the buildings came crashing down, killing thousands of people and remaking the famous skyline. Especially in New York City, people would look to their elected officials for assurance about their security and safety. Hillary was now on the front lines.

With so much still unknown, Hillary scrambled to get as much information as she could and to touch base with her family. She called Bill, who was in Australia for a speech. He was watching the destruction on television and wanted to know if Chelsea was okay. Though she didn't know for sure, Hillary told him that everything was fine and not to worry.

Around the time that Hillary was calling, Chelsea had been in her friend's apartment trying to reach her mother, but she couldn't get through, either. Feeling an overwhelming need to reach her mom, Chelsea ran out to look for a pay phone, but there were long lines at each one. She returned to the apartment, and when her friend came back home, they followed the mayor's advice and headed uptown.

Near Grand Central Station, people were panicking,

yelling "Fire!" and "Bomb!" and running
terminal. Though there was no fire, C
friend were frightened and crying. "For a
truly thought I was going to die," she wr

Chelsea was near Fiftieth Street and I
when her mother finally got through. J
voice, Chelsea burst into tears.

After their conversation, Hillary cal
tell him Chelsea was safe.

She also called Giuliani and the Nev
She and the other New York senator, (
spoke with President Bush, getting his a
federal government would help with t
and New York's rebuilding.

That afternoon, now wearing a more
suit, Hillary joined other senators at
headquarters, where they gathered to b
leaders. As the sun was setting, Hill
hundred members of Congress on the
leaders of both the House and Senate
port, and called for a moment of silen
to walk away, some members began
America," tentatively at first, and the
ger. When they finished, many l
Hillary, the *New York Times* reporte

CNN sought her out for an in
President Bush was to speak to the
she would stand behind the pres

Hillary joins New York City Mayor Rudy Giuliani and New York Governor George Pataki *(left)* for a tour of the World Trade Centre site after September 11, 2001.

"The TV images I'd seen the night before didn't capture the full horror," she wrote later. It felt like she was looking into "the jaws of hell."

On 13th September she and Schumer met with President Bush. They knew the administration planned to set aside $20 billion in emergency aid for Washington, New York, and Pennsylvania. They decided to ask for twice that, with $20 billion going to New York alone.

To their surprise, Bush said yes.

She and the Republican president were in agreement on rebuilding New York. She would later support him in responding to another perceived terrorist threat—a position that would carry a stiff political cost.

30

WAR

Hillary had expected to work six days a week as a senator. But in the aftermath of September 11, 2001, she worked seven days a week for months. A reporter who spent a couple of days shadowing her that autumn noted that their conversations on the way to and from events were "punctuated with deep yawns."

Over several trips to what became known as Ground Zero, she grew concerned about the air quality and working conditions around the World Trade Centre site. She worried about the health of workers and nearby residents, especially whether the contaminated air was damaging their lungs. She lobbied her colleagues for funding to monitor the situation and then brought in an expert to study it. Eventually, the Environmental Protection Agency agreed to track the impact on health, and Congress approved funds to support it.

She wasn't always successful or popular. Though she

and Schumer had worked to get New York $20 billion in aid, New York was ultimately allotted $11.1 billion. Hillary promised to keep fighting for more. "It's important that we recognize that this is a long-term effort," she said. "We've got a good down payment."

At an October concert to benefit police and firefighters, Hillary was booed when she went up on stage to thank the crowd for supporting New York. Neither group had supported her candidacy, and she was under fire for appearing uninterested during a Bush speech. Hecklers told her to get off the stage and shouted, "We don't want you here!" (Bill, by contrast, got a warm reception.)

She shrugged it off as something that happens to those in politics, something that wasn't personal. It was "almost part of the healing process," she said. "They can blow off steam any way they want to."

Still, the loss of life was hard on her—and it continued. In November, an American Airlines plane headed for the Dominican Republic crashed minutes after takeoff from New York's John F. Kennedy International Airport, killing 265 passengers, crew members, and people on the ground. After meeting with family members who lost loved ones, she was overwhelmed. "I feel like I'm drowning in tragedy," she said.

Bill saw the painful impact as well. "The heartbreak of it was almost too much for her," he said. "She's tough, but she's also incredibly human."

In responding to the tragedy of September 11, Hillary

would soon be seen as a "hawk," an advocate for aggressive action against possible sources of terrorism. Days after the terrorist attack, Congress passed a joint resolution allowing the use of force against those responsible, and Bush signed it. In October 2001, less than a month after 9/11, the United States retaliated with an attack on Afghanistan, home to the terrorist group al Qaeda and its leader Osama bin Laden, who took credit for the attacks. Within weeks, the country's Taliban regime began to retreat, collapsing in early December. Efforts to capture bin Laden, however, were unsuccessful.

President George W. Bush and Hillary after the president signs a law giving tax benefits to families of 9/11 victims.

Shortly after the terrorist attacks, the Bush administration also turned its focus to Iraq and its leader, Saddam Hussein. The administration accused that country of ongoing efforts to build weapons of mass destruction, flouting a United Nations ban, and of harbouring terrorists, hinting at a link between Saddam Hussein and al Qaeda. Seeing the country as a threat to international security, the United States and its European allies called on Iraq to allow the United Nations to inspect the country for evidence of chemical and biological weapons and nuclear capability.

When Iraq didn't fully comply with the inspections in 2002, officials in the Bush administration began to push for an invasion of the country, capitalizing on the still-raw emotions, fear, and patriotism heightened by the 2001 attacks. The administration lobbied lawmakers intensely in the autumn. In September, President Bush asked Congress for broad authority to use military force against Saddam Hussein.

It was a controversial request and one of the most arduous and weighty decisions that Congress had been asked to make since the early days of the Vietnam War. Some reports disputed that Iraq actually had weapons of mass destruction or that there were links between Saddam Hussein and al Qaeda. Others claimed to be more certain of the connections.

Hillary was already familiar with the potential threat: In late 1998, Bill had ordered a four-day U.S. and British air assault on Iraqi weapon and military sites because of its failure to cooperate with U.N. inspectors. Ahead of the vote, she attended classified briefings and studied reports. She quizzed Bush officials and asked pointed questions about how it would deal with governing a rudderless Iraq after it toppled Saddam.

Across the country, antiwar protests popped up, and some experts warned that taking military action would disrupt the careful balance in the Middle East, with long-term implications. But in Congress, most of the votes were with the president.

On 10th October 2002, the Republican-controlled House voted 296 to 133 to give Bush the power to use force against Iraq. Out of 208 Democrats, 126 voted no. Then the Democrat-controlled Senate wrestled with the question.

In comments on the floor that day, Hillary took a harder line against Saddam than most of her Democrat colleagues, saying that if he was left unchecked, he would continue to rebuild his chemical and biological weapons and continue to try to develop nuclear capability. She also argued that he aided al Qaeda, a position that other Democrats disputed.

She said she preferred more efforts at diplomacy. But, "I take the President at his word," she said, "that he will try hard to pass a United Nations resolution and seek to avoid war, if possible."

The decision was a difficult one, "probably the hardest decision I have ever had to make," she said. "Any vote that may lead to war should be hard." But she said she was voting in favour because she wanted the president to be in a strong position to lead the country, because she wanted to support the military, and because she wanted Saddam Hussein to know that the country was unified.

"I support this resolution as being in the best interests of our nation," she said. But she added, "it is not a vote to rush to war; it is a vote that puts awesome responsibility in the hands of our president. And we say to him: Use these powers wisely and as a last resort."

The debate in the Democrat-led Senate went on into the night. At 1:15 a.m. on 11th October, the Senate voted 77-23 to give Bush the authority he sought.

In March 2003, the United States and its allies invaded Iraq, entering into a costly second war.

Both the new war and the ongoing conflict in Afghanistan would drag on far longer than most imagined, and in time Iraq would become a source of considerable disagreement. Though Saddam Hussein's government would be toppled, and the nation ultimately would hold elections, a stable democracy would prove elusive. Weapons of mass destruction were never found. The claims of ties to al Qaeda turned out to be false. While early opponents of the war predicted those results, the facts weren't fully evident for some time. Hillary remained a supporter of the war for several years and refused to apologize for her vote for it.

In January 2003, she was appointed to the Senate Armed Services Committee, the first New York senator to serve on the committee that oversees national security programmes. In giving up her seat on the Budget Committee, Hillary said she wanted the new assignment because she wanted to oversee the military response to terrorism; since the current administration was spending so much on defense, she wanted to know where the money was going.

Others saw a different reason: They believed she was buffing up her political résumé by adding credentials in national security and showing that a woman could be as tough and informed as a man.

The move fed a perception held by many in Washington and elsewhere: Hillary was prepping for a presidential run. Ever since she had been elected, she was constantly asked the same question: Will you run for president?

Over and over, she told friends, reporters, and others that she was happy being the senator from New York, that she would not run in 2004, and that she had no plans to do so in 2008. One scribe found more than 130 magazine and newspaper stories in which she had told interviewers the same thing between early 2001 and autumn 2003. Still, the question kept coming.

In June 2003, her autobiography *Living History* was published, giving a first personal glimpse into the Clinton White House. She and aides had worked on it at night and on weekends, little by little. The book was far from a tell-all about her life and the White House. But sterile though it was, it offered a deeper look into her background and her perspective than she had shared before, and it quickly became a bestseller. More than a million copies flew off the shelves in the first month alone.

Autographing her autobiography, *Living History*, in New York in June 2003.

As she toured the country, fans encouraged her to run. So did big Democratic supporters, executives, and politicians. In part because she was so well known, polls showed her well ahead of any other potential Democratic candidate, and not far behind the incumbent president.

Publicly, she responded, "I am absolutely ruling it out." In a meeting with a former congressman from Arkansas, she almost gushed about her job in the Senate, wrote Kolbert in the *New Yorker*. "I'm having the time of my life," Hillary said. "I pinch myself every morning."

But privately, according to authors and political reporters John Heilemann and Mark Halperin, she seriously considered jumping into the race. Over three months, she participated in meetings and conference calls looking at the competition and whether she could be elected. One staffer collected details about filing fees and deadlines. Others worked on the language she might use after saying for so long that she was committed to finishing her Senate term.

In November 2003, she was the master of ceremonies at the Jefferson Jackson Dinner in Des Moines, Iowa. The closely watched Democratic fund-raiser featured the potential candidates—but Hillary took the spotlight. Iowans were so excited to see her that they snapped up a record 7,500 tickets, selling out. When she came up to the stage, the attendees chanted her name.

"Star of the Show," read one headline in the *Des Moines Register*, which noted that many there wished out loud that she would run.

A few weeks later, she gathered her inner circle, including top aides from the White House and Bill and Chelsea, to make a final decision. Bill and her aides all thought she could win if she ran. She was sorely tempted. But Hillary couldn't get past her promise to serve New York for a full term—and Chelsea agreed, believing voters wouldn't forgive her if she changed her mind.

As Hillary saw it, running in 2004 would make true everything that her fiercest critics said about her—that she was hypocritical and dishonest, that she was blindly ambitious, and that her ambition was all that motivated her. She wouldn't run.

She did, however, campaign for a promising young African American candidate named Barack Obama, who was running for the Senate from Illinois. She appeared at his fund-raisers in Chicago and held a fund-raiser for him at her home in Washington. Her political action committee supported his campaign. "There's a superstar in Chicago," she told aides.

Hillary with former First Lady Barbara Bush, Houston Mayor Bill White, and first-year Senator Barack Obama at a Houston press conference following the devastation of Hurricane Katrina.

In 2004, Bush was reelected—and the up-and-coming Obama was elected to the U.S. Senate, where he and Hillary became colleagues.

With a few years of experience under her belt, Hillary began to speak out more on social issues, often taking a middle-of-the-road position and joining with Republican lawmakers. For instance, she slammed the sex and violence in video games—singling out *Grand Theft Auto*—and called for a uniform rating system like the one for movies. Joining Republicans Sam Brownback and Rick Santorum, she co-sponsored Democrat Joe Lieberman's bill calling for the government to study the impact of video games, television, and the Internet on child development. (The bill didn't pass.)

She supported civil unions for gay couples, but opposed gay marriage, drawing criticism from gay-rights advocates. She continued to argue for health-care reform, pushed for automated health-care records, and sponsored legislation requiring that prescription drugs prescribed for adults and children be tested for children as well as adults.

She was especially active in military matters, calling for higher pay for soldiers and expanded health-care services for National Guard members. As the Iraq war dragged on and public opinion began to turn against it, she grew critical of the Bush administration's management of the war, but she was slow to call for a withdrawal of troops. When she did vote for pulling out of Iraq, she wanted a gradual withdrawal rather than a set timetable.

"I am cursed with the responsibility gene," she told the *New York Times* after returning from a weekend trip to Iraq in early 2007. "I am. I admit to that. You've got to be very careful in how you proceed with any combat situation in which American lives are at stake."

Pundits tried to paint her centrist opinions as a shift intended to prepare for a presidential bid in 2008. In truth, most of her positions on social issues were consistent with her comments during the White House years and her Senate campaign—but fewer people were listening to her then. Though she was often painted as a far-left liberal, there was still a bit of the Goldwater Girl left in Hillary, who was at heart a pragmatic, moderate Democrat.

Her position on the Iraq war was more politically troublesome. By 2006, Americans "were overwhelmingly against the war," she said later. That November, voters threw out many Bush allies who supported the war. Democrats again won control of both the House and the Senate.

Still, Hillary was easily re-elected to her second term as New York's senator, trouncing an antiwar opponent in the primary and the Republican candidate in November. She had done what she promised to do: serve New York as the junior senator for at least one term.

As soon as the midterm elections ended, attention turned to a wide-open race for president in 2008. In poll after poll, Hillary was the Democratic front-runner. Everyone assumed she would run. She just had to say so.

31

CANDIDATE

On Saturday, 20th January 2007, Hillary issued a statement and put a short video message on her website. She was taking the initial step toward running for president and, she said, "I'm in to win."

She noted the upcoming big questions for voters. How could the United States end the war in Iraq? How could every American have health insurance? How could America clean up the environment and find energy independence?

She shared her qualifications—her work on education reform in Arkansas, her push to expand health-care coverage for children, and her efforts to help victims of 9/11. And she invited Americans to have a conversation with her, through Web chats over the next few days.

Though the announcement was widely expected, the decision to make it had not come easily. Now approaching her sixtieth birthday, Hillary knew the race would be demanding and exhausting, and she would be opening the door again to every issue and criticism that had dogged her during the White House years. Plus, she had picked up a few new ones, especially her vote allowing Bush to invade Iraq. And she had never really become comfortable at playing along with the media.

Bill was a wild card as well, someone who could hurt her chances as easily as he could help them. With his political experience and stature, he could be her best ally. But voters had not forgotten his tomcatting (along with gossip that it had continued). The former president's desire to do things his way, ignoring her aides, also posed a threat to her campaign.

As late as December 2006, she was still wrestling with whether she should jump in. Hillary and Bill spent the holidays in Anguilla, and on the beach on New Year's Day, Hillary asked Bill what he thought she should do.

He told her to ask herself one key question: Would she be the best president of all the people running? If so, she should run. If not, she shouldn't.

Not long after, she called Patti Solis Doyle, one of her closest, longtime aides. "Bill said that if I really feel like I can do this and do a good job and be the best one, then I should do it," Hillary told her. "And I *do* believe that."

The decision to enter the race came with another challenge: the young superstar senator, Barack Obama. Other Democratic senators, worrying that Hillary might not be able to win a national election, had encouraged the youthful and eloquent politician to run. At forty-five years old, he lacked her national experience, but he was smart, upbeat, and charismatic, and especially appealing to young people, who were willing to knock on doors and work the phones for his campaign.

Obama announced his interest just before Hillary did, making the 2008 election perhaps the most historic of modern times. Hillary wasn't the first woman to run, nor was Obama the first black candidate, but neither a woman nor an African American had ever had such a good shot at becoming president.

While Hillary had been focused on her Senate reelection campaign in 2006, Obama and another Democratic candidate, John Edwards, had begun making speeches and appearances in Iowa and New Hampshire, the sites of the highly influential first votes of the presidential race.

From the moment she became the only woman in the Democratic race, gender was on the agenda. Male candidates might offer a discussion with voters without much extra analysis. But when Hillary used the slogan, "Let the

In April 2007, all the Democratic hopefuls participate in the first debate of the 2008 campaign.

Conversation Begin," it took on a different meaning, as Jon Stewart joked on *The Daily Show* shortly after her announcement.

"I don't think that slogan's going to help you with men," he suggested, noting the stereotypes about how men and women communicate. "You might as well get on your campaign bus, the I Think We Really Need to Talk Express, to unveil your new Iraq policy: America, let's pull over and just ask for directions."

Hillary's chief strategist and pollster, Mark Penn, wanted her to portray herself as tough, a formidable commander in chief in the style of Margaret Thatcher, Britain's long-serving prime minister who was nicknamed the Iron Lady. "Being human is overrated," he said. And, in fact, around the world, many female leaders had come off more as battle-axes than as kindly figures.

But portraying Hillary as tough and in control hid Hillary's more human side, her empathy, and her sense of humour, and reinforced the caricature that she was cold, pushy, and robotic. By contrast, successful candidates like Ronald Reagan and Bill Clinton had come across as warm and caring; even George W. Bush had run as a "compassionate conservative."

Hillary got off to a strong start. In late March 2007, at a union-sponsored candidate forum, Obama tried to bluster through a question about his health-care plan. Hillary was sharp and passionate, calling health care "the number one voting issue in the '08 election." In a series of debates, she was more focused and more on point, showing up Obama's inexperience.

On the Iraq issue, however, Hillary was under fire. Iraq had become the most controversial war since Vietnam, and more and more voters were angry about it and wanted the United States out quickly. Obama had been an Illinois state senator when the crucial vote was taken, and he had come out strongly against the war then. It turned out to be the right call. Hillary had been increasingly voicing opposition to the war; in 2006, she said that if she had known at the time of the vote what she knew now, she wouldn't have voted for it.

That wasn't enough for antiwar voters. They wanted her to admit she had erred, something Hillary had long avoided for fear of looking vulnerable. So she simply said she had changed her position, which frustrated potential supporters. (She didn't truly admit to making a mistake until the publication of her book *Hard Choices* in 2014, saying that she had learned that admitting mistakes can also reflect strength and growth. "I should have stated my regret sooner and in the plainest, most direct language possible," she wrote, adding that she "got it wrong. Plain and simple.")

Hillary was also struggling to connect to Iowans. Citizens there take their role seriously and make an effort to see and hear candidates' positions. Instead of a primary, where people privately cast a vote at polls that are open from morning until evening, Iowa holds caucuses. People attend a meeting that might last a few hours and declare their vote publicly, in front of friends and neighbours. If candidates don't get enough votes, those who voted for them can switch to someone else. The process can be confusing and intimidating, and many people either can't attend because of work or family responsibilities or don't go because of the time commitment. Presidential hopefuls have to find a way to reach those dedicated voters who will go to a caucus.

While Obama built an extensive regional team in Iowa, Hillary's team hadn't committed many people to campaign in the state. Bill had been able to skip Iowa in 1992, and despite Hillary's popularity at the Jefferson Jackson Dinner in 2003, the Clintons weren't well connected there. In spring 2007, a campaign aide wrote a memo suggesting that she skip Iowa. It would cost millions of dollars to put enough people on the ground to reach the potential voters, and those funds could go to bigger states, where early voting was starting around the same time as the Iowa caucuses.

The memo was leaked to the *New York Times*, and the embarrassing disclosure forced Hillary's hand. Now, she *had* to go to Iowa to prove she was a strong candidate and could compete there. She also would have to work harder there to win over Iowans who were offended that her campaign considered passing on their state. Gradually, she built a team, but she resisted making personal phone calls, which were time-consuming though valuable, and she balked at visits to small counties to meet just a few dozen voters.

Some saw her attitude as cocky and smug, a sign that she believed that she should and would win just because she was the early leader. At the same time, she had reason for optimism. An early October ABC News–*Washington Post* poll showed her with a whopping lead over Obama nationally, 53 per cent to 20 per cent. A strong majority of voters polled believed she was the most likely Democratic candidate to win the election.

Iowa, however, stood in her way. The Hawkeye State had never elected a woman to Congress, and polls in the state showed her, at best, in a tight race. Her campaign tallied her efforts there in comparison with her opponents and found Hillary had attended sixty-nine events in just over a third of the state's counties. By contrast, Obama had made a hundred stops in about half the counties, and John Edwards had been to nearly all ninety-nine counties.

As the caucuses drew near, she began to stumble. At a debate at Drexel University in Philadelphia, she fumbled her answer to a question about whether she supported

Hillary and Obama face off during a debate at Drexel University in Philadelphia, where Hillary fluffed an answer about driver's licences for illegal immigrants.

driver's licences for illegal immigrants, giving a wordy response that was unclear. Another candidate, Chris Dodd, called her on it, and her efforts to explain it only added to the confusion. Edwards and Obama jumped on her response. "I can't tell whether she was for it or against it," Obama said.

Even her campaign had a hard time fixing the gaffe, clarifying the initial clarification to say that she supported the idea in the absence of immigration reform. Suddenly, her opponents had a line of attack: This was a familiar Hillary, the one from the White House who couldn't seem to give a simple answer and stick with it.

At the Jefferson Jackson Dinner in November, neither she nor Obama were able to speak until late in the

evening, after many Hillary supporters had left. Obama seized the moment with a dazzling oration, offering hope and promising change while working in a few jabs at Hillary. "I am not in the race to fulfill some long-held ambitions or because I believe it's somehow owed to me," he said.

As the Iowa race came down to the wire, Hillary won the endorsement from the state's leading newspaper, the *Des Moines Register.* Iowans admired her experience but still weren't sure they liked her. So in December, she and Bill went on what the *New York Times* dubbed a "likability

Campaigning in Iowa, November 2007.

tour," working their way across Iowa via helicopter. Her campaign ran humanizing ads featuring her mother and Chelsea, who also joined the campaign trail. It seemed to help, but not enough to make up for her slow start and lack of early organization in the state—or Obama's momentum.

On Thursday 3rd January 2008, a record number of Iowans went to caucuses to support a Democratic candidate. The campaigns had expected 150,000 to 180,000 people to attend a caucus. But 240,000 came to cast a vote, almost twice as many as in 2004. When the dust settled, Obama had won almost 38 per cent of the vote, and Hillary had come in third, just barely behind John Edwards, who got about 30 per cent. It was a crushing loss, like a sports team that has a near-perfect season and then dissolves in the playoffs. Yet again, a presidential race suddenly looked like it might end before it had even really begun.

32

2008

To stay in the race, Hillary needed a turnaround—and quickly.

The New Hampshire primary was 8th January 2008, just five days away. If she wanted to save her campaign, she had to make a better showing there. Though Iowa and New Hampshire delivered only a fraction of the delegates needed to win the nomination, donor money would vanish if she wasn't a viable candidate. And, as predicted, her campaign had spent heavily in Iowa, sapping much of her war chest.

She gave her concession speech and then pulled her staff together in a single room. Climbing up on a chair, she vowed that they would keep going.

That night, she and her top team flew to New Hampshire, arriving at 4:00 a.m.

Bill had kept a low profile during Iowa. But as a veteran of New Hampshire, he urged Hillary to do what he had done years before: connect directly with voters.

Rather than speaking and running to the next event, she stayed to take questions, at least leaving the impression of being more open.

At a debate among the Democratic candidates that Saturday night, she pushed back when she felt like Obama and Edwards were teaming up against her. Then, a moderator asked her why New Hampshire voters admired her experience, yet seemed to like Obama more. "Well, that hurts my feelings," she responded with a big smile, drawing laughter from the audience.

"But I'll try to go on," Hillary said, getting another laugh. "He's very likable. I agree with that. . . . I don't think I'm *that* bad."

Obama looked up from taking notes and said dryly, "You're likable enough, Hillary." He, too, got a laugh at the time—though his comment later was criticized as cutting and cocky.

Boosted by his big Iowa victory and the enthusiastic crowds that met him, Obama began to cruise. Hillary's campaign cranked up the phone banks, and an estimated 4,000 volunteers knocked on doors, while she continued to work the crowds.

The day before the primary, Hillary met with her campaign manager. Patti Solis Doyle had bad news: The campaign's polling data showed Hillary badly trailing Obama in New Hampshire. She probably was going to lose the upcoming primary in South Carolina, and maybe the caucus in Nevada, too. There was some money in the campaign coffers to help with the slew of primaries on Super Tuesday in early February, but probably not enough.

With the grim picture still in her head, Hillary headed to a coffee shop to meet with a group of women. In the conversation, one of them asked a friendly question: "How do you do it?" she asked, referring both to staying upbeat and also managing to look good every day.

Hillary acknowledged that she got some help on the appearance part; then, as she addressed the rest of the question, her feelings bubbled to the surface. "It's not easy, and I couldn't do it if I didn't passionately believe it was the right thing to do," she said.

"I have so many opportunities from this country," she added, her eyes tearing and her voice softening. "I just don't want to see us fall backwards.

"You know, this is very personal for me," she went on, blinking hard. "It's not just political. It's not just public. I see what's happening. We have to reverse it.

"Some people think elections are a game, they think it's like who's up or who's down," she added, her voice full of emotion. "It's about our country. It's about our kids' futures. And it's really about all of us together."

It was a rare moment for Hillary—and a dicey one. In previous years, other candidates had lost credibility after crying on the campaign trail. Hillary didn't actually cry, but letting her feelings show could have been seen as a sign of weakness. The press pounced on her very personal response, debating the impact.

The verdict came quickly. When New Hampshire's votes were counted the next day, she had won. She had reached voters, she had stood up to her opponents, and in showing a soft side, she had also proved her toughness. All of that had convinced women, in particular, to vote for her. A Clinton had again staged a comeback in New Hampshire.

In her victory speech, she told her supporters, "Over the last week, I listened to you, and in the process I found my own voice."

With the support of female voters, Hillary wins the New Hampshire primary.

She also earned a new place in American history, becoming the first woman to win a binding presidential primary. Backstage, she was all smiles, high-fiving aides and looking, according to one account, "like a quarterback who'd just completed a last-second Hail Mary pass in overtime."

She was back in the race—but there was much to do. Roughly half the states were voting in the next month.

The campaign moved on to the Nevada caucuses, and Hillary's Nevada team had learned from Iowa that turnout matters. They focused on boosting the turnout for Hillary and succeeded, with more than 117,000 voters turning out—twelve times the number that voted four years before. Hillary won 51 per cent of the vote.

Her team hadn't planned much campaigning in South Carolina. Bill, however, believed he could help her in a Southern state and began to stump for her there. But as he spoke out aggressively against Obama, he angered black voters and brought her campaign more headaches than help. Ultimately, her campaign reined Bill in, involving him more in internal issues like advertising and sending him primarily to rural areas.

In part because of Bill, Obama demolished Hillary in South Carolina, winning 55 per cent of the vote to her 27 per cent. Donors big and small poured money into his campaign, through both the Internet and traditional means.

John Edwards, lagging behind, dropped out of the race at the end of January.

All along, Hillary's campaign had zeroed in on Super Tuesday—5th February—when twenty-two states would cast votes. Back in the fall, her camp thought she might wrap up the nomination on that day. But now, the campaign was teetering on disaster—trailing Obama and losing momentum.

Her campaign's experienced and seasoned managers—whom she hoped would be a team of rivals who challenged and pushed each other—instead were disorganized and fighting internally. Most troubling, fund-raising had slowed, and cash was tight. At the end of January, the Clintons personally loaned $5 million to the campaign.

The infusion helped. Hillary won nine states in all, including four of the five largest states voting: California, New York, New Jersey, and Massachusetts. The Massachusetts victory was especially sweet because the state's highly respected senator, Ted Kennedy, had recently endorsed Obama. Obama won thirteen states, including his home state of Illinois, and a host of small states. Overall, Hillary won the popular vote—but just barely.

But the race for the Democratic nomination was only partly about votes. At its heart, it was a race for delegates, the folks who actually vote for a candidate at the Democratic National Convention. Candidates won delegate support based on both the popular vote and on a state's congressional districts, with each district typically getting three to six delegates. In addition, there were superdelegates: governors, party leaders, and other elected officials who can choose to vote however they wish.

Hillary's campaign had concentrated on big states that could deliver the most delegates, which were often states—as her aides would argue later—that the Democrats would need to carry to win the general election in November. Because neither Hillary nor Bill really trusted the caucus process, they avoided most of the caucusing states, including six states that voted on Super Tuesday.

Not only was Obama smart, charismatic, and likable, but also more tactical. Back in the summer, dozens of lawyers had studied the rules for each state primary or caucus. They concluded that Obama could pick up a large number of delegates with a modest amount of campaigning in caucus states, small states, and even Hillary states like New York, where he was sure to lose. Each state was a simple maths problem: For instance, based on the rules, he could win 40 per cent of New York's delegates if he won just 30.1 per cent of the popular vote.

By adding up the possibilities, the Obama campaign realized that he didn't have to win a big majority to win the nomination. Picking up delegates in states he lost could give him an edge in his delegate tally.

The process was so messy, however, that the press had trouble interpreting it. The *New York Times* only counted delegates who were officially selected and bound to a vote. Based on that, it said Hillary was leading the race after Super Tuesday. The Associated Press—counting the delegates another way—reported that Obama was ahead.

The strategy would become clearer during the rest of February. With fresh cash in his campaign, Obama was able to outspend Hillary and soar past her, winning eight states and the District of Columbia, including caucus states that Hillary had ignored. With that streak, he moved firmly ahead.

Hillary was down, but not out. If she had doubts, her aides said she never shared them. Travelling with a hair-stylist, a makeup artist, and a personal assistant who had a gift for fashion and jewellery, she looked like a celebrity and sounded like a star athlete. "I just take it a day at a time—it's a good policy for life as well as politics," she told reporters.

Some on Obama's team calculated—correctly—that she could never catch up. But determined and optimistic, Hillary believed she could still win, especially if she could bring more superdelegates to her side. Early on, she had balked at calling them for support, and she and Bill now had to try to regain lost ground.

Her campaign brought in more than $30 million after Super Tuesday, and she turned her attention to two key states, Texas and Ohio, which had primaries on 4th March. The Clintons' ties in the Lone Star State dated back to their days campaigning for McGovern in the 1970s, and they still had strong connections there. The economy was faltering, the early rumbles of what would explode into a full-fledged financial earthquake later in the year, and Hillary's message about restoring jobs and righting the economy resonated in Ohio.

She also poked fun at herself. After *Saturday Night Live* made light of how the press seemed to fawn over Obama, she slipped away from campaigning to do a live guest appearance on the show. Standing next to Amy Poehler, who was made up just like Hillary and wearing a nearly identical suit, she asked, "Do I really laugh like that?"

Hillary takes a quick break from the campaign trail to have a little fun with Amy Poehler on *Saturday Night Live*.

The next day, in a partly filled high school gym in Austintown, Ohio, she found a new voice—that of an underdog. "I'm a fighter, and I will get up every day in the White House, and I will fight for you," she told the crowd. She joined arms with a local prize-fighter. "This guy knows what it's like to get knocked down. He also knows what it's like to get back up and fight," she said. "You know, in life you get knocked down from time to time. Sometimes, you don't know it's coming."

She began to share stories about people denied health care, about those who had lost jobs. She began to connect. On 4th March, she won both Texas and Ohio. "For everyone here in Ohio and across America who's ever been counted out but refused to be knocked out, and for everyone who has stumbled but stood right back up, and for everyone who works hard and never gives up, this one is for you!" she declared in a triumphant victory speech.

Suddenly, she was on a roll. She won easily in Pennsylvania in April, though both candidates had faced some setbacks. In late March, Hillary had to drop a story she told on the campaign trail: She had been saying that she and Chelsea had come under sniper fire during a trip to Bosnia in 1996, and they had to run from their plane to avoid it. However, a video from the trip was found showing that she and Chelsea calmly exited the plane and met with dignitaries.

Obama also took a hit after a video surfaced of his longtime pastor making incendiary comments. Obama responded with a passionate speech about race in America. (Hillary had wanted to speak about women, but the opportunity never presented itself.)

Many political experts thought Hillary was at her best in the last three months of the campaign, rallying crowds, sharing her passion, and winning votes. Even so, her slow start and earlier miscalculations were too great to overcome. After Obama won in North Carolina and she barely eked out a victory in Indiana in early May, it was painfully clear that she couldn't catch up unless something truly dramatic happened. Many people in the party urged her to concede, yet she refused. From March through to June, she won more contests and collected more delegates, though that wouldn't be enough. Even so, she stayed in the race until the last primary.

At rallies, she had called it "the longest job interview in the world," and fought for it until the bitter end. "Bill and I share a character trait of being determined and committed and not easily deterred or discouraged," she told the *New York Times* in an apparent understatement.

When all the votes were added up, the race had been incredibly close. Out of an estimated 35.5 million votes cast, Obama had won perhaps 150,000 more votes than Hillary, with less than half a percentage point separating them.

Finally, on 7th June Hillary thanked her supporters and endorsed Obama in her rousing concession speech. For the first time, she also played up her historic role as the first female presidential candidate in American history to actually have a chance. Though "the highest, hardest glass ceiling" wasn't broken, "thanks to you, it's got about eighteen million cracks in it," she said, to cheers and applause.

Though many Hillary supporters wanted her to be Obama's running mate, Obama didn't seriously consider her as a candidate for vice president. He had doubts that she would be a good fit for the number-two position—and he didn't want a former president hanging out so close to the White House.

In September and October, several major financial-

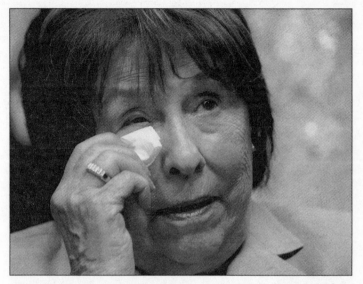
Hillary's mom, Dorothy Rodham, wipes away a tear as she listens to Hillary's concession speech in June 2008.

services companies failed or nearly failed, sending the economy tumbling into the worst financial crisis since the crash of 1929. The stock market plunged, slashing the value of Americans' savings, retirement accounts, and college funds, and the number of unemployed workers soared. In November, Obama soundly defeated John McCain, becoming the nation's first African American president.

As he put together his cabinet, Obama knew he wanted Hillary on his team. He just had to convince her.

33

SECRETARY

The first time Barack Obama suggested Hillary should be his secretary of state, she said no. The second time he asked, she said no again.

Obama first mentioned the job in a face-to-face meeting in Chicago shortly after the November 2008 election. Hillary was stunned. She had expected to be offered a lesser cabinet post, like secretary of Health and Human Services, which she would turn down. But this was a plum position, an influential cabinet post that was fourth in the line of succession to the president, after the vice president and the leaders of the House and the Senate.

Obama told her that he had been thinking of her to lead the State Department for some time. He and his advisers believed an aggressive Bush administration had sullied the reputation of the United States abroad as it had taken the country to war in Iraq as well as Afghanistan. In the meantime, the serious financial troubles meant the economy was going to need much more attention than the new president had expected.

As a result, Obama told her, he needed his chief foreign-affairs adviser to have standing with leaders around the world. He needed someone who was smart and tough and disciplined. In his mind, he needed Hillary.

But Hillary wasn't so sure. She told the president-elect that she was happy in the Senate, where she could work on a new effort to overhaul health care and try to create new jobs to replace the millions that were being lost.

She was worried about repaying leftover campaign debts, which had topped $25 million in the summer. She and Bill had loaned the campaign about $13 million of their own money, which they lost when her campaign wasn't able to pay it back by a required deadline. By the end of 2008, she still owed about $6 million. She felt a moral obligation to pay it all back, but she wouldn't be able to actively raise funds as a cabinet member. (She finally repaid the last bit in early 2013.)

And then—again—there was Bill. His foundation had donors and programmes all over the world. He would have to disclose them and take steps to restrict donations from foreign countries that might be made in hopes of influencing Hillary. Further, Obama would have to accept that she couldn't control what Bill said.

On top of all that, the sixty-one-year-old said, she was tired and wanted to be home more.

Obama said he understood her concerns, but he needed

her and the country needed her. He asked her to think it over.

Bill quickly got on board, agreeing to share his donor list and take steps to make her appointment possible. He urged her to take the job, saying, "The good you can do as secretary of state will more than outweigh whatever work I have to cut back on."

In true Hillary fashion, she did her homework. She spoke with aides, Senate colleagues, and longtime friends. She called Madeleine Albright, who had served as the first female secretary of state during Bill's administration. She listened as Joe Biden, the vice president-elect, and Obama's aides lobbied her. She weighed her options in the Senate, where she still didn't have much seniority. She had been a team player, but far from a superstar. In nearly eight years, she had sponsored more than 700 bills, but only three minor efforts had become law: naming a highway and a post office and creating an historic site. Of the more than 2,600 bills she cosponsored, seventy-four became law.

Still, she decided she wanted to stay a senator. Her staff prepared a statement, and she tried to call Obama to tell him no.

Cleverly, he refused to take her call. An afternoon call was rescheduled until later, and then rescheduled again. Finally, around midnight, she reached him. He listened to her concerns and then brought up the work ahead navigating two wars amid other foreign challenges. And he refused to take no for an answer, suggesting she sleep on it.

She didn't sleep much, though. She replayed the conversation in her mind, and weighed the teachings of her faith that had led her to public service. She imagined if the tables were turned: What if she thought he was the best candidate for a position? Wouldn't she want him to accept? Finally, she decided, "When your president asks you to serve, you should say yes."

The next morning, she did.

The learning curve was steep. Though Hillary had travelled around the world and met with world leaders as First Lady and a senator, she had never actually negotiated with them. She didn't speak a foreign language. Predecessors like Albright and Condoleezza Rice, the most recent secretary of state, had both previously worked for the National Security Council and had diplomatic experience.

Amid almost constant travel, Hillary would have to learn about dozens of countries, their leaders, and details of America's relationship with them. But she brought other experience to the job. "The art of diplomacy is to get other people to want what you want," Albright told a reporter. Hillary "knows how to do what I think is essential: putting herself in other people's shoes."

Or, as Hillary said in an interview, "Having come to this job from the political world, I have a certain level of understanding or sensitivity to what people's political problems are, even in authoritarian regimes, because everybody's got politics."

By February 2009, she was putting those skills to use. Rather than head to Europe or the endlessly complex Middle East, she chose to go first to Asia for visits to Japan, Indonesia, South Korea, and China. It was an unusual, thought-out choice: Under her leadership, the Obama administration would try to, in her words, "pivot" toward Asia and especially China, an economic power-house intertwined with the United States financially, but worlds apart politically. In the past, the region had received far less attention; she believed it would continue to grow in importance.

Her first trip was notable as much for her comments and style as for the location. She was blunt and direct, so much so that one reporter called the trip the "Clinton Straight Talk Express." She spoke openly about the possible impact of a battle for leadership in North Korea. She told reporters travelling with her that she would be focusing on climate change and the financial crisis in China and would give less airtime to human rights. On the last subject, "we pretty much know what they're going to say," she said.

Though her comment was true, it infuriated human rights activists, who didn't want to see that important issue downplayed. Once again, she was reminded that she needed to think about how others heard her. "Now that I was America's chief diplomat, every utterance would be subjected to a whole new level of scrutiny, and even seemingly self-evident observations could set off a feeding frenzy in the media," she wrote later.

Rather than just meet with top leaders, Hillary also tried to connect with regular people and the local press, with the hope that she might shift public opinion about the United States and, in turn, influence foreign governments. An aide dubbed the sessions "townterviews," a combination of town hall meetings and interviews; along with her effort to visit U.S. staff abroad, these became a regular part of her overseas trips.

In Seoul, she talked to nearly 3,000 female students. In Japan, she visited the University of Tokyo. In Beijing, she met with women lawyers, doctors, and academics. Their questions were all over the map. Who were her favourite musicians? The Beatles and the Rolling Stones, she admitted to a television host in Indonesia. How did she become strong? "Well, I played a lot of baseball, and I played with

On her swing through Asia as the new secretary of state, Hillary appears on a variety television show aimed at teens in Jakarta, Indonesia.

a lot of boys." How did she know she had fallen in love with her husband? "I feel more like an advice columnist than a secretary of state," she quipped, before adding that her husband was her best friend.

Though she had long had a strained relationship with the press, she began to let her hair down—quite literally—with the group of reporters who spent hours on the same aeroplane. She chatted over drinks after the workday and on the many long plane rides—off-the-record, of course, which meant she couldn't be quoted.

When she was in the air, she often changed into a comfortable top and sweats and pulled her hair into a ponytail, or clipped it with one of the binder clips from the briefing report she was studying. Her hairstylist stayed in Washington, so she was on her own on the road, and sometimes she skipped the makeup as well. At one point, an unflattering photo of her at a press conference wearing only lipstick and sporting her eyeglasses went viral, with the caption, "Hillary Au Naturale."

Over the years, Hillary had learned to grab sleep wherever she could, crammed into a campaign plane, in a car, or in the little time she might have between meetings. Aides said she could snooze all the way through a landing. The intensive travel was as exhausting as it was engaging, and Hillary sometimes dug her fingernails into her palm to stay awake during meetings and conference calls.

While dealing again with the double standard she had

long faced over her hair and clothing, she also made a point of highlighting women's issues around the world, such as voting rights, violence against women, and school and job opportunities. She appointed her former White House chief of staff as ambassador-at-large for global women's issues. And while men sometimes started to check their email and tune out when she broached women's issues, she was passionate about even seemingly insignificant matters such as smoky cookstoves. Nearly two million women and children die each year, she said, from pneumonia or other side effects of smoke and toxins from cooking over open fires or with poorly ventilated stoves. Available, inexpensive options could transform lives, she told one audience, adding, "We are excited because we think this is actually a problem we can solve."

In her first three months, she visited more than twenty countries. But more surprising to Washington's political scorekeepers, she and her new boss seemed to be getting along just fine. They met weekly, often on Thursday afternoons. Though they were never close, he found her to be low maintenance and a team player. And he had some pressing foreign issues to address, most notably Afghanistan.

When Obama took office, he pledged to resolve the two wars that had dragged on for years. Although the United States had attacked Afghanistan for harbouring Osama bin Laden and other terrorists, the Bush administration had taken its focus off that war when it went into Iraq. Over the years, the Taliban had regrouped, and

Taking advantage of a pretty day in Washington, Hillary and President Barack Obama hold one of their weekly meetings at a White House picnic table.

more than seven years after 9/11, bin Laden still hadn't been captured.

Early in his new job, Obama had agreed to send more troops and additional trainers to Afghanistan to finish the job, and also pay more attention to Pakistan, which shared a border. He promised "a clear and focused goal" for what seemed to be an open-ended effort: "to disrupt, dismantle, and defeat al Qaeda in Pakistan and Afghanistan, and to prevent their return to either country in the future."

By late summer, it appeared that his first steps hadn't been enough. The army commander on the ground, Stanley McChrystal, began asking for even more troops—

up to 40,000 more—which would put about 100,000 soldiers in the country.

Over several months, Obama pulled together his top military and foreign advisers, including Hillary, Defense Secretary Robert Gates, and Vice President Biden, to debate the request. Biden was strongly against more military in the region and wanted the president to try an alternative approach zeroing in on al Qaeda. Hillary, however, sided with Gates and much of the military in calling for thousands more troops. They also wanted more civilians who would work to improve conditions for the people in the country and try to wean it from the poppy trade, the source of drug money that funded insurgents. It would be her job to negotiate with Afghan leaders.

The alignment was unusual; often the secretary of defense is at odds with the person carrying out foreign policy. But Hillary and Gates were seen as "moderate pragmatists," who found common ground on this issue. That surprised Gates, who had served in the Bush administration and who initially had a less-than-positive view of Hillary. "I quickly learned I had been badly misinformed," he said later. As a colleague, he found her smart, funny, tough-minded, and "idealistic but pragmatic."

Her support for more military presence wasn't surprising, given her previous positions on Iraq. In one meeting with the national security team, Hillary argued that the status quo just wasn't working. She believed more troops were needed, as well as more civilians. The plan "comes with enormous cost, but if we go halfhearted, we'll achieve nothing. We must act like we're going to win."

That stance, said investigative reporter Bob Woodward, mirrored a philosophy Hillary first adopted in the White House years: "Fake it until you make it." Used by those trying to overcome addiction, the phrase means trying to adopt certain behaviours while figuring out how to make them real. She wanted an approach that would prove the nation was serious about reaching its goal.

Obama is joined by Hillary, *(from left)* National Security Advisor Gen. James Jones, Admiral Michael Mullen of the Joint Chiefs of Staff, and Defense Secretary Robert Gates on the Marine One flight to the U.S. Military Academy at West Point in New York.

After nine meetings with his national security experts, Obama finally made a decision, siding largely with Hillary and Gates—but with a couple of twists. In a 2nd December speech at the U.S. Military Academy in West Point, New York, he said that the United States would be sending

30,000 more soldiers into Afghanistan, with the hope that allies would send 10,000 more. And then, he said, he would begin to withdraw troops in mid-2011.

Ultimately, the surge would be less than successful. Obama did begin to reduce troops in 2011, but the region remained volatile. He didn't fully end the combat mission in Afghanistan until the end of 2014, and even then, about 10,000 U.S. soldiers remained. Officially, the war lasted thirteen years, making it the longest war ever in U.S. history. More difficult foreign decisions loomed ahead.

34

MOTB

Hillary and Bill got some happy news near the end of 2009: Chelsea was engaged to her longtime boyfriend, Marc Mezvinsky. Wedding planning was added to the secretary of state's schedule.

Though her job kept her on the road, Hillary stayed in close touch with Chelsea, now twenty-nine, through email. That wasn't always simple: In countries like Russia, where political relationships were delicate, she was advised to leave her BlackBerry and laptop on the plane, with the batteries removed. In a hotel room, she was supposed to read sensitive material inside an opaque tent or, if that wasn't available, under a blanket. "I felt like I was ten years old again, reading by flashlight under the covers after bedtime," she said.

Bill didn't use email, but he and Hillary talked on the phone every day when they weren't together. To the surprise and satisfaction of the Obama administration, Bill had stayed out of her business, and she rarely mentioned him at work.

Seeing him, however, was something of a challenge. "We're like Talmudic scholars trying to figure out" a schedule, she said. "Once a month, maybe more if I'm lucky, I go home," flying a commercial airline to New York and driving to Chappaqua. When they were there, they played with their new dog, Seamus, and sometimes liked to house hunt just for fun. (Buddy, Bill's loyal White House dog, was killed by a car in January 2002 while the Clintons were on holiday.)

Occasionally, they got lucky and found themselves in the same city. Once, they were able to have an evening out in Bogotá, Colombia—but then, because of logistical complications, they had to return to separate hotels. When they both attended a funeral, they got a whole day together. "We just take whatever time we can," she said.

She had a scare in February 2010 when Bill went to the hospital with chest pains. The first time he had experienced that kind of discomfort, in 2004 at age fifty-eight, the former president ended up having major heart-bypass surgery. That recovery was long and made more complex when complications required a second surgery.

This time, doctors were able to place stents in an artery to open it back up and prevent a possible heart attack. Hillary was meeting with President Obama in Washington at the time and hurried to New York later that day. Bill recovered quickly enough that she went ahead with a trip to the Persian Gulf.

Amid Bill's recovery, work on China, and another trip to Vietnam, Hillary was helping Chelsea plan her special weekend in Rhinebeck, New York. Chelsea gave her a necklace with the letters *MOTB*, for mother of the bride, and Hillary even signed a Mother's Day email to her staff as *MOTB*. She checked out flower arrangements and dresses via email, while also working on issues with North Korea and Iran; she squeezed in trips back home for tastings and dress selection. (It was later revealed that, in a highly unusual arrangement, Hillary had used only her personal email account during her entire time as secretary of state, never adopting a government email address. The decision would prove to be very controversial.)

Hillary and Bill with Marc Mezvinsky and Chelsea on their wedding day.

The press couldn't stop quizzing her about the wedding, and she confessed in July to a Polish interviewer that the big event "truly is the most important thing in my life right now." She even had a diplomat's answer when asked about the interfaith marriage, since Chelsea's fiancé was Jewish. What's important isn't race or faith or ethnicity, she answered, but "are you making a responsible decision? Have you thought it through? Do you understand the consequences? And I think in the world that we're in today, we need more of that."

Before 400 guests on 31st July 2010, both a minister and a rabbi married Chelsea and Marc. Bill walked her down the aisle. Hillary was overcome with emotion seeing her beautiful, grown-up daughter take this big step, and she and Bill welcomed Marc into their family. "It was one of the happiest and proudest moments of my life," Hillary said later.

She was especially happy that her ninety-one-year-old mother, Dorothy, was there to enjoy the day. Her mother had moved into Hillary and Bill's Washington home when Hillary was a senator and was there when Hillary came home tired or frustrated after the 2008 campaign or a long day in Washington. They would sit together in the breakfast nook. Dorothy would ask if she was eating right, if she was getting enough rest. Hillary would "let everything pour out."

In the year after the wedding, however, Dorothy had heart trouble and grew frail. Hillary was just about to

Ninety-one-year-old Dorothy Rodham celebrates with Chelsea and Hillary. She would pass away about sixteen months later.

take off for London and Turkey when Dorothy was rushed to the hospital. Hillary hurried to her side to hold her hand one last time. The next day, on 1st November 2011, her mom—her confidante and her rock—passed away. The loss was excruciating.

Dorothy had overcome a terrible childhood to live a full and vibrant life. She had taught Hillary about the resilience of the human spirit. Because adults had believed in her, Dorothy said, she had risen above her circumstances, a true testament to the power of kindness.

"No one had a bigger influence on my life nor did more to shape the person I became," Hillary said later. She was heartbroken, weeping "for how much I would miss her." In the days after, she sat next to the empty chair where they had shared so much time together, "wishing more than anything that I could have one more conversation, one more hug."

She took some time off after her mother's death, but not much. What was most notable about her breaks for Chelsea's wedding and to mourn her mom was how rare those days off from work were. As in the White House, the pressing business of foreign affairs didn't go on holiday. Some of the issues were as important as anything Hillary had been involved in during a lifetime of significant experiences.

One of those was in the spring of 2011. That March, Leon Panetta, now head of the Central Intelligence Agency, filled Hillary in on a top-level state secret over a private lunch. Nearly ten years after 9/11, his agency finally had a decent lead on where al Qaeda leader Osama bin Laden was living. He would need Hillary's support to go after him.

During March and April, the president held several secret meetings in the White House with his top national security team. Participants were told not to tell anyone; Hillary listed them simply as "meeting" on her schedule. The CIA believed bin Laden might be living inside a walled compound in Pakistan, just a few miles from the country's leading military academy. The intelligence gleaned from the CIA wasn't certain: Various reports put the likelihood that bin Laden was there at 40 per cent to 80 per cent. Obama called it a 50-50 possibility.

Almost immediately, Hillary was in favour of moving on a credible lead. "It was a matter of keeping faith with the people that we represented in this country," the former New York senator said. Plus, "for me, it was very personal because of what I'd lived through with what happened on 9/11."

One by one, options were considered and rejected. A joint raid with Pakistan? Hillary and others argued that the nation wasn't trustworthy enough. Bombing the compound? That could result in innocent lives lost, and there wouldn't be any proof that bin Laden was actually inside. Using drones to drop a missile? That might limit damage to the neighbourhood, but it still wouldn't allow for positive identification of bin Laden.

The best option was to send highly trained Special Operations forces into Pakistan to raid the compound. But that was also the riskiest and most dangerous. If the raid failed, American soldiers could lose their lives, and Obama and the United States would be humiliated and harshly criticized.

If the raid succeeded, it would almost certainly damage the U.S. relationship with Pakistan, and Hillary would be one of the people who would have to patch that up.

At one point, someone asked if they should consider what a raid would do to Pakistan's national honour. Hillary had no patience with that idea. "What about *our* national honour?" she asked. "What about *our* losses? What about going after a man who killed three thousand innocent people?"

On 28th April 2011, Obama gathered his team for a final go-round. There was one scheduling hitch to consider: The raid, if Obama okayed it, would happen on the night of the White House Correspondents' Dinner, a glitzy, celebrity-filled affair, where the president joins a professional comedian in making fun of politics and the White House. It seemed awkward to be making jokes while soldiers were on such a crucial mission. Others worried what the press would think if the president left early.

To Hillary, this whole discussion was absurd. National security was at stake. She ended the talk with the strongest of language, which translated loosely to "forget about the White House Correspondents' Dinner." (Later, she said she didn't remember her exact words, but she didn't dispute the expletive-deleted quote that appeared in the press.)

Obama polled the group on what to do. Biden opposed taking action for political reasons; the stakes were too high if the mission failed.

Gates, the defense secretary, also was opposed. He worried that bin Laden wasn't really there, and he feared that Pakistan might retaliate by cutting off supply routes, hurting the Afghanistan war effort. He had painful memories of three failed raids that had terrible political consequences: an unsuccessful 1970 effort to rescue prisoners of war in Vietnam, a disastrous attempt in 1980 to rescue hostages in Iran, and a dangerous cross-border mission into Pakistan in 2008. He preferred to use a drone. (A couple of days later, after meeting with his senior staffers, he changed his vote.)

Hillary offered a careful analysis of the pros and cons, acknowledging that the raid would hurt the relationship with Pakistan. But she knew from her travels that the two countries needed each other, even if they didn't trust one another. She believed Pakistani leaders would get over it. She supported the mission. "The chance to get bin Laden was worth it," she said later.

Obama, who already had been leaning towards a raid, decided to go for it.

Weather delayed the mission until Sunday 1st May, avoiding the need for any extra dramatics at the correspondents' dinner. Late that night in Afghanistan—afternoon in Washington—two Black Hawk helicopters with twenty-three Navy SEALs, a translator, and a dog left for Abbottabad, Pakistan. Transport helicopters later flew in as back-up.

Obama, Gates, Biden, Hillary, and other members of the team nervously gathered in the White House Situation Room to wait. But, Gates recalled, when Obama realized there was a video feed from the compound in a nearby conference room, he crossed the hall and grabbed a chair to watch. The others crammed into the small room behind him.

The first fuzzy images were discouraging. One of the Black Hawks made an unexpectedly hard landing inside the compound, with the tail crashing against a wall. The second helicopter was supposed to drop SEALs on the roof, but instead landed just outside the compound. Just a few minutes in, the mission seemed to be falling apart.

Hillary's heart was in her throat. "Our worst fears were coming true," she said later.

Then men started to emerge from the helicopters. They had regrouped and were ready to make their attack. Using small explosives, they blasted their way through metal doors and locked gates that protected a courtyard and the house before disappearing from the video feed.

The tension in the room is palpable as Obama, Biden, and the national security team receive an update on the mission to get Osama bin Laden.

For fifteen to twenty minutes, the team watching in Washington could only wait and hope. The translator and the dog guarded the outside of the compound to keep curious neighbours away. On the other side of the wall, the SEALs blew out gates that blocked the stairs to the home's second and third stories, looking for the man they had code-named Geronimo.

Finally, a report was relayed from SEALs on the third

floor: "For God and country—Geronimo, Geronimo, Geronimo." A pause. "Geronimo E-KIA." The enemy was killed in action, cornered in his bedroom.

It wasn't time to exhale yet. The team had to get out of Pakistan safely, including a refueling stop. Some of the SEALs grabbed flash drives, computer disks, and other intelligence from inside the house. Others moved women and children out of the way so they could blow up the damaged helicopter.

Osama bin Laden's body was loaded on a helicopter, and the whole crew took off. About four hours after the raid began, everyone had returned to Afghanistan. After bin Laden was formally identified, the government said, the most-wanted man in the world was buried at sea.

Before sharing the powerful news with the American people, Obama called the four living presidents to tell them first. When Bill answered, he said, "I assume Hillary's already told you . . ."

Bill had no idea what Obama was talking about.

Without a doubt, Hillary could keep a secret.

35

BENGHAZI

As the Obama administration was pursuing Osama bin Laden, Hillary was grappling with unprecedented upheaval in the Arab world—events that would have tremendous consequences for her last year as secretary of state and beyond.

Back in January 2011, as protests began to roil Tunisia, she had almost predicted some of what was to come. At a regional conference in Qatar, a tiny country in the Persian Gulf, she warned Arab leaders that the world was changing and political corruption, high unemployment, and a lack of democracy in their countries wouldn't be tolerated forever. "In too many places, in too many ways, the region's foundations are sinking into the sand," she told them.

Despite her warning, she couldn't begin to imagine what was just ahead. Just a day later, the president of Tunisia was ousted following weeks of protests and demonstrations. Within weeks, mass protests would break out in Egypt, Yemen, Bahrain, and Libya, in what would become known as the Arab Spring. In February, the longtime Egyptian dictator, Hosni Mubarak, resigned.

Most of the revolutions were largely peaceful. But in Libya, an oil-rich country in northern Africa, the uprising that started in mid-February quickly turned violent. That country's entrenched dictator, Mu'ammar al-Gaddhafi, never a friend to America, was responding with brutal force. By mid-March, Gaddhafi's forces were headed toward Benghazi, the eastern city where the rebellion had started; the United States and other nations worried that tens of thousands of lives might be at stake.

Hillary began to lobby for a no-fly zone, closing the skies so that Gaddhafi couldn't use planes to bomb his people. Though he hadn't yet attacked from the air, the move would send a message that the world was watching.

Defense Secretary Gates strongly opposed U.S. involvement, saying Libya's problems didn't threaten U.S. interests. A no-fly zone "begins with an attack on Libya to destroy its air defenses," he told a House subcommittee. "A no-fly zone begins with an act of war." The United States already was in two wars and stretched thin. Gates didn't think it needed to be in another. Neither did Vice President Biden.

Hillary, however, was among those who didn't want America to stand by and risk that Gaddhafi might slaughter his people. Two other women on the national security team—United Nations Ambassador Susan Rice and national security aide Samantha Power—agreed with her.

The conflict put her in the thick of negotiations around the world. Over six days, Hillary flew almost 20,000 miles—so many, wrote *Vanity Fair* reporter Jonathan Alter, that "she might just as well have used her seat belt as a fashion accessory."

Starting in Paris, France, in the second week of March, she met with European allies and Arab leaders to discuss a unified, international response. In an unusual move, the twenty-one-nation Arab League supported enforcing a no-fly zone. From Paris, she flew to Cairo, Egypt, and Tunis, Tunisia, for more talks.

While in Tunis, she spoke on the phone with the Russian foreign minister, who had been opposed to enforcing a no-fly zone. "We don't want to put troops on the ground," she assured him. "Our goal is to protect civilians from brutal and indiscriminate attacks." She knew Russia wouldn't vote for a no-fly zone, but she won his assurance that the country wouldn't veto it in the U.N. Security Council, either.

When the U.N. vote was taken later that day, ten nations supported the no-fly zone and five, including Russia, abstained.

Hillary had just returned home from Tunis when Obama sent her back to Paris to meet with top foreign leaders to sort out their joint roles. An attack was planned, but the French jumped out front, sending their planes ahead. Beginning on 19th March the U.S. Navy launched more than a hundred missiles from warships into Libya's radar and missile defense systems, destroying them and then attacking some ground forces. Gaddhafi's forces pulled back, sparing Benghazi.

The conflict lasted longer than expected, and its management was turned over to NATO, the North Atlantic Treaty Organization. Gaddhafi's government finally fell in late August.

In mid-October 2011, on a trip that included five countries in five days, Hillary stopped in Tripoli, Libya, to meet with the transitional government. In a coincidence of timing, Gaddhafi was killed two days later.

"We came. We saw. He died," Hillary told her staff.

The visit didn't produce any significant news, but there was one unexpected, lasting moment. On the military transport plane heading to Tripoli, two photographers snapped photos of Hillary in sunglasses intently reading her BlackBerry. Roughly six months later, the photo made the rounds of social media, and a pair of communications professionals in Washington got talking about it over a few drinks. "Who's she texting?" they wondered. On a lark, they created a Tumblr to answer that.

The first entry showed a photo of President Obama with his phone, and a caption, "Hey Hil, Whatchu doing?" The caption on her photo: "Running the world."

Within hours, the Tumblr went viral. One photo showed Condoleezza Rice telling President Bush, "So then

The photo that went viral: Hillary looks intently at her BlackBerry on a military plane headed to Libya.

I sent her a text saying I think I left my favorite sunglasses in the desk." The caption on Hillary, wearing sunglasses: "Sorry Condi, haven't seen them."

"Hey girl . . ." purred actor Ryan Gosling into his phone.

". . . It's Madame Secretary," Hillary answered.

As the gag caught on, an increasing number of exchanges were added, making Texts with Hillary an Internet meme. After a few days, Hillary responded with her own: "ROFL @ ur tumblr! g2g—scrunchie time. ttyl?"

Loosely translated, she said, it meant, "Love your site."

Taking advantage of her cool, new image among so-called digital natives who had grown up with the Internet, Hillary invited the creators, Adam Smith and Stacy Lambe, to meet her at the State Department, where they all posed for a photo with their phones.

Though she was far from a digital native herself—she didn't even know how to use a personal computer—Hillary embraced the use of Twitter, Tumblr, Facebook, and other social media as tools of modern-day diplomacy. During her tenure, the State Department created more than 300 official Twitter accounts, offering up tweets in Arabic, Chinese, Farsi, Russian, and other languages. Diplomats had the green light to create Facebook pages and were encouraged to monitor what average people were saying on social media. Chelsea nicknamed her Techno Mom.

After the Gaddhafi government fell, many different factions still competed for power there, especially in Benghazi, the centre of the original rebellion. A popular diplomat, Chris Stevens, was named ambassador to Libya, based in Tripoli.

In September 2012, Stevens traveled to Benghazi, intending to stay a week. Before becoming ambassador, he had been the State Department's special envoy there, working with the rebels as they formed a new government. The fifty-two-year-old had plenty of contacts in Libya's second-largest city and worked from a temporary State Department compound, which didn't have the security of a typical embassy. In a diary found later, Stevens noted that the conditions were "dicey," with "never ending security threats," but he seemed happy to be there.

On September 11, Stevens finished work around 9:00 p.m. Within the hour, a group of well-armed attackers swarmed the compound, breaking through the main gate and storming the mission's buildings. Local militias planned at least part of the attack, investigations found later. But an American-made video that mocked the prophet Muhammad may have also fueled the anger of some of the participants.

As the attackers opened fire on various parts of the compound, a diplomatic security officer herded Stevens and Sean Smith, a thirty-four-year-old information officer, into a safe room in the main villa.

The invaders weren't far behind. Using fuel found outside one of the buildings, they set the villa on fire, sending thick black smoke into the safe room. As the smoke saturated the space, the trio tried to find refuge in a bathroom, but the smoke followed them. Finally, the security officer tried to lead Stevens and Smith to a single emergency window in an adjacent room. But when he finally got there, the two men were no longer behind him. He went back in towards the high heat and heavy smoke several times, but couldn't locate them.

Eventually, he and other Americans made it to a secret Central Intelligence Agency annex less than a mile away. But later that night, the annex was also attacked, killing two CIA operatives and wounding others. Stevens and Smith were found back at the mission; both had died from smoke inhalation.

It was the first time since 1979 that an ambassador had been murdered in the line of duty and it was a devastating loss—occurring on Hillary's watch.

From the time she was notified that the compound was under attack, Hillary helped coordinate the response while staying in touch with the White House, the CIA, and the Defense Department. The embassy in Tripoli moved to send in reinforcements, and Hillary called the Libyan president to insist on immediate help to protect Americans in Tripoli and Benghazi. After a harrowing night, the remaining Americans and the bodies of the dead men were evacuated from Benghazi the next morning.

The next day, she called Stevens's sister and Smith's wife to say that "our hearts were broken at their loss" and to tell them how much the department and the nation honoured the men's service. Then, appearing before the press, Hillary publicly condemned "this senseless act of violence."

Untangling the chaotic attack took some time. Within two weeks, an accountability review board was created to investigate what happened. In a scathing report issued in December 2012, it found that security at the compound was "grossly inadequate," especially considering that the mission had twice been the target of small explosives in the six months before the attack. While some improvements had been made, including adding concrete barriers and extending the height of the outer walls, other requests for more and better security had been denied by senior State Department officials.

The report didn't address the State Department's top leadership. However, Hillary did pledge to adopt all the panel's recommendations, and took steps to increase

Obama grasps Hillary's hand after speaking at a Joint Base Andrews ceremony marking the return of the bodies of four Americans killed in Benghazi, Libya.

military security at some embassies and to appoint a senior person to specifically oversee potentially high-threat posts.

Congress also revved into high gear. Altogether, seven House and Senate investigations were launched to investigate what happened, who was responsible, and whether the Obama administration initially misled the public about the attackers.

In November 2012, Obama was elected to a second term, and he asked Hillary if she would consider staying on. She declined. She had always planned on serving for only one term and was ready for a break.

She was scheduled to testify before the House Foreign Affairs Committee about Benghazi in mid-December. But she had fainted during a bout with a stomach virus earlier in the month, and the fall caused a concussion, as well as double vision and dizziness, which took some time to go away. She sent two deputies instead, and some accused her of mysteriously developing the "Benghazi flu."

Then, in late December, she was hospitalized for three days after further tests revealed a dangerous blood clot behind her right ear, which could have caused a stroke or brain hemorrhage. Doctors put her on blood thinners, which she was required to take indefinitely to prevent future clots.

Finally, in January, she testified before both the House Foreign Affairs and the Senate Foreign Relations Committees, wearing—as the press dutifully noted—her glasses instead of contact lenses. In opening statements, she told both committees, "I take responsibility, and nobody is more committed to getting this right. I am determined to leave the State Department and our country safer, stronger, and more secure."

She choked up when she described the four flag-draped coffins arriving at Joint Base Andrews, where family and close friends waited, along with Obama and Biden. "For me this is not just a matter of policy. It's personal," she said. "I put my arms around the mothers and fathers, the sisters and brothers, the sons and daughters, and the wives left alone to raise their children."

She wouldn't be pushed into a corner about what she could have or should have done. She made clear that she didn't make the decisions about security requests for the compound, neither approving nor denying them.

The senators quizzed her relentlessly about why the Obama administration initially said the attackers were protesters angry about the video when the violence was a more organized terrorist attack. She responded that the administration shared what it knew at the time. When the questions continued, Hillary grew angry.

Hillary responds forcefully during testimony to Congress about the Benghazi attacks in January 2013.

"With all due respect, the fact is we had four dead Americans," she said, her voice rising. "Was it because of a protest? Or was it because of guys out for a walk one night who decided they'd go kill some Americans? What difference, at this point, does it make?" she asked. "It is our job to figure out what happened and do everything we can to prevent it from ever happening again, Senator."

None of the investigations found wrongdoing by the Secretary of State. Still, in May 2014, the speaker of the House of Representatives ordered an eighth investigation into the Benghazi attack, one that would create significant headaches for Hillary.

It was not the way she had hoped to end a generally well-regarded four-year tour. She had traveled nearly a million miles and visited 112 countries, more countries than any other secretary of state. Benghazi was, without a doubt, her biggest regret.

There had also been successes: an Israeli-Hamas cease-fire in Gaza; freeing a Chinese dissident; and efforts to open up and bring reform to Burma, a country with a troubled human rights record. But the Arab states were still search-ing for their future course, and Israel and the Palestinians were still at odds. There had been no world-changing home runs, no nuclear disarmament agreements or significant shifts in relations with China, or even permanent improve-ments for women worldwide.

Hillary told people she wanted to rest, but hardly any-one really believed that. She genuinely relished hard work—and liked to keep her cards close to her vest. Even as a young woman, she claimed she had never mapped out a long-term plan for her future. As she left her job in 2013, she was sticking to the same script. "I'm some-body who gets up every day and says, 'What am I going to do today, and how am I going to do it?'" she said. "I think it moves me toward some outcome I'm hoping for and has some, you know, some joy attached to it."

She wouldn't say what her future days would include. But just about everyone in the political world had a pretty good idea.

36

2016?

Even before Barack Obama was reelected in 2012, political pundits were talking about Hillary Rodham Clinton making another run for president in 2016.

Hillary, of course, wasn't joining the discussion.

Would she like to be president? CNN's Wolf Blitzer asked her in 2011.

"No," she said.

When she left the secretary of state job in early 2013 to become a plain old private citizen for the first time in thirty years, she said she wanted to take some time off, work on a new book, pursue philanthropy. But pollsters and pundits already were naming her the Democratic front-runner for the next election. Former staffers and volunteers started a political action committee, Ready for Hillary. She made headlines with a politically charged announcement: For the first time, she supported the right of gay couples to marry.

And she set up a Twitter account that left open her

future plans, listing all her former jobs. Her @Hillary-Clinton profile at the time: "Wife, mom, lawyer, women & kids advocate, FLOAR, FLOTUS, US Senator, SecState, author, dog owner, hair icon, pantsuit aficionado, glass ceiling cracker, TBD . . ."

Even so, she told everyone who asked that she hadn't made a decision. Instead, she painted a picture of a quiet, almost boring life after so many years of being in the public eye. She organized her closets ("very calming," she told *People*). She caught up on *Dancing with the Stars*, one of her mom's favourite shows.

With a less frenetic schedule, she and Bill spent more time together. They talked and told jokes and binge-watched *House of Cards*. "We have a great time; we laugh at our dogs; we watch stupid movies; we take long walks; we go for a swim," she told *New York* magazine.

In truth, she didn't stay still for very long. In 2013, she and Chelsea joined Bill's charitable foundation, and it was renamed the Bill, Hillary & Chelsea Clinton Foundation. Hillary began work on programs to support women and children, including one aimed at helping young children and another aimed at advancing opportunities for women and girls around the world.

Like Bill, she joined the speaker's circuit, earning around $200,000 an appearance, with the funds often donated to the Clinton Foundation.

She also finished that book she promised. *Hard Choices*, a 596-page region-by-region account of her time as secretary of state, was published in June 2014. The sixty-six-year-old headed out on an extensive book tour, starting with a television interview with ABC's Diane Sawyer. For the most part, Hillary was the careful statesman, admitting that her campaign strategy fell short in 2008, refusing to accept personal blame for the Benghazi disaster, and declining to talk about Monica Lewinsky, who was back in the news.

Then the couple's huge speaking fees came up. Sawyer noted reports that Hillary had made $5 million from speeches and that Bill had made much more. In fact, according to tax returns released during the 2008 campaign, the couple had made a total of $109 million in the previous eight years, largely from book royalties and Bill's speaking fees.

"You have no reason to remember," Hillary told her, "but we came out of the White House not only dead broke, but in debt. We had no money when we got there, and we struggled to piece together the resources for mortgages, for houses, for Chelsea's education. You know, it was not easy."

In a flash, it was as if the other Hillary had returned, the one with a tin ear that sometimes made her sound out of tune. True, the Clintons left the White House millions of dollars in debt. But they also had the friends and connections to quickly purchase two homes for more than $1 million each and the ability to earn with a single appearance or speech way more than an average family makes in a year.

The comment crash-landed like so many had before, prompting endless talk-show commentary, columns, and criticism. At best, she was rusty in her political skills. At worst, she could be seen as dishonest, spinning a story to get sympathy.

Three weeks later, Hillary said she regretted her description of their finances. Though it was accurate, "it was inartful," she said. "We are so successful and so blessed by the success we've had."

If the book tour was a dry run for what would be ahead in a campaign, it highlighted the challenges Hillary would have. Reporters pointed out that the book's sales were anaemic compared with her previous book; *Hard Choices* sold about 260,000 copies over six months, ending 2014 as twentieth on the nonfiction bestseller list. She had the stamina to dart from city to city and appearance to appearance, but she hadn't yet begun to define her vision for America.

Hillary and Bill with their new granddaughter, Charlotte Clinton Mezvinsky, in September 2014.

The busy summer was followed by a life-changing event: In September, Chelsea gave birth to a daughter, Charlotte Clinton Mezvinsky, making Hillary a grandma. Hillary said she was looking forward to reading to the baby and to being there as she grew up. The experience would change her, she said, giving her more reason to focus on the future.

As the expectations for a presidential run grew, yet another scandal emerged: During her four years as secretary of state, Hillary had used only her personal email, rather than a government address. The move, at the least, sidestepped the requirement that work emails and other records be archived, a practice that makes the government accountable to citizens. It also raised questions about how secure her communications were, since she bypassed government safeguards.

After many months of speculation, Hillary finally announces in April 2015 that she is running for president in 2016.

The State Department in October 2014 had asked Hillary and other former secretaries of state to turn over any records or work-related personal emails. That December, Hillary's advisers gave the department more than 30,000 emails. At the same time, they deleted more than 32,000 that were considered personal.

Her unusual email setup came to light in March 2015

via another controversy: The House Select Committee set up the year before to dig further into the Benghazi attack had subpoenaed numerous emails related to the Libyan embassy and discovered the @clintonemail.com address.

The news was shocking to those who believe in government transparency, but Hillary took several days to respond. At a press conference held a week after the news broke, Hillary said that she "opted for convenience" in using one account, instead of a work and a private email, which she said was within the rules. She insisted that she had not sent or received classified materials from that email, set up on a server at her Chappaqua home.

She also said that the deleted emails included communications about Chelsea's wedding, her mother's funeral arrangements, and yoga routines. "No one wants their personal emails made public, and I think most people understand that and respect that privacy," she said.

"Looking back," she added, "it would have been better if I'd simply used a second email account and carried a second phone." But she hadn't.

The disclosure didn't deter her plans. On 12th April, 2015, after months of speculation, she finally declared her candidacy for president of the United States. "Everyday

Americans need a champion. And I want to be that champion," she said in a video announcement.

Quickly, she became the front-runner for the Democratic nomination—but she had plenty of work to do to win it. She was hoping to position herself as a supporter of the middle class, but she would have to run a better campaign than she had in 2008. Telling her mother's story of a rough start that benefited from the support and kindness of others, she hoped to show that she understood regular Americans, even as she and Bill had become truly rich.

Hillary would need to win and keep voters' trust, which seemed to be a constant challenge. Almost as soon as she entered the race, she was under fire. The Clinton Foundation admitted that it hadn't followed all the rules about disclosures and foreign donations while she was secretary of state. There were ongoing questions about her high-priced speeches, especially those to big Wall Street firms, and about her use of a private email account. Once again, her long history of conflict over her personal privacy and her personal finances continued to dog her.

Then there was the issue of Clinton fatigue. She had been a Washington fixture since many millennials were babies, and she was still married to Bill, who was still her best asset and her greatest liability. She could face backlash from voters who wanted a new face.

Beyond that, was she likeable enough? Would she seem energetic and with-it enough? Was she too liberal or not liberal enough? If elected, she would be sixty-nine when she took office, the second-oldest president in U.S. history behind Ronald Reagan.

In 2008, Hillary said, voters had addressed the question, "Could a woman really serve as commander in chief?"

As the 2016 elections approached, another question remained for voters to answer: Could *this* woman be America's next commander in chief?

37

FRONT-RUNNER

Despite her early initial lead, Hillary once again struggled to find her footing. And once again, she was facing an unexpected major challenger who would make her run for the White House far more difficult.

In late April 2015, two weeks after Hillary announced her candidacy, Bernie Sanders threw his hat in the ring. The 73-year-old senator from Vermont, known for his gruff demeanour, rumpled appearance, and unruly tufts of white hair, served sixteen years as Vermont's only member of the U.S. House of Representatives before becoming a senator from Vermont in 2007. Sanders wasn't a Democrat, but an independent who called himself a democratic socialist, favouring more regulation and more taxation to level the playing field between the rich and poor.

Though little known outside of Washington and Vermont, Sanders concluded that running in the Democratic primary was the best way to speak to potential voters about income inequality, the increasingly high cost of college, and the brazen Wall Street behaviour that had led to the financial crisis in 2008–09.

In joining the race, he tapped into a growing anger and frustration among many liberal Americans who felt left out of a U.S. economic system that seemed to favour the wealthy over the millions struggling to live on modest paychecks. The U.S. unemployment rate was almost as low as it was before the 2008–09 financial crisis. But some people had never returned to the workforce and others, young people especially, struggled to find good jobs. They were tired of the same-old, same-old talk from politicians.

Sanders built his campaign around the idea that "A Political Revolution is Coming," a transformation that would lead to more government benefits, like free college tuition at public universities. His bold promises began to win supporters and attention.

By July, Sanders had raised $15 million from small donors and was gaining on Clinton in Iowa, that all-important first caucus state. Polls showed his support had more than doubled in two months, to 33 per cent, while Hillary's strong support was slipping.

Meanwhile, Hillary's decision to use a private email server again stirred up questions about whether she was trustworthy. There was one disclosure after another: The State Department said it couldn't find some emails that an adviser-friend sent her, indicating that maybe she hadn't turned over all her work emails after all. Some of her emails appeared to include such sensitive government information that they shouldn't have been on her personal system.

In July, the *New York Times* reported a shocker, saying that the Justice Department was opening a criminal investigation into how classified government information was handled. The next day, the Justice Department clarified that it was asked to open an investigation—though not a criminal one. Still, the possibility that Hillary could be accused of a serious crime hung over her and her campaign like an ominous cloud for another year.

Throughout the rough summer, Hillary continued to insist that her use of a private server was allowed. She even tried joking about it. "You may have seen that I recently launched a Snapchat account," she told Iowans at a dinner. "I love it. Those messages disappear all by themselves."

The controversy was crowding out her campaign messages and her poll numbers were still falling. Her friends and advisers urged her to apologize.

Once again, Hillary struggled with saying she had erred. In August, she admitted that using a private email account "clearly wasn't the best choice," and she took responsibility for that. But that wasn't enough. Finally, in September, she said that the decision was "a mistake."

"I'm sorry about that," she added.

On 13th October, she sparred with Sanders and three others in the first Democratic debate. He attacked her for ties to wealthy donors and Wall Street and she criticized

Bernie Sanders and Hillary spar over policies at the first Democratic primary debate in October 2015.

him for failing to support stricter gun laws. When the email issue came up, she apologized again. And then Sanders expressed his own exasperation.

"Let me say something that may not be great politics," he said. "And that is, the American people are sick and tired of hearing about your damn emails!" There were bigger, more important problems, he said. "Enough of the emails! Let's talk about the real issues facing America."

But that didn't quiet the controversy. In October, she was called to testify, again, about the Benghazi tragedy.

Over eleven hours, House Select Committee members grilled her about security at the compound, her role in the attacks and the aftermath, and her emails.

But this time, she kept her cool. In fact, during one exchange, she dropped her chin into the palm of her hand

and watched with a bored look as two congressmen argued at length.

Having survived both the hearing and the first debate without any serious gaffes, she returned to the campaign trail. She was most effective when she met with people in small groups or pressed the flesh after a talk or event, listening carefully to individual stories. But in 2016, even that had changed.

For years, right through to 2008, people she met on the road would hand her notes, some handwritten on scraps of paper, some more formal, sharing their deepest concerns. She also wrote down what people told her and collected articles. Then every once in a while, she would schedule two hours of "card-table time," when she and her aides sorted through all the scraps and papers to see what people really cared about.

In the social media age, though, no one wanted to stop to tell a story or pass along a note. They wanted selfies instead. She understood. People preferred a record for Facebook or Instagram. But, she said, "It's a loss."

As it was, the first two states to vote, Iowa and New Hampshire, would be challenging for Hillary, especially with Sanders making impressive gains among young people, the more liberal wing of the party, and white voters.

Iowa, a mostly white state where Democrats tilt to the left, had been difficult for her in 2008, and remained so in 2016, even though she eventually had more than one hundred staffers there. Hillary had started campaigning in earnest in April 2015, driving a van across the state and holding small meetings with fifteen to twenty voters at a time, hoping to build committed supporters.

Sanders had more time in Congress, but Hillary was seen as part of the "establishment." As a former secretary of state, she had substantial experience in foreign policy, while Sanders had virtually none. But, echoing what would become a theme of the 2016 election, one Iowa political consultant noted, "Experience is not something voters are dying for right now."

By contrast, Sanders' intense delivery at rallies came across as passionate and authentic. His straightforward proposals for government-run health insurance for all and universal public preschool were idealistic and appealing; her policy proposals were more complex and far too detailed to fit on a T-shirt. And she still had the responsibility gene, refusing to make promises that she knew couldn't be delivered.

In short, Hillary appealed to the head. Bernie appealed to the heart.

On 1st February, 2016, about 171,000 Iowa voters showed up to caucus with their neighbours, a turnout second only to 2008. The race was so close that it wasn't decided until early the next morning. But when all the precinct results were tallied, Hillary won by a nose, 49.8 per cent to 49.6 per cent. It wasn't a great showing, but it was good enough.

She immediately headed to New Hampshire, another

mostly white state, which was holding its primary 9th February. Though the state had given Hillary a boost in 2008 and had been Bill's comeback state in 1992, Sanders lived in neighbouring Vermont and had a strong lead. Worried about upcoming races, her campaign sent Bill to Nevada, a much more diverse state that was holding its caucus 20th February.

Though Hillary knew she was a long shot, the results were bitter to swallow. Sanders won more than 60 per cent of the vote to her 38 per cent. He was raising more money than Hillary, almost entirely from very small donations, and he won majorities from a range of the state's voters, including working class men, young men and women, and those who wanted someone "honest and trustworthy."

The close race in Iowa and the big loss in New Hampshire against an unexpected rival brought back memories of her 2008 defeat. Hillary worried, as she had then, about whether she had the right strategy or the right people. But she had learned from 2008 that trying to bring in new people could be more disruptive than helpful. Instead, she let them know she would stay with them.

After the defeat, she exchanged her regular plane for a larger jet and urged her aides to fly home with her. As more than two dozen staffers came on board, she and Bill stood in the doorway to greet them and shake hands and share hugs. Over and over, she told her team that she appreciated their work.

Campaigning in Nevada and South Carolina, Hillary

reached out to black and Latino voters. There she had an edge over Sanders. He spoke about racism in broad terms—how drug penalties are different for blacks and whites, and how many black men are in prison. She told personal stories.

Sanders had marched for civil rights in the 1960s. But starting in the 1970s, Hillary and Bill had worked side-by-side with African American leaders. Said Representative John Lewis, a civil rights legend, "I never saw him; I never met him." But, he said, "I met Hillary."

As the Nevada caucus neared, Hillary's team braced for another tie, or even a loss. But her outreach had worked. She beat Sanders by five percentage points, winning moderates, blacks, and older voters.

Then it was back to South Carolina, the state where Barack Obama had embarrassed her in 2008. Sanders had more than 200 staffers there and had ploughed $2 million into advertising. But again, Hillary focused on individuals. At an event in tiny Bennettsville, the mother of Dontre Hamilton, who was killed by a Milwaukee police officer in 2014; the mother of Eric Garner, who died after a New York police officer choked him the same year; and other mothers of young, unarmed black victims told their personal stories. They had received letters or phone calls from Hillary or had met with her for hours.

"Hillary heard my cry," Maria Hamilton said.

This time, Hillary took the state resoundingly, winning every county and more than 73 per cent of the state vote.

The victory revved up her campaign going into Super Tuesday, when eleven states voted. Hillary reigned, winning big in Texas, Georgia, and Virginia and taking seven states overall. Sanders captured Minnesota, Colorado, Oklahoma, and his home state, Vermont.

Sanders had led the delegate race after New Hampshire, but he would not lead again. After Super Tuesday, Hillary had nearly six of every ten delegates who were pledged so far, as well as a commanding lead in so-called superdelegates, elected officials and other Democrats who were free to vote as they wished.

Over the next couple of weeks, the momentum would seesaw. Sanders won several states, including a surprise victory in Michigan, where young people and independents turned out in unexpectedly high numbers. But then Hillary rebounded, capturing Florida, Illinois, and Ohio, each with a large block of delegates. By mid-March, she had a solid lead that was getting harder and harder to overcome.

In ordinary years, that would have been enough to send a challenger packing. But this was no ordinary year. Sanders' base of fervent young people and liberals was growing. He had raised more money than Hillary three months in a row and large numbers of enthusiastic voters were still coming to his rallies. He believed he could still beat her—and mathematically it was possible. In short, he did to Hillary what Hillary had done to Obama in 2008: He refused to concede and promised to stay in the race until the very end.

As the battle continued, it grew more testy and combative. In April, Sanders fumbled an interview with the *New York Daily News* editorial board. When pressed on how he would carry out his promises, he was unable to give specifics and he didn't appear to even know how the government might break up big banks.

In response to his stumble, Hillary was asked if he was qualified to be president. She said the interview "raised a lot of serious questions," but didn't answer the question. She didn't want to anger his liberal base because she would need that support in the general election.

Sanders shot back. Angrily, he declared that she wasn't qualified to be president because she took money from Wall Street for speeches and voted for the war in Iraq.

By May, Sanders was claiming that the Democratic primary system, with its large number of superdelegates, was rigged in Hillary's favour. He threatened to take his battle for the nomination to the Democratic National Convention floor, where he would fight for Hillary's delegates. His unwillingness to acknowledge her lead took root with his most ardent supporters—including young men (and some women) who the media dubbed "Bernie bros"—and raised scepticism about the nominating process.

In early June, after she won the California primary, Hillary finally collected enough delegates to become the Democratic nominee for president. Two hundred and forty years after the founding of the United States of

America, a major party was about to nominate a woman for president.

Sanders had taken more caucuses, but she won more primary elections. He was more popular with independents, but she had the support of Democrats, who had voted in greater numbers. Despite complaints about the process, she whipped him by every measure: She won a total of 15.8 million votes, about 3.8 million more than he did. She won 389 more delegates from those primaries and caucuses, and she almost swept the superdelegates, garnering the support of 591 to his 48.

Even so, Sanders left his mark. In response to his populist positions, she had adopted more liberal stances, such as opposing a new trade agreement with Asia and supporting free tuition at public universities for less-wealthy families.

Still, Sanders was slow to accept the results, waiting for a month after the primaries ended to concede. He pledged to support Hillary for president, to the great disappointment of his diehard fans.

By then, Hillary had already turned towards the general election. Benghazi and her emails were once again in the news and she was facing a Republican challenger who was far more complex and aggressive than Bernie Sanders would ever be.

38

NASTY

Hillary had little time to celebrate before she was back on the griddle.

Barely two weeks after she won the very last primary, the District of Columbia, the House Select Committee on Benghazi released an 800-page report detailing every stage of the 2012 attacks in Benghazi and the response. The report took the Defense Department, the Central Intelligence Agency, and the State Department to task for failing to be in a position to respond quickly.

But the investigation, which cost nearly $7 million, didn't uncover anything new about Hillary related to the attacks.

The email inquiry that grew out of the Benghazi investigation, however, continued to reverberate. Four days after the Benghazi report, on Saturday, 2nd July, the Federal Bureau of Investigation questioned Hillary for three and a half hours about her account and her private server.

Then, on 5th July, FBI Director James B. Comey took the highly unusual step of publicly announcing his recommendation to the U.S. Justice Department and providing a play-by-play analysis of what was found and how that recommendation was reached.

In short, he said, the FBI had investigated whether Hillary had broken the law by mishandling classified information "either intentionally or in a grossly negligent way," which is a felony, or by knowingly removing classified information from "appropriate systems," a misdemeanour.

The conclusion: Hillary and her colleagues were "extremely careless in their handling of very sensitive, highly classified information." But Comey said, there wasn't enough evidence for a reasonable prosecutor to charge her with a crime.

In outlining his conclusions, Comey, a Republican and former prosecutor, also dismantled some of Hillary's defenses. For instance, she previously said she had not received or sent classified information. But the FBI found that 110 emails contained confidential, secret, or top-secret information when they were sent. Very few of them were actually marked as such, he said, but she should have known the subject matter was at least confidential.

In addition, Hillary had said she turned over all her work emails. But the FBI found several thousand more—including three containing classified information—from others' email or by searching old servers, Comey said.

The Justice Department quickly accepted Comey's

recommendation, closing the investigation. That removed lingering, unsettling concerns that a presidential nominee might be indicted. But his point-by-point assessment inflamed new ones, including persistent feelings that Hillary was not trustworthy or truthful. It also raised questions about the judgment of someone now labeled "extremely careless."

In a normal election year, that would have been a serious setback for a presidential candidate. But this wasn't any regular year, and Hillary wasn't facing a typical candidate. She was facing Donald J. Trump, a New York real-estate tycoon and a former reality TV star, whose oversize comb-over got almost as much attention as her hair had.

Trump, who turned seventy in 2016, had an unusually colourful background for a presidential candidate. Companies he controlled, including casinos in Atlantic City, had sought bankruptcy six times. He was married to his third wife, Melania, a former model from Slovenia, and had five children between the ages of ten and thirty-eight years old.

The self-proclaimed billionaire, who had never held any public office, had run roughshod through the Republican primary, dispatching sixteen potential contenders, including Florida Senator Marco Rubio, Texas Senator Ted Cruz, and Jeb Bush, former Florida governor and the brother and son of two former presidents. (Unlike the Democrats, the Republicans didn't have superdelegates, who might have opposed a candidate without experience or clear Republican positions.)

Trump won with a combination of name-calling and blustery, nationalistic declarations, including promises to tear up trade agreements, close the nation's doors to Muslim refugees, and end illegal Mexican immigration by building a giant wall along the southern border. In campaign rallies and tweets, he called opponents cutting nicknames, like "Little Marco," "Lyin' Ted," and "Low Energy Jeb."

Like Sanders, Trump bragged of his role as an outsider ready to overhaul the establishment and made big promises in broad terms. Sanders had tapped into liberal anger; Trump tapped into conservative anger and fanned it to a fiery pitch. Many found his rhetoric offensive to women, blacks, Latinos, and Muslims.

In a nation deeply divided between liberals and conservatives, both Hillary and Trump were unusually unpopular candidates. After years of hating and distrusting Hillary, many conservatives couldn't imagine voting for her. Yet, Trump set new standards for statements that crossed the line. For instance, for years, he tried to discredit President Obama by falsely claiming he wasn't really born in the U.S. Trump was widely criticized for insisting, without evidence, that Mexico was forcing its people into the U.S., saying "they're bringing drugs. They're bringing crime. They're rapists." At one point, he also mocked a disabled reporter by imitating his physical disabilty.

Starting in April 2016, Trump began to take aim at

Hillary. He began calling her "Crooked Hillary" or just "Crooked" on Twitter and in speeches. Soon after, he set off a new gender war, declaring, "Frankly, if Hillary Clinton were a man, I don't think she'd get 5 per cent of the vote. The only thing she's got going is the woman's card."

It wasn't sexist to say that her only qualification was being a woman, he said later. "It's just a very, very true statement" because "she's a bad candidate."

Hillary picked up the ball and ran with it, quickly offering an official "Woman Card" for $5 through her campaign website. "If fighting for women's healthcare and paid family leave and equal pay is playing the woman card, then deal me in," she exclaimed at a Philadelphia rally. At later rallies, crowd members would finish the line for her, responding in unison, "Deal me in!"

Comey's report, which came shortly before the Republican and then Democratic conventions, essentially cleared Hillary, but Trump and his supporters used it as ammunition. At the Republican National Convention in Cleveland the week of 18th July, delegates adopted a new, intimidating chant: "Lock her up! Lock her up!" Outside the convention center, "Hillary for Prison" shirts sold briskly.

Hillary said she "felt sad" rather than threatened by the chants, and kept her focus on more pressing issues, including picking a vice presidential running mate to go against Trump and his running mate, Indiana Governor Mike Pence.

She considered a range of people, from established

politicians to prominent business people, and then made a safe, practical choice: Tim Kaine, a senator from Virginia who spoke Spanish and had a strong reputation, as well as a long history of public service.

At the Democratic convention in Philadelphia the last week in July, First Lady Michelle Obama set the mood. In an uplifting speech on opening night, she knocked down Trump's negative approach without ever mentioning his name. In a line later picked up by Hillary, she said that she and the president taught their daughters how to respond when someone is cruel or bullying: "Our motto is, when they go low, we go high."

On Tuesday, Hillary was officially nominated amid some deeply emotional moments. Geraldine Emmett, a 102-year-old lifelong Democrat, remembered when her own mother did not have the right to vote. She cast fifty-one votes from Arizona "for the next president of the United States, Hillary Rodham Clinton." And then she cried.

"I never cry," she said afterwards, adding, "She deserves it so much."

Betsy Johnson Ebeling, Hillary's best buddy since sixth grade, who remained a lifelong friend, cast ninety-eight votes from Illinois "in honour of Dorothy and Hugh's daughter and my sweet friend."

"This one's for you, Hill," she said, as her eyes filled with tears.

Despite the celebration for the first woman candidate, there were still tensions. Sanders' delegates frequently booed when Hillary's name was mentioned in speeches, and after the roll call, several dozen Sanders supporters left the convention hall in protest.

Thursday night was Hillary's. In accepting the nomination, she wore white, the colour worn by women seeking the right to vote a century ago, a reminder of the significance of the moment.

She thanked Sanders for putting "economic and social justice issues front and centre," and reached out to his supporters, saying, "I want you to know, I've heard you." Still, some Sanders supporters booed and jeered during her speech, prompting Hillary supporters to try to chant over them. Others simply refused to applaud.

Her prose was straightforward rather than soaring, and she was confident and poised. She acknowledged that some people doubt her motives, despite her years as First Lady, senator, and secretary of state. "The truth is," she said, "through all these years of public service, the 'service' part has always come easier to me than the 'public' part. I get it that some people just don't know what to make of me."

She shared personal stories about her mother and father, and admitted that, "More than a few times, I've had to pick myself up and get back in the game."

She made fun of her own wonkiness and love of policy. Trump, she noted, "doesn't like talking about his plans." But she added, "You might have noticed, I love talking about mine."

"It's true," she said at another point in the speech,

"I sweat the details of policy—whether we're talking about the exact level of lead in the drinking water in Flint, Michigan; the number of mental health facilities in Iowa; or the cost of your prescription drugs."

"Because it's not just a detail if it's your kid—if it's your family," she went on. "It's a big deal. And it should be a big deal to your president."

Recognizing the divisiveness of the election, she pledged to reach out to all sides, Democrats, Republicans, and independents. She debuted yet another slogan: "Stronger Together," a counterpoint to Trump's attacks on specific groups. As the delegates cheered, the room filled with confetti and balloons.

Hillary and Tim Kaine celebrate their nomination at the Democratic National Convention.

On the strength of the Republican convention, Trump had pulled into a tie or a small lead. But Hillary got a strong bounce from her convention, and by mid-August, she had pulled ahead. But staying ahead was difficult.

Following the conventions, Trump shuffled his campaign leadership and his disorganized campaign finally began running television ads, something Hillary's campaign had been doing for a while. The candidate and some of his supporters also ramped up attacks on Hillary. At one point, he referred to her as "such a nasty woman," prompting #NastyWoman to take off on social media. He also told an interviewer, "I just don't think she has a presidential look, and you need a presidential look." He declined to elaborate, though his intent was hard to miss: A female president would look different than every other president to date.

He and his supporters also challenged her health, energy, and stamina and claimed that she was physically weak, napped too much, or worse, was subject to seizures. There was a tiny grain of truth to the issue: She had been hoarse and sometimes coughing on the campaign trail, and at a Labor Day event on September 5, she suffered a massive coughing fit.

She tried to make a joke about it while hacking away, saying, "Every time I think about Trump, I get allergic."

The coughing fit was followed by one of her biggest gaffes of the campaign, disparaging a broad swath of Trump supporters. "To just be grossly generalistic," she said at an LGBT fundraiser on 9th September, "you could put half of Trump's supporters into what I call the basket of deplorables," noting that they are "racist, sexist, homophobic, xenophobic, Islamaphobic—you name it."

Though Trump's positions had, in fact, been welcomed by white supremacist groups, the cutting remark took aim at millions of people. Trump was quick to criticize her.

Later, Hillary said she regretted saying "half," but returned to her opponent, saying, "It's deplorable that Trump has built his campaign largely on prejudice and paranoia and given a national platform to hateful views and voices."

Still, like the "woman card," the "deplorable" comment struck a nerve. Trump's website offered $35 "I'm a Deplorable" T-shirts and the label became a point of pride for his biggest supporters.

Her health also became a bigger issue. Nearly a week after the coughing fit, she left a ceremony remembering 9/11, blaming the heat on a modestly warm day. Video caught her nearly collapsing and requiring help to get into a van.

She was taken to Chelsea's apartment, where her doctor concluded she had been overheated and dehydrated. A couple of hours later, she emerged, waving and saying she felt fine. Only later that day did her campaign admit that she had been diagnosed with a form of pneumonia on 9th September and given antibiotics.

The delayed disclosure again raised questions about her truthfulness and tendency toward secrecy, especially after so much had been insinuated about her health.

Hillary joked about it a few days later, telling a black women's group that her illness "finally got some Republicans interested in women's health."

Frustration over the health issue, along with new stories about the Clinton Foundation and her email, hurt her standing with voters. About a week ahead of the important first presidential debate, she and Trump were running essentially neck and neck.

As was her nature, Hillary prepared, devoting most of four days to getting ready. She studied briefing books and practised handling the kinds of insults Trump excelled at hurling. She tested how much she could interrupt Trump without triggering a pushy-woman stereotype.

Trump, who was easily bored, declined to practise, preferring instead to kick around ideas with his staff.

Before a record television debate audience of 84 million viewers, her work paid off. She was confident, knowledgeable, and composed, and maybe a bit too scripted, while he rambled and jumped from subject to subject, lacking specifics. While she mostly let him talk during his turn, he interrupted her numerous times.

They sparred over her planned tax increases for the wealthy and his proposed tax cuts, primarily for the wealthy and companies. He criticized her private email— she apologized again—and she asked about his own taxes. Noting that he was the first candidate in decades to refuse to release his tax returns, she suggested that he had not paid any federal taxes in years.

"That makes me smart," Trump replied, apparently verifying her claim.

He talked about his rallies and how she had stayed home for a few days. She had a sharp response: "I think Donald just criticized me for preparing for this debate," she said. "And you know what else I prepared for?

"I prepared to be president."

While his barbs failed to rattle her, she needled him and finally got under his skin. Toward the end of the debate, she noted that he had called various women "pigs," "slobs," and "dogs," and then brought up a former beauty queen, Alicia Machado, who won a pageant he owned. Trump had called her "Miss Piggy" after she gained weight, Hillary said. Trump, taken aback, demanded, "Where did you find this?"

Formal polls gave Hillary a resounding win.

But rather than return to the issues, Trump stewed about Machado, telling people how she had gained "a massive amount of weight." A few days later, he took to Twitter in the early morning hours to call Machado a "con" and "disgusting."

Hillary reclaimed her lead.

Then, within hours on Friday, 7th October, two days before the second debate, both campaigns faced unexpected developments. WikiLeaks, a site that discloses private or confidential information from unknown sources, began to publish thousands of emails hacked from Hillary's campaign chairman John Podesta, dribbling them out over several weeks. The emails raised questions about more potential conflicts of interest at the Clinton Foundation and revealed catty internal discussions and blunt commentary. There were no real bombshells, but the disclosures were embarrassing and distracting for the campaign. (Even more troubling: The Clinton camp believed the emails had been hacked by groups with ties to the Russian government, who were believed to have hacked and released Democratic National Committee emails in July.)

The same day, a scandal truly exploded on the Trump side. *Access Hollywood* found a 2005 outtake in which Trump described, in stunningly lewd terms, how he treated beautiful women. The tape, which was leaked to David Fahrenthold of the *Washington Post*, starts while Trump is on a bus, talking into a working microphone to the show co-host Billy Bush. Then Trump spots an attractive actress waiting for him to tape a short soap opera segment.

"I better use some Tic Tacs just in case I start kissing her," he tells Bush. "You know, I'm automatically attracted to beautiful—I just start kissing them. It's like a magnet." On the tape, Bush laughed.

"I don't even wait. And when you're a star, they let you do it. You can do anything," Trump went on enthusiastically. "Grab 'em by the pussy. You can do anything."

The response sent a collective shiver through both parties and many voters. On Twitter, Hillary called Trump's words "horrific." Prominent Republicans called them "sickening" and "vile" and some withdrew their support.

Trump was defiant. In an initial statement, he called the words "locker room banter." In a video apology that night, he said he had changed since then. Then, he tried to redirect blame, alleging that Bill Clinton had done worse by abusing women and that Hillary had "bullied, attacked, shamed, and intimidated" those women.

As low as that was, he went lower. Ahead of the debate that Sunday in St. Louis, he rounded up three women who had accused Bill Clinton of assaulting them, including Paula Jones, whose sexual harassment lawsuit had been dismissed. He reached back into Hillary's time in Fayetteville, Arkansas, when she was asked to represent a man charged with raping a girl. That victim and the three others appeared with Trump at a brief press conference and were his guests at the debate.

When they walked onto the stage, the candidates did not shake hands. Moderator Anderson Cooper pointedly asked Trump if he had assaulted women as he had described. Trump said he hadn't. But over the next several days, a number of women came forward to share their stories of how he had kissed or groped them without permission on an airplane, in an office building, at a nightclub, and during a magazine interview.

During the debate, Trump attacked Hillary, saying that if he won, he would appoint a special prosecutor to investigate her email use.

Hillary responded that it was "awfully good that someone with the temperament of Donald Trump is not in charge of the law in our country." Trump interrupted.

"Because you'd be in jail," he said, making a threat that was more appropriate for a dictatorship than a democracy.

Over and over, he responded angrily and tried to bait her, but she kept her composure. She stuck to her plan, dodging some of his most pointed accusations and speaking directly to those who asked the questions in the town hall–style debate.

As a final question, a voter asked them to say something positive about the other. Hillary complimented Trump's children.

Trump, in return, noted that she was a fighter. "I will say this about Hillary," he said. "She doesn't quit. She doesn't give up. I respect that."

It may have been the truest thing he said all night. In fact, she *had* fought hard. She had fought hard in Little Rock, Arkansas, to become the first female partner at her law firm, and she fought for Bill after his painful 1980 defeat. She had fought to change the role of First Lady and fought to speak up for women and families. After being knocked down, she fought again for Bill when his presidency was on the line and for Democrats who needed her. She fought for New York after 9/11 and for America as secretary of state.

Now it was up to voters to decide if she would win her biggest fight of all.

39

ELECTION

After winning the second debate on 9th October and then the third on 19th October, Hillary's lead in the polls grew. She seemed to be on a roll.

But once again, her email problems came back to hurt her.

Hillary and her campaign staff were flying to Cedar Rapids, Iowa, on 28th October when some of her top advisers got wind that FBI Director James Comey had said something new.

Upon landing, Jennifer Palmieri, Hillary's communications director, delivered the news.

"It's not good," she said.

In fact, it was terrible. Just eleven days before the election, Comey had sent a vague letter to Congress that said he was revisiting the email investigation.

"In connection with an unrelated case," he wrote, "the FBI has learned of the existence of emails that appear to be pertinent to the investigation." He didn't know if the material was significant, how long an investigation would take, or even what was in the emails. But, he said, he wanted Congress to know.

The extraordinary disclosure—made without any solid information—completely blindsided Hillary and seemed to fly in the face of a law forbidding federal officials from using their positions to interfere with an election.

The emails had been discovered during an investigation into inappropriate sexting by the estranged husband of Hillary's close aide, Huma Abedin. The laptop was his, but Abedin had backed up emails on that computer.

Hillary took the news with a slight smile, saying, "I knew there'd be another twist in the road."

It was more like a sinkhole. Once again, voters were reminded of her trust issues. Trump hammered her on the disclosure, renewing his accusations that she was a criminal. Within days, polls showed her lead shrinking.

To journalists, historians, political scientists, and political pundits, that seemed almost impossible. Hillary was without a doubt more qualified than the ill-prepared and impulsive Republican nominee. More than fifty of the nation's major newspapers had said as much; some had always endorsed a Republican for president, but were now saying they believed Trump wasn't qualified.

Despite Trump's significant shortcomings, he presented himself to angry voters as an outsider and an agent of change. Hillary struggled to offer herself as an alternative, especially to white voters without college degrees who felt left behind by a global economy and an increasingly diverse society.

She had been around so long that she seemed to define the establishment. She hadn't offered a clear core message, or a path to real change. She didn't have the eloquence or grace of Barack Obama, the charisma of her husband, or the gritty passion of Bernie Sanders. And she still had her blind spots when it came to her personal finances and her privacy.

Her campaign may also have made a tactical mistake. Believing it could expand her reach, it spent heavily in swing states that her advisers wanted to win, including Florida, Ohio, and North Carolina, while spending little money or time in long-time Democratic strongholds with lots of blue-collar voters, like Michigan and Wisconsin. She was playing an aggressive offense, said *The Atlantic's* Ronald Brownstein, leaving her vulnerable to Trump's inroads in those states.

As 8th November neared, she brought big names to her rallies. Jennifer Lopez and Marc Anthony joined Hillary in Florida, and Beyoncé and her husband, Jay Z, headlined a rally in Ohio that included back-up dancers in blue trouser suits. At one point during Beyoncé's set, a quote from 1992 flashed on the screen, underscoring how far Hillary had come from a First Lady candidate to a serious contender: "I suppose I could have stayed home and baked cookies and had teas, but what I decided to do was to fulfill my profession."

Just two days before the election, Comey had another surprise. After comparing the new emails to ones already reviewed, the FBI found most of the emails were duplicates or personal communications. There was nothing new. As a result, he said in another letter to Congress, "We have not changed our conclusions that we expressed in July."

By then the race had narrowed. On Monday, 7th November, both candidates stumped across the country. Trump visited five states and offered a dark message about a rigged election system, a crooked media, and a corrupt Washington.

She hit five events in four states, including Michigan, North Carolina, and Pennsylvania, holding her largest rally yet in Philadelphia, with the Obamas, Bruce Springsteen, and Jon Bon Jovi.

"Tomorrow, you can vote for a hopeful, inclusive, big-hearted America," she said. "Let's make history together."

Her most enthusiastic supporters, especially women, were ready to do so. They left "I voted" stickers on suffragette Susan B. Anthony's grave, and on Election Day, they planned to don white or trouser suits with high hopes that their dream of a female president would become a reality. They were convinced it was possible.

Finally, more than eighteen months after she first declared her candidacy, 8th November arrived. That morning, Hillary and Bill voted at a local elementary school in Chappaqua, New York. She returned home to do interviews encouraging people to vote, and then worked on two versions of her speech. An election night party was scheduled at New York's Javits Center, known for its glass ceiling.

She never made it there.

Soon after polls began to close, the results began to point to a tight race. States that should have quickly become hers wavered between red and blue, as did key swing states. In the Midwest, a Democratic stronghold, Trump picked up even stronger than expected support from rural white voters, especially those without college degrees, highlighting a festering national divide.

Hillary did well with women, minorities, young people, and college graduates, as well as with voters who wanted experience or good judgment. But it wasn't enough. Those who wanted change overwhelmingly voted for Trump.

There were other possible reasons, too. Political parties rarely hold on to the White House for more than eight years at a time. And some Americans were still uncomfortable with the notion of a female commander in chief.

As the night wore on, the map turned increasingly red as she lost Michigan and Wisconsin and the swing states of Florida, Ohio, and North Carolina. In the early hours of 9th November, Donald J. Trump earned the 270 electoral college votes he needed to win. For the first time in American history, a president without any political or military experience was elected.

In the popular vote, Hillary actually collected more votes than Trump did—only the fifth time in American history that a candidate won the popular vote, but lost the race.

Hillary called Trump to concede around 2:45 a.m.

The next morning, fighting emotion, she gave a powerful and uplifting concession speech to her staff and supporters. She said she was sorry she didn't win, admitting how deeply disappointing and terribly painful her loss was.

But, she said, "I still believe in America—and I always will. And if you do, then we must accept this result—and then look to the future."

She had a special message for young people reeling from the loss. She had faced successes and painful set-

With Bill and Tim Kaine behind her, Hillary concedes the hard-fought race to Donald Trump.

backs in her life, and they would, too. But, she went on, "please never stop believing that fighting for what's right is worth it.

"It is worth it."

And she added, in reference to the sexist and demeaning words about women spoken during the campaign, "to all the little girls who are watching this, never doubt that you are valuable and powerful and deserving of every chance and opportunity in the world to pursue and achieve your own dreams."

There was another message unsaid. The first pioneer clears the way, but often doesn't get to the goal. Susan B. Anthony dedicated her life to winning the vote for women, but died before the Nineteenth Amendment was adopted in 1920. Alice Paul devoted another half-century, with only some success, to winning equal rights for women.

So it was for Hillary Diane Rodham Clinton. She was a trailblazer for women in politics. She redefined a First Lady's role, became the first female senator from New York, and became the first woman to win a major party's presidential nomination. She had come far closer to taking America's top job than any woman ever had.

But it wasn't meant to be, not in this year of outsiders, not at a time when experience and familiarity was distrusted and anger and dissatisfaction ruled. Now it would be up to another woman, in another day, to crack that highest, hardest ceiling and become the first female president of the United States.

Drawn and Quartered

As a presidential candidate, the secretary of state, and a candidate again, Hillary was regularly in the public eye—and the editorial pages—from 2007 on.

"Admit it, Hillary makes you feel like you forgot to pick up the dry cleaning."

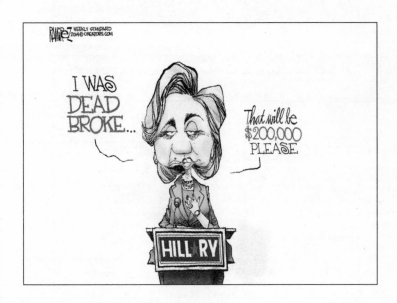

TIME LINE

19th August 1946:
William Jefferson Blythe III, who later took the surname Clinton, is born in Hope, Arkansas.

26th October 1947:
Hillary Diane Rodham is born.

1950: The Rodham family moves to Park Ridge, Illinois.

5-8th August 1968:
The Republican National Convention is held in Miami Beach, Florida.

8th November 1960:
Democrat John F. Kennedy is elected president, defeating Republican Richard Nixon.

February 1968:
Hillary is elected president of Wellesley College Government.

22nd November 1963:
Kennedy is assassinated in Dallas. Vice President Lyndon B. Johnson is sworn in as president.

3rd November 1964:
Democratic President Johnson is elected for another term, defeating Republican Barry Goldwater.

5th November 1968:
Nixon is elected president, defeating Democrat Hubert Humphrey and George Wallace of the American Independent Party.

26-29th August 1968:
Violence breaks out at the Democratic National Convention in Chicago.

6th June 1968:
Senator Robert Kennedy, Democratic candidate for president, is assassinated in Los Angeles.

4th April 1968:
Martin Luther King Jr. is assassinated in Memphis, Tennessee.

September 1965:
Hillary enters Wellesley College.

31st May 1969: Hillary is Wellesley's first student graduation speaker.

Fall 1969: Hillary enters Yale Law School.

30th April 1970: Nixon announces expansion of the Vietnam War into Cambodia.

1st May 1970: Thousands rally in New Haven, Connecticut, on behalf of accused Black Panthers.

4th May 1970: National Guardsmen kill four and wound nine during an antiwar demonstration at Kent State University in Ohio.

7th May 1970: Hillary speaks at the fiftieth-anniversary convention of the League of Women Voters.

11th June 1974: Bill wins the Democratic primary for U.S. House, setting up a race against Republican incumbent John Paul Hammerschmidt.

January 1974: Hillary joins the House Judiciary Committee legal staff to work on the Nixon inquiry.

Spring 1971: Hillary Rodham and Bill Clinton meet in the Yale Law Library.

Fall 1973: Hillary goes to work for the new Children's Defense Fund in Cambridge, Massachusetts. Bill begins teaching law at the University of Arkansas in Fayetteville.

April 1972: Hillary and Bill compete in Yale's Prize Trial.

17th June 1972: Five men are arrested while attempting to wiretap the Democratic National Committee offices at the Watergate office complex.

June 1973: A top Nixon aide tells a Senate committee that the president was involved for months in trying to cover up the Watergate scandal.

Fall 1972: Bill works on the campaign for George McGovern in Texas, and Hillary works to register voters there.

7th November 1972: Nixon is re-elected president, defeating Democrat George McGovern in a landslide.

23rd January 1973: Nixon announces the end of U.S. involvement in Vietnam.

2nd November 1982: —
Bill is re-elected as
Arkansas governor;
he will win again
in 1984, 1986,
and 1990.

— 27th July 1974:
The House
Judiciary
Committee adopts
the first of three
articles of
impeachment.

—27th February 1982:
Bill announces he is
running for governor
again, and Hillary says
she now will be Mrs.
Bill Clinton.

9th August 1974: —
Nixon resigns, and
Vice President Gerald
Ford is sworn in as
president.

—Late August 1974:
Hillary moves to
Fayetteville to join
Bill and teach at the
University of
Arkansas Law School.

4th November 1980: —
Bill is defeated in his
re-election bid, and
Republican Ronald
Reagan is elected
president, defeating
incumbent Democrat
Jimmy Carter.

5th November 1974: —
Bill loses a close race
to Hammerschmidt.

— 27th February 1980:
Chelsea Victoria
Clinton is born.

Summer 1975: —
Hillary and Bill
are engaged.

11th October 1975: —
Hillary and Bill wed.

7th November 1978: —
Bill is elected governor
of Arkansas.

—October 1978:
Hillary begins
trading in
commodities with
friend Jim Blair,
making about
$100,000 in profit
in less than a year.

Spring 1976: —
Bill runs for
Arkansas attorney
general and wins
the Democratic
primary.

Summer 1978: —
Hillary and Bill
invest in a real-
estate deal that will
become known as
Whitewater.

—30th May 1978:
Bill wins the
Democratic
primary for
Arkansas
governor.

— Fall 1976:
Hillary becomes
field
co-ordinator in
Indiana for the
Jimmy Carter
campaign; Bill
runs Carter's
Arkansas
campaign.

2nd November 1976: —
Bill is elected
Arkansas attorney
general, and Democrat
Jimmy Carter is elected
U.S. president, defeating
incumbent Republican
Gerald Ford.

January 1977: —
Hillary and Bill move
to Little Rock, where
she joins the Rose
Law Firm.

22nd April 1983: Bill announces Hillary will lead the effort to overhaul the state's education system.

20th January 1994: A special counsel is appointed to investigate questions about Whitewater.

6th January 1994: Bill's mom, Virginia Kelley, dies.

March 1984: Arkansas State Board of Education adopts "Hillary committee" recommendations.

27th October 1993: Hillary and team deliver 1,342-page health-care bill to Congress.

22nd September 1993: Bill presents his broad plan to reform health care to Congress and the nation.

14th July 1987: After gathering family and friends, Bill decides he won't run for president in 1988.

20th July 1993: Hillary's friend and White House counsel Vince Foster commits suicide.

1988 and 1991: Hillary is named one of one hundred most influential U.S. lawyers by *National Law Journal*.

7th April 1993: Hillary's father, Hugh Rodham, dies, a few weeks after suffering a stroke.

3rd October 1991: Bill joins the race for the Democratic nomination for president.

26th January 1992: Hillary and Bill appear on *60 Minutes* to address stories about Bill's alleged extramarital affairs.

18th February 1992: After sliding in polls, Bill comes in second in New Hampshire primary; he gains momentum and wins the nomination.

26th January 1993: Bill announces Hillary will lead the effort to reform health care.

20th January 1993: Bill Clinton is inaugurated as the USA's forty-second president.

July 16, 1992: Bill accepts the nomination for president at the Democratic National Convention.

3rd November 1992: Democrat Bill Clinton is elected president, defeating incumbent Republican George H. W. Bush and independent H. Ross Perot.

September 1997:
Chelsea enters Stanford University.

March 1994:
Hillary's 1978 commodities profits cause controversy.

22nd April 1994:
Hillary holds her first, and only, general press conference as First Lady.

6th June 1997:
Chelsea graduates from Sidwell Friends.

May 1997:
U.S. Supreme Court rules Paula Jones case can go forward.

6th May 1994:
Paula Jones sues Bill for alleged sexual harassment.

5th November 1996:
Bill is re-elected president, defeating Republican Bob Dole and independent Ross Perot.

27th August 1996:
Hillary gives her own speech at the Democratic National Convention, where Bill is again the Democratic nominee.

Summer 1994:
Health-care reforms fail to get out of committee, essentially dying without a vote.

August 1994:
Ken Starr becomes special Whitewater counsel.

8th November 1994: Election gains give Republicans control of Congress for the first time since 1954.

26th January 1996:
Hillary testifies before a federal grand jury.

19th January 1996:
Hillary is subpoenaed to testify about possible criminal misconduct related to the missing files.

10th January 1996:
Hillary's book *It Takes a Village* is published.

4th January 1996:
Hillary's long-missing billing records related to Whitewater are found.

Late March 1995:
Hillary speaks up for women during a trip to South Asia with Chelsea

19th April 1995:
Oklahoma City federal building is bombed, killing 168.

November 1995:
The federal government shuts down from November 14 to 19 and December 16 to January 6, 1996, because of budget struggles between Congress and the White House.

5th September 1995:
Hillary breaks ground with speech about women's rights at a United Nations conference in Beijing.

— 17th January 1998:
Bill gives a deposition in the Paula Jones case, which includes questions about Monica Lewinsky.

26th January 1998: —
Bill publicly denies having sex with Lewinsky at a White House event.

— 27th January 1998:
Hillary appears on the *Today* show and says media should look into "a vast right-wing conspiracy."

1st April 1998: A federal judge dismisses Paula Jones's lawsuit as without merit.

— 17th August 1998:
Bill testifies before Starr's grand jury and then confesses to the nation that he had a relationship with Lewinsky that was "not appropriate."

9th September 1998:
Starr's report is delivered to Congress.

— 15th September 1998:
Democratic women ask Hillary to campaign on their behalf.

3rd November 1998:
Democrats pick up more seats in the House.

— 13th November 1998:
Bill agrees to pay Paula Jones $850,000 to settle her sexual harassment lawsuit.

19th December 1998:—
Bill Clinton is impeached on charges of perjury and obstruction of justice.

— 12th February 1999:
The U.S. Senate acquits Bill after a trial. Hillary meets with adviser to discuss a possible Senate run.

7th July, 1999: —
Hillary announces an exploratory committee to consider running for the Senate from New York.

September 1999: Hillary and Bill buy a $1.7 million home in Chappaqua, New York.

— 7th October 2001:
The United States retaliates, attacking Afghanistan.

September 11, 2001:
Nearly 3,000 people are killed in New York, Washington, and Pennsylvania in the worst terrorist attack ever on U.S. soil.

3rd January 2001:
The First Lady is sworn in as senator from New York.

— 7th November 2000:
Hillary is elected to the U.S. Senate, defeating Republican Rick Lazio.

— 20th September 2000:
The Whitewater real-estate investigation ends without any charges against Hillary or Bill.

— 26th June 2000:
Hillary's friend Diane Blair passes away.

May 2000: —
Rudy Giuliani withdraws from the New York Senate race, citing marital and health issues.

6th February 2000:
Hillary formally announces her Senate candidacy.

11th October 2002: Hillary votes in favour of a resolution allowing the Bush administration to use force against Iraq's leader Saddam Hussein.

8th November 2016: America votes.

20th March 2003: The United States invades Iraq.

July 28, 2016: Hillary accepts the presidential nomination at the Democratic National Convention.

12th April, 2015: Hillary Rodham Clinton announces she is running for president.

June 2003: Hillary's autobiography, *Living History*, is published.

26th September 2014: Hillary's first grandchild, Charlotte Clinton Mezvinsky, is born.

10th June 2014: *Hard Choices* is published.

1st February 2013: Hillary ends her term as secretary of state.

23rd January 2013: Hillary testifies before Congress about Benghazi.

December 2012: Hillary delays testimony about Benghazi because of a concussion; she is then hospitalized for a blood clot in her head.

7th November 2006: Hillary is re-elected to the Senate.

20th January 2007: Hillary announces she is running for president.

11th September 2012: Four Americans die in an attack on the U.S. consulate in Benghazi, Libya.

8th January 2008: Hillary wins the New Hampshire primary after coming in third in Iowa caucuses.

February 2008: Hillary falls behind Barack Obama.

1st November 2011: Hillary's mother, Dorothy Howell Rodham, dies.

7th June 2008: Hillary finally concedes.

1st May 2011: U.S. Navy SEALs kill Osama bin Laden.

4th November 2008: Obama is elected president, defeating Republican John McCain.

Late November 2008: Hillary accepts Obama's offer to be secretary of state.

31st July 2010: Chelsea Clinton weds Marc Mezvinsky.

BIBLIOGRAPHY

There was no shortage of material on Hillary Rodham Clinton. After more than three decades in the public eye, she has been the subject of dozens of books and thousands of articles, from just about every point of view and on almost every topic imaginable.

There was a shortage, however, of reliable, accurate, or complete information. Because she's a politician, much of her own story has been carefully controlled and crafted over the years. The Clintons' own books were helpful in detailing their point of view. But while Hillary's lengthy tomes chronicled her comings and goings, they were not especially insightful or revealing. In part because Hillary has worked to keep part of her life private, and also because she's a celebrity, many others have filled the void by speaking for her and about her, sometimes illuminating her experiences and sometimes creating entire story lines based only on slim bits of information.

Wading through the muck made this one of the most difficult research projects I've ever encountered. There were some great storytellers—except their stories didn't hold up to scrutiny. Others wrote hundreds of pages that didn't seem to reveal much of anything.

Simple facts were often wrong. One small example: A prominent magazine reported in 1992 that Hillary helped lead a Wellesley team to multiple wins on the College Bowl, then a televised quiz show. The College Bowl website shows that Wellesley didn't compete until the year after Hillary graduated. Hillary was actually on her high school's *It's Academic* team, which won a couple of rounds on a locally televised quiz show—but she was an alternate not a contestant. Yet the College Bowl "fact" is often reported.

That said, some writers were thorough and detailed, including *Washington Post* writers Donnie Radcliffe and Martha Sherrill in the early 1990s and later work by political reporters Dan Balz, James Bennet, Ann Devroy, John Harris, Anne Kornblut, Mark Leibovich, David Maraniss, Robin Toner, and Bob Woodward.

I did my best to verify facts, dates, and anecdotes. If possible, quotations reported from speeches were matched up with the text of speeches online. In addition to reading more books and articles than I could count, I tapped three sets of oral histories—interviews at the Richard Nixon Presidential Library with the House Judiciary Committee legal staff, interviews conducted by Diane Blair about the 1992 campaign, and interviews with members of the Clinton administration at the Miller Center at the University of Virginia. I also visited the University of Arkansas Special Collections in Fayetteville, the William J. Clinton Presidential Library archives in Little Rock, and the Bill Clinton State Government Project at the Butler Center for Arkansas Studies, also in Little Rock.

The Clinton Library has a large digital database, including Hillary's daily schedules during the White House years, photographs, and many speeches and interview transcripts. I made extensive use of this, though changes to the site in early 2015 made navigating it much more difficult.

Hillary Clinton did not agree to an interview. In a phone conversation and numerous e-mails over sixteen months, I requested an interview or answers to specific questions from her traveling press secretary Nick Merrill. None of those questions were answered, but Merrill did help with Clinton permissions to use some photographs.

The books, articles, websites, and videos that follow are the ones that I found most useful. You will find additional sources mentioned in the notes. If you have questions about sources, feel free to contact me through my website, www.karenblumenthal.com.

Clinton Writings

Clinton, Bill. *My Life*. New York: Alfred A. Knopf, 2004.
Clinton, Hillary Rodham. *An Invitation to the White House: At Home with History*. New York: Simon & Schuster, 2000.

————. *Dear Socks, Dear Buddy: Kids' Letters to the First Pets.* New York: Simon & Schuster, 1998.

————. *Hard Choices.* New York: Simon & Schuster, 2014.

————. *It Takes a Village: And Other Lessons Children Teach Us.* New York: Simon & Schuster, 1996.

————. *Living History.* New York: Simon & Schuster, 2003.

Rodham, Hillary. "Children's Rights: A Legal Perspective." In *Children's Rights: Contemporary Perspectives*, edited by Patricia A. Vardin and Ilene N. Brody. New York: Teachers College Press, 1979.

————. "Children Under the Law." *Harvard Educational Review* 43 (Winter 1973): 487–514.

Biographies

Allen, Charles F. and Jonathan Portis. *The Comeback Kid: The Life and Career of Bill Clinton.* New York: Birch Lane Press, 1992.

Bernstein, Carl. *A Woman in Charge: The Life of Hillary Rodham Clinton.* New York: Alfred A. Knopf, 2007.

Bombardieri, Marcella. "From Conservative Roots Sprang a Call for Change." *Boston Globe*, Oct. 21, 2007.

Brock, David. *The Seduction of Hillary Rodham.* New York: Free Press, 1996.

Bruck, Connie. "Hillary the Pol." *New Yorker*, May 30, 1994.

"Hillary: An American Life." *Time* special issue, 2014.

Kelley, Virginia, with James Morgan. *Leading with My Heart.* New York: Simon & Schuster, 1994.

Kenney, Charles. "Hillary: The Wellesley Years." *Boston Globe*, Jan. 12, 1993.

King, Norman. *The Woman in the White House: The Remarkable Story of Hillary Rodham Clinton.* New York: Birch Lane Press, 1996.

Leveritt, Mara. "Hillary On Her Own Terms." *Arkansas Times*, Oct. 1989.

Maraniss, David. *First in His Class: A Biography of Bill Clinton.* New York: Simon & Schuster, 1995.

Milton, Joyce. *The First Partner: Hillary Rodham Clinton.* New York: William Morrow, 1999.

Nelson, Rex, and Philip Martin. *The Hillary Factor: The Story of America's First Lady.* New York: Gallen, 1993.

Oakley, Meredith L. *On the Make: The Rise of Bill Clinton.* Washington, D.C.: Regnery, 1994.

Radcliffe, Donnie. *Hillary Rodham Clinton: A First Lady for Our Time.* New York: Warner Books, 1993.

Sheehy, Gail. *Hillary's Choice.* New York: Random House, 1999.

———. "What Hillary Wants." *Vanity Fair,* May 1992.

Sherrill, Martha. "The Education of Hillary Clinton." *Washington Post,* Jan. 11, 1993.

———. "The Rising Lawyer's Detour to Arkansas." *Washington Post,* Jan. 12, 1993.

Warner, Judith. *Hillary Clinton: The Inside Story.* New York: Signet, 1993.

Before the White House Years

Bass, Carole. "The Education of Hillary Rodham Clinton." *Legal Times,* Oct. 19, 1992, pp. 2, 15–17.

Blair, Diane D. Project. Pryor Center for Arkansas Oral and Visual History. Special Collections, University of Arkansas, Fayetteville. http://pryorcenter.uark.edu/projects.php.

Clinton, Bill. State Government Project. Butler Center for Arkansas Studies, Little Rock, Ark.

Duff, Audrey. "Is a Rose a Rose?" *American Lawyer,* July–Aug. 1992.

Dumas, Ernest, ed. *The Clintons of Arkansas: An Introduction by Those Who Know Them Best.* Fayetteville, Ark.: University of Arkansas Press, 1993.

Goldwater, Barry. *The Conscience of a Conservative.* Shepherdsville, Ky.: Victor, 1960.

Horn, Miriam. *Rebels in White Gloves: Coming of Age with Hillary's Class—Wellesley '69.* New York: Times Books, 1999.

Hubbell, Webb. *Friends in High Places: Our Journey from Little Rock to Washington, D.C.* New York: William Morrow, 1997.

Kalman, Laura. *Yale Law School and the Sixties: Revolt and Reverberations.* Chapel Hill, N.C.: University of North Carolina Press, 2005.

Leibovich, Mark. "In Turmoil of '68, Clinton Found a New Voice." *New York Times*, Sept. 5, 2007.

Merriweather, James. "Hillary Clinton Forges Own Passage Forward." *Arkansas Gazette*, July 22, 1990.

"The 90's Election Specials Raw: Clintons at Maine South High School #2." Media Burn video, 1:00:59. March 12, 1992. http://mediaburn.org/video/the-90s-election-specials-raw-clintons-at-maine-south-high-school-2/.

U.S. House of Representatives Committee on the Judiciary Members and Impeachment Inquiry Staff. Oral Histories. Nixon Presidential Library and Museum. http://www.nixonlibrary.gov/forresearchers/find/histories/hcj.php.

Washington Post. "The Watergate Story." http://www.washington-post.com/wp-srv/politics/special/watergate/coverage.html.

Woods, Betty. "Ms. Rodham? Just an Old-Fashioned Girl." *Arkansas Democrat*, Feb. 11, 1979.

White House Years

Baker, Peter. *The Breach: Inside the Impeachment and Trial of William Jefferson Clinton.* New York: Scribner, 2000.

Bennet, James. "The Next Clinton." *New York Times Magazine*, May 30, 1999.

Blair, Diane D., Papers (MC 1632). Special Collections, University of Arkansas Libraries, University of Arkansas, Fayetteville.

Blumenthal, Sidney. *The Clinton Wars.* New York: Farrar, Straus and Giroux, 2003.

Branch, Taylor. *The Clinton Tapes: Wrestling History with the President.* New York: Simon and Schuster, 2009.

Cawley, Janet. "First Lady 'Has Nose for Goal Line.'" *Arkansas Democrat-Gazette*, May 26, 1993.

Chua-Eoan, Howard G. "Power Mom." *People*, Jan. 25, 1993.

Drew, Elizabeth. *On the Edge: The Clinton Presidency.* New York: Touchstone, 1995.

Gergen, David. *Eyewitness to Power: The Essence of Leadership Nixon to Clinton.* New York: Simon & Schuster, 2000.

Goldman, Peter, Thomas M. DeFrank, Mark Miller, Andrew Murr, Tom Matthews, with Patrick Rogers and Melanie Cooper. *Quest for the Presidency 1992.* College Station, Tex.: Texas A&M University Press, 1994.

Halley, Patrick S. *On the Road with Hillary: A Behind-the-Scenes Look at the Journey from Arkansas to the U.S. Senate.* New York: Viking, 2002.

Harris, John F. *The Survivor: Bill Clinton in the White House.* New York: Random House, 2005.

"Hillary Rodham Clinton: Changing the Rules." *Biography.* A&E Home Video, 1996. Videocassette, 60 min.

"Hillary Rodham Clinton 50th Birthday." Interview by Carl S. Anthony, Chicago Historical Society, Oct. 27, 1997. Videocassette.

Johnson, Haynes, and David S. Broder. *The System: The American Way of Politics at the Breaking Point.* Boston: Little, Brown, 1997.

Maraniss, David. *The Clinton Enigma: A Four-and-a-Half-Minute Speech Reveals This President's Entire Life.* New York: Simon & Schuster, 1998.

————. "First Lady of Paradox." *Washington Post,* Jan. 15, 1995.

National First Ladies' Library. www.firstladies.org.

Stephanopoulos, George. *All Too Human: A Political Education.* Boston: Little, Brown, 1999.

Toobin, Jeffrey. *A Vast Conspiracy: The Real Story of the Sex Scandal That Nearly Brought Down a President.* New York: Random House, 1999.

Washington Post. "Whitewater Special Report," "Clinton Accused," and "Jones v. Clinton." http://www.washingtonpost.com/wp-srv/politics/special/whitewater/whitewater.htm.

William J. Clinton Presidential History Project. Miller Center, University of Virginia. http://millercenter.org/president/clinton/oralhistory.

Woodward, Bob. *The Agenda: Inside the Clinton White House.* New York: Simon & Schuster, 1994.

————. *Shadow: Five Presidents and the Legacy of Watergate.* New York: Touchstone, 1999.

After the White House

Allen, Jonathan, and Amie Parnes. *HRC: State Secrets and the Rebirth of Hillary Clinton*. New York: Crown, 2014.

Bai, Matt. "Mrs. Triangulation." *New York Times*, Oct. 2, 2005.

Balz, Dan, and Haynes Johnson. *The Battle for America 2008: The Story of an Extraordinary Election*. New York: Viking, 2009.

Gates, Robert M. *Duty: Memoirs of a Secretary at War*. New York: Alfred A. Knopf, 2014.

Gerth, Jeff, and Dona Van Natta Jr. *Her Way: The Hopes and Ambitions of Hillary Rodham Clinton*. New York: Little, Brown, 2007.

Harpaz, Beth J. *The Girls in the Van: A Reporter's Diary of the Campaign Trail*. New York: Thomas Dunne Books, 2001.

Heilemann, John, and Mark Halperin. *Game Change: Obama and the Clintons, McCain and Palin, and the Race of a Lifetime*. New York: Harper, 2010.

Tomasky, Michael. *Hillary's Turn: Inside Her Improbable Victorious Senate Campaign*. New York: Free Press, 2001.

Traister, Rebecca. *Big Girls Don't Cry: The Election That Changed Everything for American Women*. New York: Free Press, 2010.

Woodward, Bob. *Obama's Wars*. New York: Simon & Schuster, 2010.

Newspapers and Magazines

New York Times, Washington Post, Arkansas Democrat-Gazette, Arkansas Gazette, Time, People, New Yorker, Newsweek, Southwords, Wellesley News, Vanity Fair

Election Results

Information on all U.S. elections:

The American Presidency Project. "Presidential Elections Data." http://www.presidency.ucsb.edu/elections.php.

2008 election results:

CNN. "Election Center 2008." http://www.cnn.com/ELECTION /2008/primaries/results/scorecard/.

New York Times. "Election 2008." http://politics.nytimes.com/election-guide/2008/results/votes/index.html.

2016 election results:

Andrews, Wilson, Kitty Bennett, and Alicia Parlapiano, "2016 Delegate Count and Primary Results." *New York Times,* http://www.nytimes.com/interactive/2016/us/elections/primary-calendar-and-results.html.

New York Times. "Who is Running for President?" http://www.nytimes.com/interactive/2016/us/elections/2016-presidential-candidates.html.

Wall Street Journal. "2016 Election: Polls, Calendar, Money, and More." http://graphics.wsj.com/elections/2016/.

NOTES

Introduction

IN LOSING, HILLARY: Adam Nagourney and Jeff Zeleny, "Ending Her Bid, Clinton Backs Obama," *New York Times*, June 7, 2008; "Transcript: Hillary Clinton Endorses Barack Obama," *New York Times*, June 7, 2008; "Hillary Clinton's Concession Speech," YouTube video, 29:02, from C-Span, June 7, 2008, https://www.youtube.com/watch?v=zgi_kIYx_bY; Jeffrey M. Jones, "Barack Obama, Hillary Clinton Extend Run as Most Admired," Gallup, Dec. 29, 2014, http://www.gallup.com/poll/180365/barack-obama-hillary-clinton-extend-run-admired.aspx; "Most Admired Man and Woman," Gallup, http://www.gallup.com/poll/1678/most-admired-man-woman.aspx.

Chapter 1: Roots

THE FIRST CHILD OF: Sherrill, "The Education of Hillary Clinton"; Clinton, *Living History*, pp. 2–13; Sheehy, *Hillary's Choice*, pp. 20–26; "Hillary Rodham 50th Birthday," interview by Anthony, Oct. 27, 1997; Kim Hubbard, "Happy Return," *People*, Nov. 10, 1997; Sheehy, "What Hillary Wants"; Radcliffe, *Hillary Rodham Clinton*, pp. 25–36; Chua-Eoan, "Power Mom"; Sally Jenkins, "Growing Up Rodham," *Washington Post*, Dec. 9, 2007; Clinton, *It Takes a Village*," pp. 20–25; *Park Ridge Public Schools Progress Report*, 1956, William J. Clinton Presidential Library, Little Rock, Ark.; Elizabeth Gleick, "Brothers-in-Law," *People*, Dec. 14, 1992.

IN SCHOOL, SHE WAS ELECTED: *Living History*, pp. 12–16, 20; Bonnie Miller Rubin and Ginger Thompson, "First Lady's 50th: Cake, Pizza, Memories," *Chicago Tribune*, Oct. 28, 1997; Hillary Rodham Clinton, "Hillary's Chicago," *George*, Sept. 1996, pp. 132–134; Cynthia Hanson, "I Was a Teenage Republican," *Chicago*, Sept. 1994, p. 73; Hillary Rodham, "My Future," 1959, William J. Clinton Presidential Library, Little Rock, Ark.; "Sputnik and the Dawn of the Space Age," NASA, http://history.nasa.gov/sputnik/; "The Decision to Go to the Moon: John F. Kennedy's May 25, 1961 Speech Before a Joint Session of Congress," NASA, http://history.nasa.gov/moondec.html; *It Takes a Village*, p. 206; Sheehy, "What Hillary Wants"; Lloyd Grove, "Hillary Clinton, Trying to Have It All," *Washington Post*, March 10, 1992. Some versions of the NASA story say she was fourteen, others twelve or thirteen, when she wrote to the agency.

Chapter 2: Groundwork

THE 1960 PRESIDENTIAL RACE: Gerald Posner, "The Fallacy of Nixon's Graceful Exit," Salon, Nov. 10, 2000, http://www.salon.com/2000/11/10/nixon_4/; David Greenberg, "Was Nixon Robbed?" Slate, Oct. 16, 2000, http://www.slate.com/articles/news_and_politics/history_lesson/2000/10/was_nixon_robbed.html; *Living History*, pp. 16–17, 21–23, 48; *It Takes a Village*, p. 156; Sheehy, *Hillary's Choice*, pp. 30–38; Goldwater, *The Conscience of a Conservative*, pp. 13, 37; Rubin and Thompson, *Chicago Tribune*, Oct. 28, 1997; Sherrill, "The Education of Hillary Clinton"; Radcliffe, pp. 44–49; Warner, *Hillary Clinton*, p. 20; Clinton, *Hard Choices*, p. 18; Martha Brant and Evan Thomas, "First Fighter," *Newsweek*, Jan. 15, 1996, p. 23; Hillary Clinton, interview by Martha Sherrill, April 28, 1993, FLOTUS Press Office Interview Transcripts, Vol. I, Clinton Digital Library, http://clinton.presidentialli-braries.us/items/show/7374; E. E. Cummings, "dying is fine) but Death," *E. E. Cummings: Complete Poems, 1913–1962*, p. 604, used by permission of Liveright Publishing Corp.; Hanson, *Chicago*, Sept. 1994, pp. 101–102.

Chapter 3: Park Ridge

As a sophomore, Hillary: Frank Marafiote, "Hillary Rodham Clinton's High School Yearbook," *Hillary Clinton Quarterly* (blog), Feb. 5, 2013, http://www.hillaryclintonquarterly.com/hillary-rodham-clintons-high-school-yearbook/; Rubin and Thompson, *Chicago Tribune*, Oct. 28, 1997; *Living History*, pp. 18–20, 24–26, 162; Bombardieri, "From Conservative Roots Sprang a Call for Change"; Sherrill, "The Education of Hillary Clinton"; Hanson, *Chicago*, Sept. 1994, pp. 101–106; "The 90's Election Specials raw: Clintons at Maine South High School #2," Media Burn video, 1:00:59, from Hillary Clinton's talk to students on March 12, 1992, http://mediaburn.org/video/the-90s-election-specials-raw-clintons-at-maine-south-high-school-2/.

Between her junior and senior year: Bombardieri, "From Conservative Roots Sprang a Call for Change"; *Living History*, pp. 20–26; Radcliffe, pp. 20–28, 38, 41–42, 50–52; Sherrill, "The Education of Hillary Clinton"; "Lawyer Hillary Reviews Career," *Southwords* (newspaper of Maine Township High School South), Dec. 22, 1964; "Beginning Wasn't at Bottom," "Outstanding 65ers Receive Honors at Assembly Today," and "'65 Alums Reminisce Over the Good Ol' Days," *Southwords*, June 7, 1965; Wellesley College, "Fees and Expenses," *Bulletin of Wellesley College Catalogue Numbers 1965–1966, 1966–67, 1967–68, 1968–69*, Wellesley College Catalogs, Books 49, 78, 77, 76, http://repository.wellesley.edu/catalogs.

Chapter 4: Wellesley

The school that Hillary: Radcliffe, pp. 55–61; Miriam Horn, *Rebels in White Gloves*, pp. xiii–xiv, 9–11; Chua-Eoan, "Power Mom"; *Living History*, pp. 27–33; Wellesley College, *Bulletin of Wellesley College Catalogue Number 1965–1966*, Wellesley College Catalogs, Book 49, http://repository.wellesley.edu/catalogs/49; "Wellesley Traditions: Hooprolling," Wellesley College, http://www.wellesley.edu/about/collegehistory/traditions/hooprolling. Among the more bizarre practices at Wellesley and other Seven Sisters and Ivy League schools: Freshmen were required to pose in the nude for "posture pictures." By the time Hillary attended Wellesley, women could wear their underwear. For more details, see Ron Rosenbaum, "The Great Ivy League Nude Posture Photo Scandal," *New York Times Magazine*, Jan. 15, 1995. "Colleges: A Point in Time at Wellesley," *Time*, Aug. 20, 1965; Kenney, "Hillary: The Wellesley Years"; Hillary Clinton, "Remarks on Student Activism at Wellesley College," Nov. 1, 2007, American Presidency Project, http://www.presidency.ucsb.edu/ws/?pid=77072; Wendy Wyse, "Young Republicans, Democrats Seek Student Aid in Fall Political Campaigns," *Wellesley News*, Oct. 13, 1966; "Why a Republican?" *Wellesley News*, Jan. 12, 1967. *Wellesley News* stories were accessed through the Wellesley College Archives and http://repository.wellesley.edu/news/.

AT THE SAME TIME, SHE: Francie Latour, "The Basis of Our Ethos," *Wellesley*, Spring 2008, pp. 23–29; Radcliffe, pp. 58–65; *Living History*, pp. 30–35; Sheehy, *Hillary's Choice*, pp. 45–51; Clinton, interview by Sherrill, April 28, 1993; Kenney, "Hillary: The Wellesley Years"; Chua-Eoan, "Power Mom"; Warner, p. 32; David Maraniss, *First in His Class*, pp. 255–257, 259; Bernstein, *A Woman in Charge*, pp. 46–51; Horn, pp. 24–25; "Vietnam War Protests," History.com, 2010, http://www.history.com/topics/vietnam-war/vietnam-war-protests; Mark Leibovich, "In the '60s, a Future Candidate Poured Her Heart Out in Letters," *New York Times*, July 29, 2007; Radcliffe offers a slightly different quote about the heart and mind: "I wonder if it's possible to be a mental conservative and a heart liberal?"; Robert L. Ward, "Wellesley Students Fight 'Restrictive' Curricula," *Boston Globe*, March 1, 1967.

Chapter 5: Making Possible

IN EARLY 1968: "In Dubious Battle" and "Election Support" (letter to the editor), *Wellesley News*, Feb. 15, 1968; Bernstein, pp. 51–58; Sheehy, *Hillary's Choice*, pp. 56, 62–64, 68–69,

71–74; Kenney, "Hillary: The Wellesley Years"; " 'Back Room' Politics," *Wellesley News*, April 10, 1969; Mark Leibovich, "In Turmoil of '68, Clinton Found a New Voice"; *Living History*, pp. 30–38; Radcliffe, pp. 68–74, 77–83; Latour, *Wellesley*, Spring 2008, pp. 27–29; Hillary Rodham, "Speech to Freshmen," 1968, Wellesley College Archives; Chua-Eoan, "Power Mom"; Warner, p. 33.

TOWARDS THE END OF HER INTERNSHIP: *Living History*, pp. 35–38; Leibovich, "In Turmoil of '68"; Sherrill, "The Rising Lawyer's Detour to Arkansas"; Radcliffe, p. 74; Sheehy, *Hillary's Choice*, pp. 54–55; Hillary D. Rodham, "There Is Only the Fight: An Analysis of the Alinsky Model," (honors thesis, Wellesley, 1969), http://blogs.chicagotribune.com/ news_columnists_ezorn/2012/01/hillary-clintons-secret- alinsky-thesis-exposed.html; Michael Levenson, "A Student's Words, a Candidate's Struggle," *Boston Globe*, March 4, 2007. When Bill Clinton was in the White House, Wellesley College removed access to the thesis, leading some Clinton critics to assume that young Rodham must have taken a very liberal stance in her work. The Clintons later indicated they were concerned that the paper might be perceived as critical of Senator Daniel Patrick Moynihan of New York, who was still in office; Cindi Leive, "Hillary off the High Wire," *Glamour*, Sept. 2014, p. 341; Henry Louis Gates, "Hating Hillary," *New Yorker*, Feb. 26, 1996; Radcliffe, p. 79; Clinton, "Remarks on Student Activism at Wellesley College," Nov. 1, 2007; George W. Pierson, *A Yale Book of Numbers: Historical Statistics of the College and University, 1701–1976* (New Haven: Yale, 1983), pp. 594–596; Kenney, "Hillary: The Wellesley Years."

AS WELLESLEY'S GRADUATION NEARED: *Living History*, pp. 38–43; Edward W. Brooke, "Progress in the Uptight Society: Real Problems and Wrong Procedures" (speech, Wellesley College, May 31, 1969), http://www.wellesley.edu/events/ commencement/archives/1969commencement/commence mentaddress; Hillary D. Rodham, "Remarks on the Occasion of Wellesley's 91st Commencement" (speech, Wellesley College, May 31, 1969), FLOTUS Statements and Speeches

5/31/69–10/12/92, Clinton Digital Library, http://clinton. presidentiallibraries.us/items/show/7685; James Stack, "Sen. Brooke Upstaged at Wellesley Commencement," *Boston Globe*, June 1, 1969; Judith Martin, "Wellesley Revisited: Bit of a Rebuttal at Commencement," *Washington Post*, June 8, 1969; United Press International, "Park Ridge Girl Raps Brooke," *Chicago Tribune*, June 2, 1969; "Two Commencement Speakers," *Chicago Tribune*, June 3, 1969; Raymond R. Coffey, "Blast at Brooke Brought Instant Fame," *Boston Globe*, June 5, 1969; Robert Pinsky, "When Hillary Was Already Hillary," Slate, July 2, 2013, http://www.slate.com/articles/news_and _politics/history/2013/07/hillary_clinton_wesleyan_com-mencement_speech_robert_pinsky_on_the_politician.html.

Chapter 6: Yale

EVEN AT YALE LAW SCHOOL: "Breakdown of Class of 1972 (October 1, 1969)," *Yale Law Report*, Fall 1969, p. 13; *Living History*, pp. 44–48; Radcliffe, pp. 90–98; Milton, *The First Partner*, pp. 34–42; Bernstein, pp. 63–74; Kalman, *Yale Law School and the Sixties*, pp. 167–176, 210–211, 218–219; Paul Bass and Doug Rae, "The Panther and the Bulldog: The Story of May Day 1970," *Yale Alumni Magazine*, July/Aug. 2006; Homer Bigart, "Yale to Open Gates This Weekend to Protesters Assembling to Support Black Panthers," *New York Times*, April 30, 1970; Michael T. Kaufman, "Boarded Windows and Greased Flagpole Greet Panther Protest in New Haven," *New York Times*, May 2, 1970; Bass, "The Education of Hillary Rodham Clinton," pp. 2, 15–16; Nancy L. Ross, "League Rejects Cambodia, Lib Issues," *Washington Post*, May 5, 1970; Nancy L. Ross, "League Deplores 'Crisis,'" *Washington Post*, May 8, 1970; Hillary Rodham Clinton, "What I Learned in Law School" (speech, Yale Law School, Oct. 2, 1992), *Yale Law Report*, Fall 1992.

Chapter 7: Bill

ON THE FIRST DAY OF HER SECOND YEAR: "Interview: Robert Reich," WGBH American Experience, http://www.pbs.org/

wgbh/americanexperience/features/interview/clinton-reich/; Bass, "The Education of Hillary Rodham Clinton"; *Living History*, p. 52–57; Clinton, *My Life*, pp. 4–63, 181–185; Robert Reich, Facebook post, June 27, 2013, ; Maraniss, *First in His Class*, pp. 21–47, 246–249. This is Hillary's version of their first meeting. Bill tells a similar story, with slightly different wording, in his book, *My Life*, pp. 181–182. Lisa DePaulo, "Hillary Clinton's Secret Weapon," *More*, April 2012; Sheehy, *Hillary's Choice*, pp. 71–74, 83. Bill biographer David Maraniss raised questions about Bill's true father, noting that his father was still stationed in Italy when he would have been conceived; Bill's mother later said that her son came early, *First in His Class*, pp. 27–28. Bernstein, p. 61; Josh Gerstein, "Hillary Clinton's Radical Summer," *New York Sun*, Nov. 26, 2007; Robert Farley, "Truth-O-Meter: She's No Red," Feb. 15, 2008, PolitiFact.com, http://www.politifact.com/truth-o-meter/statements/2008/feb/15/chain-email/shes-no-red/.

Chapter 8: Courtship

AS DOROTHY RODHAM TELLS IT: There is some disagreement over when this first visit to Park Ridge took place. Dorothy Rodham and Hillary remember it over Christmas. In his book, Bill Clinton recalls stopping by Park Ridge on the way to California, and one of Hillary's brothers says he was mowing the lawn when Bill arrived, which would put the visit in summer, rather than during a Chicago winter. Radcliffe, pp. 102–108; *Living History*, pp. 49–51, 56–57; *My Life*, pp. 188–189, 209; Bass, "The Education of Hillary Rodham Clinton," pp. 16–17; Maraniss, *First in His Class*, pp. 226, 263–264, 277; Bernstein, pp. 84–87, 92; Sheehy, *Hillary's Choice*, p. 85; Sheehy, "What Hillary Wants"; Hillary Clinton, speech at Chautauqua Institution, New York, June 28, 1991, FLOTUS Statements and Speeches 5/31/69–10/12/92, *Clinton Digital Library*, **http:**//clinton.presidentiallibraries.us/items/show/7697; Kelley, *Leading with My Heart*, pp. 190–192.

Chapter 9: Children

HILLARY RENTED THE TOP FLOOR: *Living History,* pp. 63–66;
Hillary Rodham, "Children Under the Law," pp. 487–514;
Bass, "The Education of Hillary Rodham Clinton," p. 17;
Hillary Rodham, "Children's Rights: A Legal Perspective";
Children's Defense Fund, "Children's Defense Fund Honors
Hillary Rodham Clinton at 40th Anniversary Celebration,"
news release, Sept. 30, 2013; *My Life,* pp. 209–211; Jeffrey
Toobin, "Terms of Impeachment," *New Yorker,* Sept. 14, 1998,
p. 33; Ronald Garay, "Watergate," Museum of Broadcast
Communications, http://www.museum.tv/eotv/watergate.
htm; "The Watergate Story," Timeline, *Washington Post,*
http://www.washingtonpost.com/wp-srv/politics/special/
watergate/timeline.html; Constitution of the United States of
America, Article II, Section 4; "Impeachment," U.S. House of
Representatives and U.S. Senate, http://history.house.gov/
Institution/Origins-Development/Impeachment/ and http://
www.senate.gov/artandhistory/history/common/briefing/
Senate_Impeachment_Role.htm; "The Watergate Files," Gerald
R. Ford Library & Museum, http://www.fordlibrarymuseum.
gov/museum/exhibits/watergate_files/; "Senate Hears
Impeachment Charges Against Andrew Johnson," History.com,
2009, http://www.history.com/this-day-in-history/senate-
hears-impeachment-charges-against-andrew-johnson.

Chapter 10: Nixon

AS THE WATERGATE SCANDAL GAINED STEAM: "The Watergate
Story" timeline, *Washington Post;* William Weld, interview by
Timothy Naftali, Sept. 28, 2011, Richard Nixon Oral History
Project, Richard Nixon Presidential Library and Museum;
Living History, pp. 65–70; Maraniss, *First in His Class,*
pp. 307–315; Radcliffe, pp. 119–130; William M. Welch,
"Hillary Clinton Recalls Watergate Role as 'Unbelievable,' "
Arkansas Democrat-Gazette, July 14, 1992; Joseph Woods,
interview by Timothy Naftali, Oct. 27, 2011, Richard Nixon
Oral History Project; Richard Gill, interview by Timothy
Naftali, Sept. 30, 2011, Richard Nixon Oral History Project;

Bernard Nussbaum, interview by Timothy Naftali, Oct. 1, 2011, Richard Nixon Oral History Project. Nixon Oral History Project interviews accessed at http://www.nixonlibrary.gov /forresearchers/find/histories/hcj.php

AS THE INQUIRY PROGRESSED: Merriweather, "Hillary Clinton Forges Own Passage Forward"; *Living History*, pp. 65–70; Radcliffe, pp. 126–137; Maraniss, *First in His Class*, pp. 314–318; Liza Mundy, "The Hillary Dilemma," *Washington Post Magazine*, March 21, 1999; Clinton, speech at Chautauqua, June 28, 1991.

Chapter 11: Fayetteville

JUST A COUPLE OF DAYS: Maraniss, *First in His Class*, pp. 316–338; *Living History*, pp. 69–75; Gleick, *People*, Dec. 14, 1992; *My Life*, pp. 220–235; Radcliffe, pp. 134, 137–150; Hillary Clinton, interview by Victor Geminiani, July 21, 1991, National Equal Justice Library Oral History Collection, Georgetown Law Library, https://repository.library. georgetown.edu/handle/10822/709428; Glenn Thrush, "Election 2008: For Young Clinton, a Case of Clashing Ideals," *Newsday*, Feb. 24, 2008; Warner, pp. 91–92; Sheehy, "What Hillary Wants"; Bernstein, pp. 118–123; Kelley, pp. 199–200, 219–220; "Bill Clinton, Miss Rodham Are Wed," *Arkansas Gazette*, Oct. 17, 1975; Clinton, speech at Chautauqua, June 28, 1991.

Chapter 12: Lawyer

HILLARY AND BILL NEVER GOT AROUND: Gleick, *People*, Dec. 14, 1992; *My Life*, p. 235–243; Radcliffe, pp. 155–170; *Living History*, pp. 76–83; "Carter Picks LR Lawyer for Legal Services Post," *Arkansas Gazette*, Dec. 13, 1977; Clinton, interview by Geminiani, July 21, 1991; Bennett H. Beach, "Law: One More Narrow Escape," *Time*, Nov. 23, 1981; Hubbell, *Friends in High Places*, pp. 4, 46–56, 64–67; Warner, pp. 95–97; Bruck, "Hillary the Pol," p. 63; Jonathan Van Meter, "Waiting in the Wings: An Exclusive Interview with Chelsea Clinton," *Vogue*, Aug. 13, 2012; Maraniss, *First in His Class*,

pp. 354–355; Nelson and Martin, *The Hillary Factor,*
pp. 202–208; "Bill Clinton: Wants Mandate," *Arkansas Gazette,*
May 28, 1978; Bob Lancaster, "'Whiz-Kid' Gets 60% of the
Vote," *Arkansas Democrat,* May 31, 1978.

Chapter 13: Governor

WITH THE YOUTHFUL BILL CLINTON: Steven V. Roberts, "New
Faces on the National Political Scene," *New York Times,*
Nov. 9, 1978; "A New Face for Arkansas," *Newsday,* Jan. 8,
1979; Woods, "Ms. Rodham? Just an Old-Fashioned Girl";
Radcliffe, p. 170; *Living History,* pp. 83–91; *My Life,*
pp. 272–273; Clinton, speech at Chautauqua, June 28, 1991;
Merriweather, "Hillary Clinton Forges Own Passage
Forward"; Walter Isaacson, "Hillary Clinton: We're Hoping
That We Have Another Child," *Time,* June 3, 1996; "Girl
Born to Clinton and Wife," *Arkansas Gazette,* Feb. 29, 1980;
"The First Family at the Governor's Mansion," photo,
Arkansas Gazette, March 5, 1980; Leveritt, "Hillary on Her
Own Terms."

HILLARY DIDN'T CONSIDER: Sharon LaFraniere and Charles R.
Babcock, "Whitewater Study Shows How Clintons' Burden
Eased," *Washington Post,* June 29, 1995; Gerth and Van Natta,
Her Way, pp. 105–112; *Living History,* pp. 86–91; Ruth Marcus
and Charles R. Babcock, "How $1,000 Stake Netted
$100,000," *Washington Post,* March 30, 1994; "Statement of
Lisa Caputo, Press Secretary for the First Lady," Office of the
Press Secretary, White House, March 29, 1994, http://
clinton6.nara.gov/1994/03/1994-03-30-statement-by
-lisa-caputo-on-first-ladys-commodity-trading.html; Cawley,
"First Lady 'Has Nose for Goal Line'"; George Bentley and
Wayne Jordan, "Clinton, Wife Assess in Wrong County; Car
Not on Books," *Arkansas Gazette,* March 22, 1979; Brenda
Tirey, "Clinton Says Mistake Let Him Get License," *Arkansas
Gazette,* March 23, 1979; "Clinton Pays Car Tax, Assessment
Penalties," *Arkansas Gazette,* March 24, 1979; Maraniss, *First
in His Class,* pp. 370–389; *My Life,* pp. 264–285; Nelson and
Martin, pp. 216–220.

Chapter 14: Comeback

IN 1981, HILLARY AND BILL: Leveritt, "Hillary on Her Own Terms," p. 35; Merriweather, "Hillary Clinton Forges Own Passage Forward"; *Living History*, pp. 93–94; *My Life*, pp. 290–295; Sheehy, "What Hillary Wants"; Bruck, "Hillary the Pol," pp. 65–66; John Brummett, "Clinton Announces for 'Hot' Campaign," *Arkansas Gazette*, Feb. 28, 1982; "Rodham Takes Leave to Join Campaign as 'Mrs. Bill Clinton,'" *Arkansas Gazette*, Feb. 28, 1982; "'Biggest Supporter' Is Asset to Clinton," *Arkansas Gazette*, Oct. 24, 1982; Oakley, *On the Make*, p. 271.

REJUVENATED AND HUMBLED: *Living History*, pp. 94–95; *My Life*, pp. 307–313; Roy Reed, "I Just Went to School in Arkansas," and Paul Root, "Lessons from the Student," both in Dumas, *The Clintons of Arkansas*, pp. 95–115; press release, Education series, Don Ernst Collection, box 33, Bill Clinton State Government Project, Butler Center for Arkansas Studies; Allen and Portis, *The Comeback Kid*, pp. 82–102; Oakley, pp. 280–293; Merriweather, "Hillary Clinton Forges Own Passage Forward"; Radcliffe, pp. 201–214; Leveritt, "Hillary on Her Own Terms"; "Mrs. Clinton Outlines Plan for Upgrading Education," *Arkansas Gazette*, July 28, 1983; Marion Fulk, "Mrs. Clinton Says She Found No One Happy with Schools," *Arkansas Gazette*, Aug. 24, 1983; John Brummett, "Mrs. Clinton Wins Praise from Panel," *Arkansas Gazette*, July 29, 1983; Landon Y. Jones, "Road Warriors," *People*, July 20, 1992; Marion Fulk, "From Low-Key Beginning, Mrs. Clinton Became Leader on Standards Committee," *Arkansas Gazette*, Dec. 25, 1983; Marc J. Holley, "Education Reform," *Encyclopedia of Arkansas History & Culture*, Sept. 8, 2014, http://www.encyclopediaofarkansas. net; David Davies, "Israeli-Begun Program for Preschoolers Gains Attention in Arkansas," *Arkansas Gazette*, Feb. 9, 1986 in Ann Kamps Collection, box 5, file 1, Bill Clinton State Government Project, Butler Center for Arkansas Studies; James Merriweather, "Clintons Report Net Worth of $418,692," *Arkansas Gazette*, July 24, 1990.

Chapter 15: Mom

ALTHOUGH HILLARY WAS BUSY: *It Takes a Village*, pp. 92,
102–103, 105–106,150–151, 220; Cawley, "First Lady 'Has
Nose for Goal Line'"; Jones, "Road Warriors"; Bai, "Mrs.
Triangulation"; Associated Press, "State's 'First Couple'
Makes Esquire List of Best, Brightest in U.S. Under Age 40,"
Arkansas Gazette, Nov. 11, 1984; résumé of Hillary Rodham
Clinton, Foundation for Child Development records, series 1,
subseries 2, Rockefeller Archive Center, http://dimes.
rockarch.org; Michael Barbaro, "As a Director, Clinton
Moved Wal-Mart Board, but Only So Far," *New York Times*,
May 20, 2007; Wal-Mart Stores Inc., annual report for the
year ended Jan. 31, 1989, p. 33, http://stock.walmart.com/
investors/financial-information/annual-reports-and-proxies/
default.aspx; Wal-Mart Stores Inc., proxy statements filed
with the Securities and Exchange Commission, May 4, 1987,
p. 10, and April 28, 1992, p. 6, obtained via a Freedom of
Information Act request.

WHILE SERVING ON OTHER: Letter from Debbie Roberts,
Augusta High School yearbook sponsor to Hillary and
Hillary response and March 1985 speaking engagements,
Ann Kamps Collection, box 1, file 2, Bill Clinton State
Goverment Project; Duff, "Is a Rose a Rose?" and sidebar,
"Hillary Clinton's Low-Key Legal Life," *American Lawyer*,
July/Aug. 1992, pp. 68–73; Leveritt, "Hillary on Her Own
Terms," p. 34; *Living History*, pp. 95–98; *My Life*, pp. 315–316,
331–335, 384; Radcliffe, p. 215; Bernstein, pp. 175–190;
"Arkansas Governor Pushing His Hat Toward Ring's Edge,"
Washington Post, July 5, 1987; Maraniss, *First in His Class*,
pp. 438–445, 450; Robin Toner, "Clinton Is Posed to Enter '88
Race," *New York Times*, July 2, 1987; Thomas B. Edsall,
"Clinton Throws Hat Out of Ring," *Washington Post*, July 15,
1987; Matt Bai, "How Gary Hart's Downfall Forever
Changed American Politics," *New York Times Magazine*,
Sept. 18, 2014; Ann Bausum, *Our Country's First Ladies*
(Washington, D.C.: National Geographic, 2007),
p. 89; Bruck, "Hillary the Pol," p. 63; Maraniss, *The Clinton*

Enigma, p. 81; Sheehy, "What Hillary Wants," and *Hillary's Choice*, pp. 182–185.

NOW IN HER EARLY FORTIES: "Women in the Law: MacCrate Names Commission," *ABA Journal*, Nov. 1, 1987, p. 148; "Mrs. Clinton Named on List of Top Lawyers," *Arkansas Gazette*, May 9, 1988; Leveritt, "Hillary on Her Own Terms," p. 33; Bernstein, pp.187–190; Sheehy, *Hillary's Choice*, pp. 186–190; Jim Nichols, "Clinton, McRae Debate," *Arkansas Gazette*, May 17, 1990; Bruck, "Hillary the Pol," pp. 75–76.

Chapter 16: Campaign

IN THE SUMMER OF 1991: Sheehy, *Hillary's Choice*, pp. 194–195; James L. "Skip" Rutherford, interview by Diane Blair, Nov. 3, 1992, Diane D. Blair Project, Pryor Center for Arkansas Oral and Visual History, Special Collections, University of Arkansas, Fayetteville, http://pryorcenter.uark.edu/projects. php, quoted with permission of Special Collections; *My Life*, pp. 341–343, 367–392; Jeffrey Stinson, "Clintons Confront Personal Question," *Arkansas Gazette*, Sept. 17, 1991; Robin Toner, "Arkansas' Clinton Enters the '92 Race for President," *New York Times*, Oct. 4, 1991; "Hillary Clinton Has Influence," *Arkansas Gazette*, Oct. 3, 1991; *Living History*, pp. 101–116; Adam Pertman, "Lawyer Hillary Clinton to Husband's Defense," *Boston Globe*, Jan. 29, 1992; Sheehy, "What Hillary Wants"; "Clinton Denounces New Report of Affair," *New York Times*, Jan. 24, 1992; Noel Oman, "Woman's Interview Renews Allegations of Clinton Infidelity," *Arkansas Democrat-Gazette*, Jan. 24, 1992; Don Johnson and Terry Lemons, "Clinton, Wife to Confront Allegations," *Arkansas Democrat-Gazette*, Jan. 25, 1992; Peter S. Canellos, "Clinton Denies Story in Appeal to U.S. Audience," *Boston Globe*, Jan. 27, 1992; Goldman et al., *Quest for the Presidency 1992*, pp. 90–101; "Hillary's first joint interview—next to Bill in '92," 60 Minutes Overtime video, 10:24, from CBS's *60 Minutes* televised Jan. 26, 1992, posted Feb. 1, 2013, http://www.cbsnews.com/news/hillarys-first-joint-interview-next-to-bill-in-92/; (years later, under oath,

Bill admitted that he had sex with Flowers once, in the late 1970s); Steve Kuykendall, "40 Million Watched Clintons on '60 Minutes,' CBS Says," *Arkansas Democrat-Gazette*, Jan. 28, 1992.

IN AN INTERVIEW WITH *PEOPLE*: Karen S. Schneider, "Running Mate," *People*, Feb. 17, 1992; Maureen Dowd, "From Nixon, Predictions on the Presidential Race," *New York Times*, Feb. 6, 1992; *My Life*, pp. 388–398; Jeffrey H. Birnbaum, "Clinton Received a Vietnam Draft Deferment for an ROTC Program That He Never Joined," *Wall Street Journal*, Feb. 6, 1992; David Wilhelm, Dec. 12, 1992, and Michael "Mickey" Kantor, Dec. 3, 1992, interviews by Diane Blair, Diane D. Blair Project, all quotations are with permission; Adam Pertman, "Clinton Sounds Comeback Theme," *Boston Globe*, Feb. 19, 1992; Lloyd Grove, "The Limited Life of a Political Wife," *Washington Post*, March 19, 1992; Duff, "Is a Rose a Rose?"; *Living History*, pp. 101–116; Dan Balz and Edward Walsh, "Clinton's Wife Finds She's Become Issue," *Washington Post*, March 17, 1992; "Mrs. Bush Sticks Up for Hillary Clinton," *Arkansas Democrat-Gazette*, March 28, 1992; Sheehy, "What Hillary Wants"; Randy Lilleston, "Hillary Clinton Cites Bush Rumor, Then Apologizes," *Arkansas Democrat-Gazette*, April 5, 1992.

ONCE AGAIN, IT WAS TIME: Maureen Dowd, "Hillary Clinton as Aspiring First Lady: Role Model, or a 'Hall Monitor' Type?" *New York Times*, May 18, 1992; Alessandra Stanley, "A Softer Image for Hillary Clinton," *New York Times*, July 13, 1992; Goldman et al., *Quest for the Presidency 1992*, pp. 43, 196–199, 662–664; *Living History*, pp. 111–116; Jones, "Road Warriors"; *My Life*, pp. 399–446; Patti Solis, interview by Diane Blair, Nov. 19, 1992, Diane D. Blair Project, quoted with permission; Van Meter, *Vogue*, Aug. 13, 2012; Lisa M. Caputo, Dec. 10, 1992, and Paul Bagala, Feb. 2, 1993, interviews by Diane Blair, Diane D. Blair Project, quoted with permission; John Aloysius Farrell, "Mrs. Clinton a Prime Target," *Boston Globe*, Aug. 19, 1992; Donnie Radcliffe, "Hillary Clinton and the Laws of the

Campaign," *Washington Post*, Oct. 30, 1992; Elizabeth Kolbert, "The Student," *New Yorker*, Oct. 13, 2003; Susan Feeney, "Attacks on Hillary Clinton Spur Debate on Women's Role," *Arkansas Democrat-Gazette*, Aug. 31, 1992; "Hillary's Chips Are the Winners," *Santa Cruz Sentinel*, Oct. 28, 1992.

Chapter 17: President

UNSEATING AN INCUMBENT: *My Life*, pp. 425, 443–451, 466–480; *Living History*, pp. 116–142, 170, 331; Virginia Culver, "Early-Risers Welcome Clinton at Stapleton," *Denver Post*, Nov. 4, 1992; Gergen, *Eyewitness to Power*, p. 256; Gwen Ifill, "On This Night, Little Rock Is One Mountain of Pride," *New York Times*, Nov. 4, 1992; Lloyd Grove and Roxanne Roberts, "Doin' the White House Rock," *Washington Post*, Nov. 4, 1992; Radcliffe, pp. 11–20; "Presidential Elections Data," American Presidency Project, http://www.presidency.ucsb.edu/elections.php; Landon Y. Jones and Garry Clifford, "Bill Clinton & Hillary Rodham Clinton," *People*, Dec. 28, 1992; Clinton, *Dear Socks, Dear Buddy*, pp. 41–43; Jerry Dean, "Clintons off to Washington 'Adventure,'" *Arkansas Democrat-Gazette*, Jan. 17, 1993; Cawley, "First Lady Has 'Nose for Goal Line'"; Marian Burros, "The First Lady Has a Second Role: Being an Ordinary Mom," *Baltimore Sun*, May 23, 1993.

Chapter 18: Firsts

AS THE FIRST LADY: Chua-Eoan, "Power Mom"; Thomas L. Friedman, "Hillary Clinton to Head Panel on Health Care," *New York Times*, Jan. 26, 1993; *My Life*, pp. 482; Alice Rogers Hager, "Candidates for the Post of First Lady," *New York Times*, Oct. 2, 1932; Carl Sferrazza Anthony, "Office Politics and the First Ladies," *Washington Post*, Jan. 25, 1993, and "First Ladylike, After All," *Washington Post*, Jan. 31, 1993; "First Lady Biography: Edith Wilson," National First Ladies Library, http://www.firstladies.org/biographies/firstladies.aspx?biography=29; "'Honorary Chairperson' Title," *Washington Post*, Feb. 18, 1977; Victor Cohn, "A First Lady's Quiet Plea on the Hill," *Washington Post*, Feb. 8, 1979.

HILLARY'S NEW JOB: Johnson and Broder, *The System*, pp. xii,
10, 61–62, 98–103; 111–114; *Living History*, pp. 143–154; ". .
. And Hillary Clinton's Job," *Washington Post*, Jan. 27, 1993;
Dana Priest, "First Lady's First Task Breaks New Ground,"
Washington Post, Jan. 27, 1993; Martha Sherrill, "The
Health Czar, at Her Other Job," *Washington Post*, Jan. 27,
1993; Marian Burros, "Hillary Clinton's New Home:
Broccoli's In, Smoking's Out," *New York Times*, Feb. 2,
1993; Margaret Carlson, "At the Center of Power," *Time*,
May 10, 1993; Michelle Green, "Her Own Woman," *People*,
May 10, 1993; "Hillary Rodham Clinton: Changing
the Rules," *Biography*, 1996; Cawley, "First Lady 'Has
Nose for Goal Line'"; Martha Sherrill, "The First
Lady's Second Wind," *Washington Post*, March 3,
1993; Bruck, "Hillary the Pol"; Gergen,
pp. 253–264.

Chapter 19: Saint Hillary

HILLARY WAS MIDWAY THROUGH: *Living History*, pp. 155–164;
My Life, pp. 500–501; Jake Sandlin, "First Lady's Father in
Serious Condition at Hospital," *Arkansas Democrat-Gazette*,
March 21, 1993; Hillary Rodham Clinton, "Remarks by First
Lady," April 7, 1993, Liz Carpenter Lecture Series, University
of Texas, Austin, Tex., http://clinton4.nara.gov/WH/EOP/
First_Lady/html/generalspeeches/1993/19930407.html;
Elizabeth Hudson, "First Lady Calls for 'Caring,'" *Washington
Post*, April 7, 1993; Henry Allen, "A New Phrase at the
White House," *Washington Post*, June 9, 1993; Priscilla
Painton, "The Politics of What?" *Time*, May 31, 1993;
Charles Krauthammer, "Home Alone 3: The White House,"
Washington Post, May 14, 1993; Michael Kelly, "Saint Hillary,"
New York Times Magazine, May 23, 1993; Martha Sherrill,
"Hillary Clinton's Inner Politics," *Washington Post*, May 6,
1993; Richard L. Berke, "Hugh Rodham Dies After Stroke,"
New York Times, April 9, 1993; Glen Chase, "Clinton
Gives Rodham Eulogy," *Arkansas Democrat-Gazette*,
April 10, 1993.

THE FAMILY THEN HEADED: *Living History,* pp. 165–168,
172–179; Margaret Carlson, "At the Center of Power";
Michelle Green, "Her Own Woman"; Letters and notes
related to Hillary's trip to Montana, FOIA Request 2006–
0023–F, Box 4, "HRC Correspondence" File, Clinton
Presidential Library; "Who Is Vincent Foster?" *Wall Street
Journal,* June 17, 1993; Hubbell, pp. 242–259; Woodward,
Shadow, pp. 230–235; Harris, *The Survivor,* pp. 70–75; *My Life,*
pp. 530–532. Both *Living History* and *My Life* quote Foster's
note as saying, "I was not meant for the job in the spotlight,"
though media outlets quoted him as saying, "I was not meant
for the job or the spotlight." "Transcript of Interview with
Senator Clinton," *New York Times,* July 6, 2007.

BILL'S BUDGET FINALLY PASSED: Johnson and Broder,
pp. 3–31, 169–188; *Living History,* pp. 182–192; *My Life,*
pp. 534–538, 547–549; Adam Clymer, "Clinton Asks Backing
for Sweeping Change in the Health System," "Transcript of
the President's Address to Congress on Health Care," and
Maureen Dowd, "Props and Fuzzy Anecdotes in a Sober,
Grown-Up Talk," all in *New York Times,* Sept. 23, 1993;
Adam Clymer, "Hillary Clinton, on Capitol Hill, Wins Raves,
if Not a Health Plan," *New York Times,* Sept. 29, 1993; Adam
Clymer, "The Clinton Health Plan Is Alive on Arrival," *New
York Times,* Oct. 3, 1993; Michael Weisskopf, "From Eyes to
Ears to Nose to Back, Specialists Battle to Be Part of Clinton
Plan," *Washington Post,* Oct. 26, 1993; "Health Plan: Out of
the Gate," *New York Times,* Oct. 31, 1993.

Chapter 20: Whitewater

THE HEALTH-CARE BILL WAS: Health Security Act, H.R. 3600,
103rd Cong. (1993-1994), http://thomas.loc.gov/cgi-bin/
query/z?c103:H.R.3600.IH; "The Clinton-Gore
Administration: A Record of Progress," historical material,
White House, http://clinton5.nara.gov/WH/
Accomplishments/eightyears-02.html; Susan Schmidt, "U.S.
Is Asked to Probe Failed Arkansas S&L," *Washington Post,*
Oct. 31, 1993; Stephanopoulos, *All Too Human,* pp. 225–243;

Gergen, pp. 286–292, 297–299, 306–310; Drew, *On the Edge*, pp. 97, 103–104; *Living History*, pp. 193–208, 230; *My Life*, pp. 571–577, 584, 594–596, 601; Ann Devroy and Susan Schmidt, "The Mystery in Foster's Office," *Washington Post*, Dec. 20, 1995; David Brock, "Living with the Clintons," *American Spectator*, Jan. 1994, pp. 18–30; William C. Rempel and Douglas Frantz, "Troopers Say Clinton Sought Silence on Personal Affairs," *Los Angeles Times*, Dec. 21, 1993; Drew, pp. 380–393; Woodward, *Shadow*, p. 231.

WITHIN THE WHITE HOUSE: Gergen, pp. 292–299, 306–310; Drew, pp. 96–104; Johnson and Broder, pp. 99–100, 263–270; Bruck, "Hillary the Pol," pp. 66, 69, 91; Stephanopoulos, pp. 96–97, 228–233, 237–241; Marian Burros, "Dreaming of a White House Christmas," *New York Times*, Dec. 15, 1993; Clinton, *An Invitation to the White House*, pp. 189–205; *Living History*, pp. 204–218; *My Life*, pp. 571–578.

Chapter 21: Pink

THROUGHOUT THE SPRING: Johnson and Broder, pp. 270–282; *Living History*, pp. 221–225; *My Life*, pp. 584; Dean Baquet, Jeff Gerth, and Stephen Labaton, "Top Arkansas Lawyer Helped Hillary Clinton Turn Big Profit," *New York Times*, March 18, 1994; Stephen Labaton, "Hillary Clinton Turned $1,000 into $99,540, White House Says," *New York Times*, March 30, 1994; Marcus and Babcock, *Washington Post*, March 30, 1994; Sharon LaFraniere and Charles R. Babcock, "Lawyer Placed Hillary Clinton's Commodity Trades, White House Says," *Washington Post*, April 10, 1994; Jeff Gerth, "Clintons Release Tax Data Showing Land Deal Losses," *New York Times*, March 26, 1994; Gwen Ifill, "Hillary Clinton Didn't Report $6,498 Profit in Commodities Account, White House Says," *New York Times*, April 12, 1994; Russell Watson, "Vince Foster's Suicide: The Rumor Mill Churns," *Newsweek*, March 20, 1994; Brant and Thomas, "First Fighter."

FINALLY, IN APRIL: *Living History*, pp. 225–233, 245–249; Hillary Rodham Clinton, press conference, April 22, 1994,

FLOTUS Statements and Speeches 12/2/93–4/26/94,
Clinton Digital Library, http://clinton.presidentiallibraries.
us/items/show/7846; Gwen Ifill, "Hillary Clinton Takes
Questions on Whitewater," *New York Times*, April 23, 1994;
"Mrs. Clinton Meets the Press," *Washington Post*, April 25,
1994; *My Life*, pp. 594–596, 601–602, 612, 620; Johnson and
Broder, pp. 460–508, 601–635; "Milestones: 1993–2000; The
War in Bosnia,1992–1995," Office of the Historian, U.S. State
Department, 2013, http://history.state.gov/mile-
stones/1993-2000/bosnia; "Harry and Louise on Clinton's
Health Plan," YouTube video, 1:00, from ads televised in
1994, posted by "danieljbmitchell," July 15, 2007, http://
www.youtube.com/watch?v=Dt31nhleeCg; Gergen,
pp. 301–309; Adam Clymer, Robert Pear, and Robin Toner,
"The Health Care Debate: What Went Wrong?" New York
Times, Aug. 29, 1994; James Fallows, "A Triumph of
Misinformation," *The Atlantic*, Jan. 1995.

Chapter 22: Eleanor Roosevelt

IN PUBLIC, HILLARY WAS COMPOSED: Diane Blair, typed notes,
Diane D. Blair Papers (MC1632), series 3, subseries 3, box 1,
file 2 and file 21, Special Collections, University of Arkansas
Libraries, Fayetteville; Jeffrey M. Jones, "Barack Obama,
Hillary Clinton Extend Run as Most Admired," Gallup, Dec.
29, 2014, http://www.gallup.com/poll/180365/barack-
obama-hillary-clinton-extend-run-admired.aspx; Johnson and
Broder, pp. 280, 462–463; Robert G. Kaiser and Ira Chinoy,
"Scaife: Funding Father of the Right," *Washington Post*, May
2, 1999; Branch, *The Clinton Tapes*, pp. 65–66, 182–183;
Federal Elections 94 (Washington, D.C.: Federal Election
Commission, March 1995), p. 30; R. W. Apple Jr., "How
Lasting a Majority?" *New York Times*, Nov. 10, 1994; *My Life*,
pp. 628–632; *Living History*, pp. 249–252, 256–261, 448;
Maraniss, "First Lady of Paradox"; Brant and Thomas, "First
Fighter."

SO DID THE SPIRIT OF ANOTHER: Green, "Her Own Woman";
Hillary Rodham Clinton, speech at dedication of Eleanor

Roosevelt College, San Diego, Jan. 26, 1995, FLOTUS Statements and Speeches 10/1/94–6/1/95, Clinton Digital Library, http://clinton.presidentiallibraries.us/items/show/7958; *Living History*, pp. 256–265; *My Life*, pp. 631–636; Carl Sferrazza Anthony, "First Ladies, Third Degree," *Washington Post*, March 24, 1994; Doris Kearns Goodwin, "Hillary and Eleanor," *Mother Jones*, Jan./Feb. 1993.

HILLARY BEGAN TO REGAIN: Harris, pp. 149–166; Barbara Vobejda, "Welfare Reform: Debate Is Shifting to Radical Changes," *Washington Post*, Nov. 17, 1994; Jason DeParle, "Momentum Builds for Cutting Back Welfare System," *New York Times*, Nov. 13, 1994; Keith Bradsher, "Many White House Employees Used Drugs, Gingrich Asserts," *New York Times*, Dec. 5, 1994; Hillary Rodham Clinton, "The Fight over Orphanages," *Newsweek*, Jan. 16, 1995; Karen De Witt, "The Speaker's Mother," *New York Times*, Jan. 5, 1995; Marian Burros, "Hillary Clinton Asks Help in Finding a Softer Image," *New York Times*, Jan. 10, 1995; Gerth and Van Natta, p. 149; *Living History*, pp. 263, 268–286, 292–296; Mary B. W. Tabor, "Meet Hillary Rodham Clinton, the Traditional First Lady," *New York Times*, April 22, 1995; Todd S. Purdum, "Hillary Clinton Finding a New Voice," *New York Times*, March 30, 1995; John M. Broder and James Risen, "Little Rock Law," *Los Angeles Times*, April 3, 1994; Peter J. Boyer, "Hope Against Hope," *New Yorker*, Jan. 8, 1996; Stephanopoulos, p. 389.

Chapter 23: Subpoena

ON THE HEELS: *Living History*, pp. 298–307; Patrick E. Tyler, "Hillary Clinton, in China, Details Abuse of Women," *New York Times*, Sept. 6, 1995; "Mrs. Clinton's Unwavering Words," *New York Times*, Sept. 6, 1995; speech as written and as it appears in *Living History* (there are some variations in speeches online); Lisa Caputo to Hillary Clinton et al., memorandum, Aug. 30, 1995, and Lisa Caputo to Maggie Williams, memorandum, Aug. 31, 1995, FOIA 2006-0198-F, Hillary Rodham Clinton on Children's Issues and Women's

Rights, Clinton Digital Library, http://clinton.
presidentiallibraries.us/items/show/14472; Farhad Manjoo,
"Jurassic Web," Slate, Feb. 24, 2009, http://www.slate.com/
articles/technology/technology/2009/02/jurassic_web.
html; "25 Years of AOL: A Timeline," *Washington Post*, May
23, 2010; "News Attracts Most Internet Users," Pew
Research Center, Dec. 16, 1996, http://www.people-press.
org/1996/12/16/news-attracts-most-internet-users/; "Our
History," New York Times Co., http://www.nytco.com/who-we
-are/culture/our-history/; "Dow Jones History," Dow Jones
& Co, http://www.dowjones.com/history.asp.

KEEPING THE GLOW FROM CHINA: *Living History*, pp. 244,
296–297, 311, 318–319, 328–337; *My Life*, pp. 653, 670–671,
682–693, 697–699; Woodward, *Shadow*, pp. 280–88, 292–321;
Toobin, *A Vast Conspiracy*, pp. 75–78, 87–91; David Maraniss,
"The Hearings End Much as They Began," *Washington Post*,
June 19, 1996; Francis X. Clines, "Sighs Sum Up D'Amato's
Verdict as Whitewater Panel Nears End," *New York Times*,
May 25, 1996; William Safire, "Blizzard of Lies," *New York
Times*, Jan. 8, 1996; "Saint or Sinner?" cover, *Newsweek*, Jan.
15, 1996; Gerth and Van Natta, pp. 156–163.

Chapter 24: Re-election

BILL WAS UP FOR REELECTION: Woodward, *Shadow*, p. 96;
Bernstein, p. 459; Margaret Carlson, "Chelsea Clinton: The
White House's Untroubled Teen," *Time*, Sept. 2, 1996; *Living
History*, pp. 248, 372–380, 386–390, 393–394; Robert Dole,
"Address Accepting the Presidential Nomination at the
Republican National Convention in San Diego," Aug. 15,
1996, American Presidency Project, http://www.presidency.
ucsb.edu/ws/index.php?pid=25960; "Election of 1996,"
American Presidency Project, http://www.presidency.ucsb.
edu/showelection.php?year=1996; Branch, pp. 365–366,
495–496; Todd S. Purdum, "Clintons Down Under: Sweet
and Sour," *New York Times*, Nov. 22, 1996; John F. Harris,
"First Lady Still Interpreting Her Role," *Washington Post*,
Nov. 27, 1996; Steven Thomma, "GOP Governors Worry

Over Welfare at Their Conference," *Philadelphia Inquirer*, Nov. 26, 1996; Typed notes, Blair Papers, series 3, subseries 3, box 1, file 21 (obvious typographical errors have been corrected, but punctuation has not been changed).

Chapter 25: Lewinsky

JUST A FEW MONTHS INTO: *Living History*, pp. 407–408, 419–421, 435–436, 440; *My Life*, pp. 596, 762, 768–769, 772–773; Joan Biskupic, "At High Court, Clinton v. Jones Raises Historic Issues," *Washington Post*, Jan. 12, 1997; "Sexual Harassment," U.S. Equal Employment Opportunity Commission, http://www.eeoc.gov/laws/types/sexual_harassment.cfm; Woodward, *Shadow*, pp. 353–355; Bob Woodward and Susan Schmidt, "Starr Probes Clinton Personal Life," *Washington Post*, June 25, 1997; Susan Schindehette, "The Ties That Bind," *People*, Feb. 15, 1999; James Bennet, "For the Clintons, Stanford Parents' Day Won't Come Soon Enough," *New York Times*, Sept. 18, 1997; Toobin, pp. 119, 195, 207–227.

SHORTLY AFTER, A LITTLE KNOWN: Toobin, pp. 229–258, 292–296, 393–396; "Newsweek Kills Story on White House Intern," Drudge Report, Jan. 17, 1998, http://www.drudg-ereportarchives.com/data/2002/01/17/20020117_175502_ml.htm; *Living History*, pp. 440–448; *My Life*, pp. 774–780; Woodward, *Shadow*, pp. 393–396; Susan Schmidt, Peter Baker, and Toni Locy, "Clinton Accused of Urging Aide to Lie," *Washington Post*, Jan. 21, 1998; "Today: Tuesday," January 27, 1998, C-Span video, 18:00, from NBC's *Today* show, http://www.c-span.org/video/?99377-1/today-tuesday; Francis X. Clines, "First Lady Attributes Inquiry to 'Right-Wing Conspiracy,'" *New York Times*, Jan. 28, 1998; David Maraniss, "First Lady Launches Counterattack," *Washington Post*, Jan. 28, 1998; Dan Balz, "In Week Two, Velocity of Allegations Slows and a Clinton Survival Strategy Emerges," *Washington Post*, Feb. 1, 1998; Baker, *The Breach*, pp. 298–299; Peter Baker, "Clinton Payment Ends Jones Suit," *Washington Post*, Jan. 13, 1999. The judge in the Jones case later found Bill in contempt of court for lying in his deposition about his relationship with Lewinsky; Bill was ordered to pay lawyers' expenses in connection with the deposition, about $90,000, Toobin, p. 398.

Chapter 26: Impeachment

STARR HAD A DEADLINE: Woodward, *Shadow*, pp. 416–435; *Living History*, pp. 465–475; *My Life*, pp. 800–809; Baker, pp. 23–49; Bernstein, p. 515–521; "Bill Clinton admits to having inappropriate relationship with Monica Lewinsky," YouTube video, 4:13, from Bill Clinton's nationally televised speech on Aug. 17, 1998, posted by "iconic," Nov. 18, 2010, http://www.youtube.com/watch?v=UEmjwR0Rs20; schedules for Hillary Rodham Clinton, Sept. 8–10, 1998, Schedules for the First Lady September 1998, Clinton Digital Library, http://clinton.presidentiallibraries.us/items/show/7303; Typed notes, Blair Papers, series 3, subseries 3, box 1, file 21; Susan Thomases, interview by Russell Riley and Darby Morrisroe, Jan. 6, 2006, William J. Clinton Presidential History Project, Miller Center, University of Virginia, Charlottesville, Va., http://millercenter.org/president/clinton/oralhistory/susan-thomases.

IN MID-SEPTEMBER: Referral to the United States House of Representatives Pursuant to Title 28, United States Code, § 595(c), submitted by the Office of the Independent Counsel, September 9, 1998, accessed on "The Starr Report," www.washingtonpost.com/wp-srv/politics/special/clinton/icreport/icreport.htm; *Living History*, pp. 475–490; *My Life*, pp. 809–811; Peter Baker and Susan Schmidt, "Starr Alleges 'Abundant' Lies," *Washington Post*, Sept. 12, 1998; Baker, pp. 105–106, 245–256; Woodward, *Shadow*, pp. 472–474; Terry M. Neal and Peter Baker, "Democratic Women Rally to First Lady," *Washington Post*, Sept. 16, 1998; Faye Fiore, "First Lady Is Center of (Political) Attention," *Los Angeles Times*, Sept. 20, 1998; Tomasky, *Hillary's Turn*, pp. 38–39; Mary McGrory, "Mr. and Mrs. Comeback Kid," *Washington Post*, Nov. 8, 1998; John Cloud, "Give 'Em Hillary," *Time*, Nov. 16, 1998; Toobin,

"Terms of Impeachment," *New Yorker*, Sept. 14, 1998; Peter Baker and Juliet Eilperin, "Clinton Impeached," *Washington Post*, Dec. 20, 1998; Melinda Henneberger, "Clinton's Top Defender Rallies Troops at Front," *New York Times*, Dec. 20, 1998; "The 25 Most Intriguing People '98: Hillary Rodham Clinton," *People*, Dec. 28, 1998.

Chapter 27: New York

THE RUMBLINGS STARTED: James Bennet, "The Next Clinton," *New York Times Magazine*, May 30, 1999; *Living History*, p. 483, 492–506; Dennis Duggan, "Election 2000: Rangel Put the Pieces Together," *Newsday*, Nov. 7, 2000; different stories cite different time periods, though there is agreement that Rangel encouraged her early on; Michael Grunwald, "A Capitol Idea for Hillary Clinton," *Washington Post*, Jan. 9, 1999; Typed notes, Blair Papers, series 3, subseries 3, box 1, file 21; Harpaz, *The Girls in the Van*, p. 253; Tomasky, pp. 19–22, 31, 44–49, 93–94. Two women were elected to at-large congressional seats in the 1930s and early 1940s, but no woman had ever been elected as a U.S. senator, or as New York governor, attorney general, or state controller. Women had been elected lieutenant governor, but lieutenant governor candidates run on a ticket with the governor, so the women candidates did not run on their own. *My Life*, pp. 811, 844–847; Harold Ickes to Hillary Clinton, memorandum, March 31, 1999, Blair Papers, series 3, subseries 4, box 2, file 6; joke from internal e-mail, First Lady Hillary Rodham Clinton's New York Senate Campaign, FOIA Request 2006-0224-F, box 2, WHO file, Clinton Presidential Library.

MOYNIHAN GENEROUSLY ALLOWED: *Living History*, pp. 506–512; Michael Grunwald, "First Lady Dives into N.Y. Bid, Carpetbag Issue," *Washington Post*, July 8, 1999; Adam Nagourney, "Hillary Clinton Begins Pre-Campaign in a New Role for Her," *New York Times*, July 8, 1999; Tomasky, pp. 50–55, 73–85; Ruth Marcus, "Clinton's Home Loan Deal Raises Questions," *Washington Post*, Sept. 4, 1999; Mandy Grunwald to Hillary Clinton, memorandum, July 6, 1999,

FOIA 2006-0198-F, Hillary Rodham Clinton on Children's
Issues and Women's Rights, Clinton Digital Library, http://
clinton.presidentiallibraries.us/items/show/14472; Harris,
pp. 378–379; Lucinda Franks, "The Intimate Hillary," *Talk*,
Sept. 1999, pp. 167–174, 248–250; William A. Orme Jr.,
"While Mrs. Clinton Looks On, Palestinian Officials Criticize
Israel," *New York Times*, Nov. 12, 1999; Joel Greenberg, "A
Day Later, Mrs. Clinton Rebukes Arafat's Wife and Explains
Herself," *New York Times*, Nov. 13, 1999; Thomas J. Lueck,
"Mrs. Clinton Explains Kiss in Middle East," *New York Times*,
July 14, 2000; Adam Nagourney, "First Lady's New
Campaign Worries," *New York Times*, Nov. 13, 1999.

Chapter 28: Winner

AFTER MONTHS OF CAMPAIGNING: "Hillary Clinton
Announcement," Feb. 6, 2000, C-Span video, 1:44:30,
http://www.c-span.org/video/?155203-1/hillary-clinton-
announcement; Harpaz, pp. 68–72, 250–262; Robin Givhan,
"Attired in Black Pantsuit, She Takes on Uniform of Power,"
New York Times, March 3, 2000; *Living History*, pp. 512–515;
Jonathan Alter, "Woman of the World," *Vanity Fair*, June 2011;
Elizabeth Kolbert, "The Lady Vanishes," *New Yorker*, June 11,
2007, p. 134; Elisabeth Bumiller, "Giuliani and His Wife of
16 Years Are Separating," *New York Times*, May 11, 2000;
Elisabeth Bumiller, "Cancer Is Concern," *New York Times*,
May 20, 2000.

ALMOST IMMEDIATELY: *Living History*, pp. 515–528; Harpaz,
pp. 10, 250–262; Tomasky, pp. 90–91, 188–205; Elisabeth
Bumiller, "It Took a Woman: How Gender Helped Elect
Hillary Clinton," *New York Times*, Nov. 12, 2000; Neil A.
Lewis, "The First Lady Is Chided, but Not Charged," and
"Statement on Travel Office Inquiry," both in *New York
Times*, June 23, 2000; Neil A. Lewis, "A Lack of Evidence Is
Cited in Case Involving Clintons," and "Statement by
Independent Counsel on Conclusions in Whitewater
Investigation," both in *New York Times*, Sept. 21, 2000; "First
Debate Clinton-Lazio, 2000 - Part 6," YouTube video, 7:71,

from debate telecast on MSNBC, Sept. 13, 2000, posted by "dacarc," Feb. 22, 2010, http://www.youtube.com/watch?v=YMJZo4UeTYQ; Adam Nagourney, "Lazio and Hillary Clinton Clash on Donations, Taxes and Trust," *New York Times*, Sept. 14, 2000; Melinda Henneberger and Don Van Natta Jr., "Once Close to Clinton, Gore Keeps a Distance," *New York Times*, Oct. 20, 2000; Patience Haggin, "Top 10 Controversial Supreme Court Cases," *Time*, Dec. 13, 2010; "Election 2000," American Presidency Project, http://www.presidency.ucsb.edu/showelection.php?year=2000; "Hillary Clinton Elected to Senate from New York," *New York Times*, Nov. 8, 2000.

Chapter 29: Senator

ON JANUARY 3, 2001: Charles Babington, "A Bittersweet Day like No Other," *Washington Post*, Jan. 4, 2001; Elaine S. Povich, "History on the Hill," *Newsday*, Jan. 4, 2001; Branch, p. 645; John F. Harris, "Clintons' Road Out Full of Bumps," *Newsday*, Jan. 30, 2001; David D. Kirkpatrick, "Hillary Clinton Book Advance, $8 Million, Is Near Record," *New York Times*, Dec. 16, 2000; Associated Press, "Hillary Inks Book Deal," *Newsday*, Dec. 16, 2000; "Senate Salaries Since 1789," U.S. Senate Historical Office, http://www.senate.gov/artandhistory/history/common/briefing/senate_salaries.htm; George Lardner Jr., "Clintons Shipped Furniture a Year Ago," *Washington Post*, Feb. 10, 2001; Jackie Calmes and Phil Kuntz, "Clinton Set to Return Some Gifts," *Wall Street Journal*, Feb. 6, 2001; Shannon McCaffrey, "Role of Sen. Clinton in Pardons Questioned," *Washington Post*, Aug. 9, 2001; Jessica Reaves, "The Rumpled, Ragtag Career of Hugh Rodham," *Time*, Feb. 22, 2001; Todd S. Purdum, "Siblings Who Often Emerge in an Unflattering Spotlight," *New York Times*, Feb. 23, 2001.

DESPITE THE NEW CONTROVERSIES: Kolbert, *New Yorker*, Oct. 13, 2003, p. 65; John Lancaster, "Sen. Clinton Plunges into New Role as Colleagues Size Her Up," *Washington Post*, Feb. 13, 2001; Lloyd Grove, "The Reliable Source," *Washington Post*, Feb. 2, 2001; Raymond Hernandez, "Senator Clinton

Settling In as Just One of 100," *New York Times*, April 13, 2001; Michael Crowley, "Dull and Duller," *New Republic*, April 9 & 16, 2001; "Transcript of Interview with Senator Clinton," *New York Times*, July 6, 2007; Joshua Green, "Take Two: Hillary's Choice," *The Atlantic*, Nov. 2006; John F. Harris, "Hillary's Big Adventure," *Washington Post Magazine*, Jan. 27, 2002; Branch, p. 646; Elaine S. Povich, "Both Clintons Exhibit Earning Power," *Newsday*, June 15, 2002; Richard A. Oppel Jr., "Mrs. Clinton Reports That Her Husband Made $9.2 Million from Speeches Last Year," *New York Times*, June 15, 2002.

SEPTEMBER 11, 2001: Harris, *Washington Post Magazine*, Jan. 27, 2002; Ann O'Leary, "Hillary Clinton during 9/11," YouTube video, 7:21, of remarks made April 20, 2008, posted by "tmbj11," April 22, 2008, http://www.youtube.com/watch?v=C7-O_XcBWMI; Gerth and Van Natta, pp. 226–239; *Hard Choices*, pp. 172–174; Hillary Clinton, transcript of NBC's *Today* show interview, Sept. 18, 2001, accessed via Factiva; Chelsea Clinton, "Before & After," *Talk*, Dec. 2001/Jan. 2002, pp. 100–103, 141; "Senator Hillary R. Clinton Comments on the 9-11 attacks 9-11-01," YouTube video, 4:41, from CNN telecast on Sept. 11, 2001, posted by "911archives," Aug. 21, 2011, http://www.youtube.com/watch?v=PZe3jL7CXPs; "Terrorist Attacks Against the United States," 107th Cong., 1st sess., *Congressional Record* 147 (Sept. 12, 2001), accessed through The Avalon Project, Yale Law School, http://avalon.law.yale.edu/sept11/senate_proc_091201.asp; "Remember New York," 107th Cong., 1st sess., *Congressional Record* 147 (Nov. 27, 2001): S12047–S12049; Frank Bruni, "Show Us the Money," *New York Times Magazine*, Dec. 16, 2001.

Chapter 30: War

HILLARY HAD EXPECTED TO WORK: Harris, *Washington Post Magazine*, Jan. 27, 2002; Bobby Cuza, "Schumer, Clinton Secure Over $11B in Federal Aid," *Newsday*, Dec. 24, 2001; Gerth and Van Natta, pp. 234–239; Bruni, *New York Times Magazine*, Dec. 16, 2001; Jeremy Sherlick and Greg Bruno, "U.S.

War in Afghanistan: 1999–Present," Council on Foreign Relations, http://www.cfr.org/afghanistan/us-war-afghanistan/p20018; "Overview of the War on Terror in Afghanistan" and "History of Iraq and the Iraq War," Ebsco Host Connection, http://www.connections.ebscohost.com; "Authorization of the Use of United States Armed Forces Against Iraq," 107th Cong., 2nd sess., *Congressional Record* 148 (Oct. 10, 2002): S10288–S10290; Jeff Gerth and Don Van Natta Jr., "Hillary's War," *New York Times Magazine,* May 29, 2007; Alison Mitchell and Carl Hulse, "Congress Authorizes Bush to Use Force Against Iraq, Creating a Broad Mandate," *New York Times,* Oct. 11, 2002; Jim VandeHei and Juliet Eilperin, "Congress Passes Iraq Resolution," *Washington Post,* Oct. 11, 2002.

IN JANUARY 2003: Kolbert, *New Yorker,* Oct. 13, 2003; Mark Leibovich, "Run? Hillary? Run?" *Washington Post,* Sept. 24, 2003; Jim VandeHei, "Clinton Develops Into a Force in the Senate," *Washington Post,* March 5, 2003; Heilemann and Halperin, *Game Change,* pp.13–20; Lynn Okamoto, "Star of the Show," *Des Moines Register,* Nov. 16, 2003; Raymond Hernandez, "Clinton Seeks Uniform Ratings in Entertainment for Children," *New York Times,* March 10, 2005; Raymond Hernandez, "Gay Rights Group Criticizes Senator Clinton's Stance on Same-Sex Marriage," *New York Times,* Feb. 22, 2006; Raymond Hernandez and Patrick D. Healy, "The Evolution of Hillary Clinton," *New York Times,* July 13, 2005; Bai, "Mrs. Triangulation"; Patrick Healy, "After Iraq Trip, Clinton Proposes War Limits," *New York Times,* Jan. 18, 2007; Dan Balz, "Clinton Is a Politician Not Easily Defined," *Washington Post,* May 30, 2006; Gerth and Van Natta, *New York Times Magazine,* May 29, 2007; *Hard Choices,* pp. 133–137; Gerth and Van Natta, *Her Way,* pp. 296–298; Anne E. Kornblut, "Clinton Dodges Political Peril for War Vote," *New York Times,* Aug. 5, 2006.

Chapter 31: Candidate

ON SATURDAY, JANUARY 20: Associated Press, "Senator Clinton's Statement About Her Candidacy for President,"

New York Times, Jan. 20, 2007; Patrick Healy, "Clinton's Announcement Makes Waves in '08 Field," *New York Times*, Jan. 20, 2007; Jon Stewart, "Let the Conversation Begin," *The Daily Show*, Jan. 29, 2007, video, 4:13, http://thedaily-show.cc.com/videos/ncn19y/let-the-conversation-begin; Heilemann and Halperin, pp. 1–10, 39–53, 80–81, 90–101, 107–112, 145–175; Dan Balz and Haynes Johnson, *The Battle for America 2008*, pp. 45–53, 71–78, 104–128; Traister, *Big Girls Don't Cry*, p. 71; Joshua Green, "The Front-Runner's Fall," *The Atlantic*, Sept. 2008; Barack Obama, speech against the Iraq War, Oct. 2, 2002, transcript posted by NPR, Jan. 20, 2009, http://www.npr.org/templates/story/story.php?storyId=99591469; *Hard Choices*, pp. 134–137; Adam Nagourney, "Clinton Staff Memo Urged Skipping Iowa," *New York Times*, May 23, 2007; Patrick Healy, "After Delay, Clinton Embarks on Likability Tour," *New York Times*, Dec. 19, 2007; Peter Baker and Anne E. Kornblut, "Turning It Around," *Washington Post*, Jan. 10, 2008; "Caucus History: Past Years' Results," *Des Moines Register*, http://caucuses.desmoines-register.com/caucus-history-past-years-results/.

Chapter 32: 2008

To stay in the race: Patrick Healy and John Broder, "A Campaign Retools to Seek Second Clinton Comeback," *New York Times*, Jan. 5, 2008; Baker and Kornblut, *Washington Post*, Jan. 10, 2008; Heilemann and Halperin, pp. 177–267, 232; Balz and Johnson, pp. 129–145, 152–153; "Transcript: The Democratic Debate in New Hampshire," *New York Times*, Jan. 5, 2008; "2008 ABC/WMUR/Facebook NH Democratic Debate (Part 6)," YouTube video, 9:33, from debate broadcast on ABC, Jan. 5, 2008, posted by "Hobobob10's Channel," Jan. 7, 2008, http://www.youtube.com/watch?v=Agly_sS9dRw; Jonathan Weisman and Alec MacGillis, "Clinton's Campaign in N.H. Touched Chord with Women," *Washington Post*, Jan. 10, 2008; Anne E. Kornblut, "'It's Not Easy,' an Emotional Clinton Says," *Washington Post*, Jan. 8, 2008; Patrick Healy and Marc Santora, "Clinton Talks About Strains of Campaign,"

New York Times, Jan. 7, 2008; "Hillary Clinton Tears Up
During Campaign Stop," Jan. 7, 2008, YouTube video, 1:58,
from ABC News, posted by "Veracifier," http://www.youtube.
com/watch?v=6qgWH89qWks; Patrick Healy and Michael
Cooper, "Clinton Stuns Obama; McCain Wins," *New York
Times*, Jan. 8, 2008; Traister, p. 101. Congresswoman Shirley
Chisholm was the first black woman to run for the
Democratic nomination, and she won a nonbinding primary
in New Jersey in 1972, which most candidates skipped; she
also won about 152 votes at the 1972 Democratic National
Convention. Patrick Healy, "Clinton's Message, and Moment,
Won the Day," *New York Times*, Jan. 10, 2008.

SHE WAS BACK IN: Balz and Johnson, pp. 155–168, 180–189;
Heilemann and Halperin, pp. 197–230, 338–343, 430;
"Primary Season Election Results," 2008, *New York Times*,
http://politics.nytimes.com/election-guide/2008/results/
votes/; "2008 Nevada Caucus," *Las Vegas Sun*, http://www.
lasvegassun.com/topics/2008caucus/; Shailagh Murray and
Matthew Mosk, "Clinton Lent Her Campaign $5 Million,"
Washington Post, Feb. 7, 2008; Gail Sheehy, "Hillaryland at
War," *Vanity Fair*, Aug. 2008; Peter Baker and Jim Rutenberg,
"The Long Road to a Clinton Exit," *New York Times*, June 8,
2008; "Election Center 2008," CNN, www.cnn.com/
ELECTION/2008/primaries/results/scorecard/; Patrick
Healy, "Obama and Clinton Brace for a Long-Distance
Run," *New York Times*, Feb. 7, 2008; "Hillary Clinton on
'SNL'" Yahoo! Screen video, 2:07, from NBC's *Saturday
Night Live*, March 1, 2008, http://screen.yahoo.com/
editorial-response-sen-clinton-000000311.html; "Clinton
Says She 'Misspoke' About Sniper Fire," CNN, March 25,
2008, http://www.cnn.com/2008/POLITICS/03/25/
campaign.wrap/index.html?iref=hpmostpop; "Transcript:
Hillary Clinton Endorses Barack Obama," *New York Times*,
June 7, 2008; "Hillary Clinton's Concession Speech,"
June 7, 2008, YouTube video, 29:02, from C-Span, posted
by "Veracifier," http://www.youtube.com/watch?v=
zgi_kIYx_bY.

Chapter 33: Secretary

THE FIRST TIME: Heilemann and Halperin, pp. 429–436; Woodward, *Obama's Wars*, pp. 26–31; *Hard Choices*, pp. 14–18, 41–51, 66–68; Robert Yoon, "Hillary Clinton's Campaign Debt Finally Paid Off," *Political Ticker* (blog), CNN, Jan. 22, 2013, http://politicalticker.blogs.cnn.com/2013/01/22/hillary-clintons-campaign-debt-finally-paid-off/; Michael Luo, "For Clinton, Millions in Debt and Few Options," *New York Times*, June 10, 2008; Senate bills come from Hillary's record at http://www.congress.gov; Allen and Parnes, *HRC*, pp. 48–60; Susan B. Glasser, "Head of State," *Foreign Policy*, June 18, 2012; Steven Lee Myers, "Hillary Clinton's Last Tour as a Rock-Star Diplomat," *New York Times Magazine*, June 27, 2012; Mark Landler, "A Clinton Listening Tour, but China Gets an Earful," *New York Times*, Feb. 23, 2009; Glenn Kessler, "Clinton's Candor Abroad Draws Mixed Reviews," *Washington Post*, Feb. 23, 2009; Mark Landler, "Clinton Reshapes Diplomacy by Tossing the Script," *New York Times*, Feb. 21, 2009; Alter, "Woman of the World"; Lisa DePaulo, "Hillary Clinton's Secret Weapon," *More*, April 2012; Suzi Parker, "Hillary Clinton, Barefaced and Bespectacled, Is a Refreshing Image in Politics," *She the People* (blog), *Washington Post*, May 8, 2012, http://www.washingtonpost.com/blogs/she-the-people/post/hillary-clinton-barefaced-and-bespectacled-is-a-refreshing-image-in-politics/2012/05/08/gIQA-wR4HAU_blog.html; Mark Landler, "A New Gender Agenda," *New York Times Magazine*, Aug. 23, 2009; Mark Landler, "Her Rival Now Her Boss, Clinton Settles into New Role," *New York Times*, May 2, 2009.

WHEN OBAMA TOOK OFFICE: Woodward, *Obama's Wars*, pp. 98–103, 113, 174–184, 291–293; *Hard Choices*, pp. 129–150; Barack Obama, "A New Strategy for Afghanistan and Pakistan" (speech, March 27, 2009), http://www.whitehouse.gov/the-press-office/remarks-president-a-new-strategy-afghanistan-and-pakistan; Helene Cooper and Eric Schmitt, "White House Debate Led to Plan to Widen Afghan Effort," *New York Times*, March 28, 2009; Mark Landler and Thom Shanker, "Clinton and Gates Join

Forces in Debate on Afghanistan Buildup," *New York Times*, Oct. 13, 2009; Gates, *Duty*, pp. 283, 290, 376; Barack Obama, "The Way Forward in Afghanistan and Pakistan," (address to the nation, Dec. 1, 2009), http://www.whitehouse.gov/the-press -office/remarks-president-address-nation-way-forward-afghan- istan-and-pakistan; Sherlick and Bruno, "U.S. War in Afghanistan: 1999–Present," Council on Foreign Relations; Mark Thompson, "U.S. Ends Its War in Afghanistan," *Time*, Dec. 28, 2014, Michael D. Shear and Mark Mazzetti, "U.S. to Delay Pullout of Troops from Afghanistan to Aid Strikes," *New York Times*, March 24, 2015.

Chapter 34: MOTB

HILLARY AND BILL GOT: *Hard Choices*, pp. 80–83, 253, 547, 586–589; Huma Khan and Kate Snow, "Chelsea Clinton Engaged to Marc Mezvinsky," ABC News, Nov. 30, 2009, http://abcnews.go.com/GMA/chelsea-clinton-engaged- marry-marc-mezvinsky-summer/story?id=9206327; Alter, "Woman of the World"; DePaulo, "Hillary Clinton's Secret Weapon"; Ann Gerhart, "A Democratic Dog That Was Everyone's Buddy," *Washington Post*, Jan. 4, 2002; Joe Hagan, "Hillary in Midair," *New York*, Sept. 22, 2013; Peter Baker, "Bill Clinton Undergoes a New Heart Procedure," *The Caucus* (blog), *New York Times*, Feb. 11, 2010, http://thecaucus.blogs. nytimes.com/2010/02/11/bill-clinton-hospitalized-for-chest- pains/; Associated Press, "Clinton: 'I Feel Great' After Heart Procedure," NBC News, Feb. 12, 2010, http://www.nbcnews. com/id/35355089/ns/politics#.VYgmg-uLR0g; Howard LaFranchi, "Hillary Clinton To-Do List: Mother of the Bride, Avoid Nuclear War," *Christian Science Monitor*, July 30, 2010; Ramin Setoodeh, "Chelsea Clinton Marries Marc Mezvinsky," *People*, July 31, 2010; Sandra Sobieraj Westfall, "Hillary Clinton: 'I Have a Decision to Make,'" *People*, June 16, 2014, p. 66.

ONE OF THOSE WAS: Allen and Parnes, pp. 225–238; *Hard Choices*, pp. 170–201; Gates, pp. 538–546; Mark Bowden, "The

Hunt for 'Geronimo,'" *Vanity Fair*, Nov. 2012; Nicholas Schmidle, "Getting Bin Laden," *New Yorker*, Aug. 8, 2011.

Chapter 35: Benghazi

AS THE OBAMA ADMINISTRATION: *Hard Choices*, pp. 334–381, 551; Greg Myre, ed., "Timeline: The Major Events of the Arab Spring," NPR, Jan. 2, 2012, http://www.npr. org/2012/01/02/144489844/timeline-the-major-events-of-the-arab-spring; Allen and Parnes, pp. 213–224, 252–253; Gates, pp. 510–523; Alter, "Woman of the World"; Massimo Calabresi, "Hillary Clinton and the Rise of Smart Power," *Time*, Nov. 7, 2011; "Former Secretary Clinton: 2011 Travel," U.S. Department of State, http://go.usa. gov/3mpzA; MJ Lee, "Hillary Clinton Likes 'Texts from Hillary' Tumblr," Politico, April 10, 2012, http://www. politico.com/news/stories/0412/74994.html; "Texts from Hillary," Tumblr, http://textsfromhillaryclinton.tumblr.com/; Robert L. Koenig, "Tweet-errific," *State Magazine*, Dec. 2013.

AFTER THE GADDHAFI: *Hard Choices*, pp. 381–416, 593; Fred Burton and Samuel M. Katz, "40 Minutes in Benghazi," *Vanity Fair*, Aug. 2013; Gates, pp. 508–523; David D. Kirkpatrick, "A Deadly Mix in Benghazi," *New York Times*, Dec. 28, 2013; "Clinton's Statement on Libya," Sept. 12, 2012, *New York Times* video, 9:13, from NBC News, http://www.nytimes. com/video/us/politics/100000001778770/secretary-clintons-statement-on-libya.html; "Accountability Review Board Report," U.S. Department of State, http://www.state. gov/arbreport/; Rachel Weiner, "Allen West: Clinton Has 'Benghazi Flu,'" *Washington Post*, Dec. 20, 2012; Ken Dilanian, "House Intelligence Committee Investigation Debunks Many Benghazi Theories," *The Rundown* (blog), PBS Newshour, Nov. 21, 2014, http://www.pbs.org/newshour/rundown/house-intelligence-committee-investigation-debunks-many-benghazi-theories/; Westfall, "Hillary Clinton: I Have a Decision"; "Hillary Clinton's Fiery Moment at Benghazi Hearing," YouTube video, 2:22, posted by ABC News, Jan. 23,

2013, http://www.youtube.com/watch?v=TC0AKNQBV80;
Jay Newton-Small, "Clinton on Benghazi: Tears and Anger,"
Time, Jan. 23, 2013, http://swampland.time.com/2013/
01/23/clinton-on-benghazi-tears-and-anger/; Michael R.
Gordon, "Facing Congress, Clinton Defends Her Actions
Before and After Libya Attack," *New York Times*, Jan. 23,
2013; Amy Chozick, "Clinton Calls Benghazi Her 'Biggest
Regret' as Secretary," *New York Times*, Jan. 27, 2014; Mark
Landler, "Scare Adds to Fears That Clinton's Work Has
Taken Toll," *New York Times*, Jan. 4, 2013; Michael E.
O'Hanlon, "State and the Stateswoman," *Foreign Affairs*, Jan.
29, 2013; Stephen M. Walt, "Is Hillary Clinton a Great
Secretary of State?" *Foreign Policy*, July 10, 2012, http://
foreignpolicy.com/2012/07/10/is-hillary-clinton-a-great-
secretary-of-state/; Hagan, "Hillary in Midair."

Chapter 36: 2016?

EVEN BEFORE BARACK OBAMA: Michael D. Shear, "2012 and
  Beyond: Clinton Says, 'No,' 'No,' and 'No,'" *New York Times*,
  March 17, 2011; Myers, "Hillary Clinton's Last Tour"; Jim
  Rutenberg, "A Clinton in 'Transition' Keeps Opponents and
  Donors Frozen," *New York Times*, March 30, 2013; Rachel
  Weiner, "How Hillary Clinton Evolved on Gay Marriage,"
  Washington Post, March 18, 2013; Myers, "Hillary Clinton's Last
  Tour"; @hillaryclinton, twitter.com, accessed in early 2015;
  Westfall, "Hillary Clinton: I Have a Decision"; Hagan, "Hillary
  in Midair"; Mike McIntire, "Clintons Made $109 Million in
  Last 8 Years," *New York Times*, April 5, 2008; Liz Kreutz,
  "Hillary Clinton Defends High-Dollar Speaking Fees," ABC
  News, June 9, 2014, http://abcnews.go.com/Politics/hillary-
  clinton-defends-high-dollar-speaking-fees/story?id=24052962;
  "Hillary Clinton with Diane Sawyer Interview," June 9, 2014,
  YouTube video, 42:59, from ABC News, posted by "The Sound,"
  http://www.youtube.com/watch?v=GdTtvXxLyY0; Sean
  Sullivan, "Hillary Clinton on 'Dead Broke' Comment,"
  Washington Post, July 29, 2014; Clare Swanson, "The Bestselling
  Books of 2014," *Publishers Weekly*, Jan. 2, 2015; "First Photos:

Bill, Hillary, Chelsea Clinton and Marc Mezvinsky with Baby Charlotte," *Washington Wire* (blog), *Wall Street Journal*, Sept. 27, 2014, http://blogs.wsj.com/washwire/2014/09/27/; Michael S. Schmidt, "Hillary Clinton Used Personal Email Account at State Dept., Possibly Breaking Rules," *New York Times*, March 2, 2015; Robert O'Harrow Jr., "How Clinton's Email Scandal Took Root," *Washington Post*, March 27, 2016; Zeke J. Miller, "Transcript: Everything Hillary Clinton Said on the Email Controversy," time.com, March 10, 2015; ABC News, "Hillary Clinton's 2016 Presidential Campaign Announcement," April 12, 2015, https://www.youtube.com/watch?v=N708P-A45D0. Annie Karni, "Hillary Clinton Formally Announces 2016 Run," Politico, April 12, 2015, http://www.politico.com/story/2015/04/hillary-clinton-2016-election-presidential-launch-116888.html. Amy Chozick, "Hillary Clinton Embraces Her Mother's Emotional Tale," *New York Times*, June 12, 2015; Wilson Andrews, Alicia Parlapiano, and Karen Yourish, "Who Is Running for President?" *New York Times*, Aug. 3, 2015, http://www.nytimes.com/interactive/2016/us/elections/2016-presidential-candidates.html; Rosalind S. Helderman, "Report: Clinton Foundation Says Not All Donations Were Disclosed," *Washington Post*, March 19, 2015; Joshua Green and Richard Rubin, "Clinton Foundation Failed to Disclose 1,100 Foreign Donations," *Bloomberg*, April 29, 2015, http://www.bloomberg.com/politics/articles/2015-04-29/clinton-foundation-failed-to-disclose-1-100-foreign-donations; Elise Labott, "Hillary Clinton to turn over private email server to Justice Department," CNN, Aug. 12, 2015, http://www.cnn.com/2015/08/11/politics/hillary-clinton-email-server-justice-department.

Chapter 37: Front-runner

Despite her early initial lead: "Meet Bernie" berniesanders.com, https://berniesanders.com/about/; Amy Chozick and Patrick Healy, "Hillary Clinton's Team is Wary as Bernie Sanders Finds Footing in Iowa," *New York Times*,

July 7, 2015; "Labor Force Statistics from the Current Population Survey," Bureau of Labor Statistics, http://data.bls.gov/timeseries/LNS14000000; Karen DeYoung, "State Department says 15 e-mails missing from pages Hillary Clinton provided," *Washington Post*, June 25, 2015; "Editors' Note: Clinton Email Coverage," *New York Times*, July 27, 2015, http://www.nytimes.com/2015/07/28/us/editors-note-clinton-email-coverage.html; Taylor Wofford, "Hillary Clinton's Emails: What You Need to Know," *Newsweek.com*, Aug. 13, 2015, http://newsweek.com/hillary-clinton-email-private-server-top-secret-362822; "Hillary Jokes About Snapchat," Real Clear Politics, Aug. 17, 2015, http://www.realclearpolitics.com/video/2015/08/17/hillary_clinton_jokes_about_snapchat_those_messages_disappear_all_by_themselves.html; Maggie Haberman and Amy Chozick, "Hillary Clinton's Long Road to 'Sorry' Over Email Use," *New York Times*, Sept. 11, 2015; "Your Damn Emails/Bernie Sanders," https://www.youtube.com/watch?v=aOOfwN0iYxM; Stephen Collinson, "Marathon Benghazi Hearing Leaves Hillary Clinton Largely Unscathed," CNN, Oct. 23, 2015, http://www.cnn.com/2015/10/22/politics/hillary-clinton-benghazi-hearing-updates/.

HAVING SURVIVED BOTH: Mark Leibovich, "I'm the Last Thing Standing Between You and the Apocalypse," *New York Times Magazine*, Oct. 16, 2016; Ezra Klein, "Understanding Hillary," Vox.com, July 11, 2016, http://www.vox.com/a/hillary-clinton-interview/the-gap-listener-leadership-quality; Wilson Andrews, Kitty Bennett, and Alicia Parlapiano, "2016 Delegate Count and Primary Results," *New York Times*, July 5, 2016, http://www.nytimes.com/interactive/2016/us/elections/primary-calendar-and-results.html?_r=0; Glenn Thrush and Annie Karni, "How Iowa Went Wrong for Hillary Clinton," Politico, Feb. 2, 2016, http://www.politico.com/story/2016/02/hillary-clinton-iowa-performance-218607; Interview with David Redlawsk, James R. Soles professor and chair of the Department of Political Science and International Relations, University of Delaware, Oct. 13,

2016; Rebecca Traister, "Hillary Clinton's Campaign Was Never Going to be Easy. But Did It Have to Get This Hard?" *New York*, May 30, 2016; Tony Leys, "Clinton Officially Nets Iowa Caucuses Win Over Sanders," *Des Moines Register*, Feb. 2, 2016; Evan Halper and Michael A. Memoli, "With New Hampshire Primary Nigh, Hillary Clinton Shifts Focus to Nevada Caucuses and Beyond," *Los Angeles Times*, Feb. 5, 2016; Patrick Healy and Jonathan Martin, "Donald Trump and Bernie Sanders Win in New Hampshire Primary," *New York Times*, Feb. 9, 2016; Glenn Thrush and Annie Karni, "How Clinton Hit the Reset Button on 2016," Politico, March 3, 2016, http://www.politico.com/story/2016/03/how-clinton-saved-her-campaign-220165; David A. Graham, "Why Clinton Is Connecting with Black Voters—and Sanders Isn't," *Atlantic*, Feb. 24, 2016; Interview with David A. Graham, Oct. 11, 2016; Chris Matthews, "Bernie Sanders Can't Explain How He'd Break up the Banks," Fortune.com, April 5, 2016, http://fortune.com/2016/04/05/bernie-sanders-big-banks/; Abby Phillip and John Wagner, "Hacked WikiLeaks Emails Show Concerns about Clinton Candidacy, Email Server," *Washington Post*, Oct. 12, 2016; Hanna Trudo and Nick Gass, "Sanders: Clinton's Not Qualified to Be President," Politico, April 7, 2016, http://www.politico.com/story/2016/04/sanders-clinton-not-qualified-to-be-president-221666; Clare Foran, "Is the Democratic Primary Really Rigged?" theatlantic.com, May 17, 2016, http://www.theatlantic.com/politics/archive/2016/05/is-the-democratic-primary-really-rigged/483168/; Harry Enten and Nate Silver, "The System Isn't 'Rigged' Against Sanders," fivethirtyeight.com, May 26, 2016, http://fivethirtyeight.com/features/the-system-isnt-rigged-against-sanders/; "2016 Democratic Popular Vote," Real Clear Politics, http://www.realclearpolitics.com/epolls/2016/president/democratic_vote_count.html; Aaron Zitner, Dante Chinni, and Brian McGill, "How Clinton Won," wsj.com, June 7, 2016, http://graphics.wsj.com/elections/2016/how-clinton-won/; MJ Lee, Dan Merica, and Jeff

Zeleny, "Bernie Sanders Endorses Hillary Clinton," CNN, July 12, 2016, http://www.cnn.com/2016/07/11/politics/hillary-clinton-bernie-sanders/.

Chapter 38: Nasty

HILLARY HAD LITTLE TIME: David M. Herszenhorn, "House Benghazi Report Finds No New Evidence of Wrongdoing by Hillary Clinton," *New York Times*, June 28, 2016; Byron Tau, "Timeline: Hillary Clinton's Email Troubles," *Wall Street Journal*, July 5, 2016; "Text of F.B.I. Director's Remarks on Investigation into Hillary Clinton's Email Use," *New York Times*, July 5, 2016; Matt Zapotosky and Rosalind S. Helderman, "FBI Recommends No Criminal Charges in Clinton Email Probe," *Washington Post*, July 5, 2016; John Santucci and Lauren Effron, "The Trump Kids," ABCnews.com, http://abcnews.go.com/Politics/trump-kids-meet-gop-candidate-donald-trumps-children/story?id=35253768; Kevin Uhrmacher, Kevin Schaul, and Ted Mellnik, "Republicans Adjusted Rules for Their Primaries After 2012," *Washington Post*, March 9, 2016; "Donald Trump Transcript: Our Country Needs a Truly Great Leader," *Wall Street Journal*, June 16, 2015; "Donald J. Trump Statement on Preventing Muslim Immigration," DonaldJTrump.com, Dec. 7, 2015, https://www.donaldjtrump.com/press-releases/donald-j.-trump-statement-on-preventing-muslim-immigration; Ben Geier, "Donald Trump Has a New Nickname for Hillary Clinton," Fortune.com, April 18, 2016, http://fortune.com/2016/04/18/trump-clinton-nickname/; Anne Gearan and Katie Zezima, "Trump's 'Woman's Card' Comment Escalates the Campaign's Gender Wars," *Washington Post*, April 27, 2016; "'Deal Me In,'" bloomberg.com, April 26, 2016, http://www.bloomberg.com/politics/videos/2016-04-27/hillary-clinton-responds-to-trump-s-woman-card-remark; Yoni Applebaum, "Trump's Promise to Jail Clinton Is a Threat to American Democracy," *The Atlantic*, Oct. 10, 2016; Kristen East, "Clinton: I was Saddened by 'Lock Her Up' Chants," Politico, July 24, 2016.

AT THE DEMOCRATIC CONVENTION: White House press release, "Remarks By the First Lady at the Democratic National Convention," July 25, 2016, https://www.whitehouse.gov/the-press-office/2016/07/25/remarks-first-lady-democratic-national-convention; "Illinois Democrats Cast Presidential Nominating Votes for Clinton," ChicagoTribune.com, July 26, 2016, http://www.chicagotribune.com/news/local/politics/ct-illinois-democrats-cast-votes-hillary-clinton-bernie-sanders-20160726-story.html; Katie Mettler, "Meet Geraldine Emmett, the 102-year-old Hillary-Booster You Saw—and Heard—at the Convention Last Night," *Washington Post*, July 27, 2006, https://www.washingtonpost.com/news/morning-mix/wp/2016/07/27/meet-jerry-emmett-102-the-arizona-democrat-born-before-american-women-could-vote/; Vanessa Friedman, "Why Hillary Wore White," *New York Times*, July 29, 2016; Patrick Healy and Amy Chozick, "Hillary Clinton Warns of 'Moment of Reckoning' in Speech Accepting Nomination," *New York Times*, July 26, 2016; Ashley Parker, "Donald Trump Says Hillary Clinton Doesn't Have 'a Presidential Look,'" *New York Times*, Sept. 6, 2016; Andrew Rafferty, "Hillary Clinton Fights Back Coughing Attack," nbcnews.com, Sept. 5, 2016, http://www.nbcnews.com/politics/2016-election/hillary-clinton-struggles-fight-back-coughing-attack-n643026; Abby Phillip, "Clinton: Half of Trump's Supporters Fit in 'Basket of Deplorables,'" *Washington Post*, Sept. 9, 2016; David A. Graham, "Gaffe Track: Hillary Clinton's 'Basket of Deplorables,'" *Atlantic.com*, Sept. 12, 2016, http://www.theatlantic.com/notes/2016/09/gaffe-track-hillary-clintons-basket-of-deplorables/499565/; Tara Golshan, "How Hillary Clinton's Health Passed from an On-line Conspiracy Theory to a Mainstream Debate," Vox.com, Sept. 13, 2016, http://www.vox.com/2016/9/12/12888498/hillary-clinton-health-conspiracy; Dan Merica, "Hillary Clinton: Pneumonia Diagnosis . . .," CNN.com, Sept. 16, 2016, http://www.cnn.com/2016/09/16/politics/hillary-clinton-obama-birther-pneumonia/; Andrew Prokop, "3 Explanations for Why Donald Trump is Suddenly Doing Better in the Polls," Vox.com, Sept. 16, 2016, http://www.vox.com/2016/9/16/12933256/donald-trump-polls-winning.

As was her nature: Patrick Healy, Amy Chozick, and Maggie Haberman, "Debate Prep? Hillary Clinton and Donald Trump Differ on That, Too," *New York Times*, Sept. 24, 2016; Stephen Battaglio, "Final Trump-Clinton Face-Off Draws 71.6 million Viewers," *Los Angeles Times*, Oct. 20, 2016; Aaron Blake, "The First Trump-Clinton Presidential Debate Transcript, Annotated," *Washingtonpost.com*, Sept. 26, 2016, https://www.washingtonpost.com/news/the-fix/wp/2016/09/26/the-first-trump-clinton-presidential-debate-transcript-annotated/; Michael Barbaro, Maggie Haberman, and Alan Rappeport, "While America Sleeps, Donald Trump Seethes On Twitter," *New York Times*, Sept. 26, 2016; Jeff Stein, "What 20,000 Pages of Hacked WikiLeaks Emails Teach Us About Hillary Clinton," Vox.com, Oct. 20, 2016, http://www.vox.com/policy-and-politics/2016/10/20/13308108/wikileaks-podesta-hillary-clinton; Annie Karni and Glenn Thrush, "22 Toxic Days for Hillary Clinton," Politico, Oct. 16., 2016, http://www.politico.com/story/2016/10/hillary-clinton-trump-wikileaks-229864; David Fahrenthold, "Trump Recorded Having Extremely Lewd Conversation About Women in 2005," *Washington Post*, Oct. 8, 2016; Alexander Burns, Maggie Haberman, and Jonathan Martin, "Donald Trump Apology Caps Day of Outrage Over Lewd Tape," *New York Times*, Oct. 7, 2106, http://www.nytimes.com/2016/10/08/us/politics/donald-trump-women.html; David Fahrenthold and Katie Zezima, "A Dark Debate," *Washington Post*, Oct. 9, 2016; Patrick Healy and Jonathan Martin, "In Second Debate, Donald Trump and Hillary Clinton Spar in Bitter, Personal Terms," *New York Times*, Oct. 9, 2016.

Chapter 39: Election

After winning the second: Edward-Isaac Dovere, "Inside the Loss Clinton Saw Coming," *Politico Magazine*, Nov. 9, 2016; Margaret Talev and Jennifer Epstein, "Clinton's

Pioneering Run Couldn't Rise Above an Angry Elector-
ate," Bloomberg.com, http://www.bloomberg.com/politics/
articles/2016-11-09/clinton-s-pioneering-run-couldn-t-rise-
above-an-angry-electorate; James B. Comey, letter to Hon.
Richard Burr and others, Oct. 28, 2016, accessed at http://
www.nytimes.com/interactive/2016/10/28/us/politics/
fbi-letter.html; Steve Vladeck, "What is the Hatch Act—and
did James Comey break it?" CNN.com, http://www.cnn.
com/2016/10/31/politics/what-is-the-hatch-act/; Emily
Guskin and Scott Clement, "Post-ABC Tracking Poll,"
Washington Post, Nov. 1, 2016, https://www.washingtonpost.
com/news/the-fix/wp/2016/11/01/post-abc-tracking-poll-
clinton-falls-behind-trump-in-enthusiasm-but-has-edge-
in-early-voting/; Cleve R. Wootson Jr., "'Imagine President
Trump.' Another Conservative Paper Can't, Endorses First
Democrat Since 1868," *Washington Post,* Oct. 2, 2016, https://
www.washingtonpost.com/news/the-fix/wp/2016/10/02/
imagine-president-trump-another-conservative-paper-cant-
endorses-first-democrat-since-1868/; Ronald Brownstein, "Is
Donald Trump Outflanking Hillary Clinton?" *The Atlantic,*
Nov. 2, 2016.

AS NOVEMBER 8 NEARED: Katie Reilly, "Beyoncé and Jay Z
Headline Rally for Hillary Clinton in Ohio," Time.com,
Nov. 5, 2016, http://time.com/4559543/hillary-clinton-rally-
beyonce-jay-z-/?iid=sr-link2; Amy Chozick tweet and photo,
@amychozick, Nov. 4, 2016; Eric Bradner, Pamela Brown, and
Evan Perez, "FBI Clears Clinton—Again," CNN.com, http://
www.cnn.com/2016/11/06/politics/comey-tells-congress-
fbi-has-not-changed-conclusions/; Michael Barbaro, Ashley
Parker, and Amy Chozick, "Optimism From Hillary Clinton
and Darkness from Donald Trump at Campaign's End," *New
York Times,* Nov. 7, 2016; Tierney McCafee, "How Clinton and
Trump Will Spend Election Day," People.com, Nov. 7, 2016;
Ronald Brownstein, "How Trump Won," *The Atlantic,* Nov. 9,
2016, http://www.theatlantic.com/politics/archive/2016/11/
how-trump-won/507053/; Presidential Election Results and
Exit Polls, nytimes.com, Nov. 9, 2016, http://www.nytimes.

com/elections/results/president; James Hohmann, "The Daily 202: Why Trump Won—and Why the Media Missed It," *Washington Post*, Nov. 9, 2016, https://www.washington-post.com/news/powerpost/paloma/daily-202/2016/11/09/daily-202-why-trump-won-and-why-the-media-missed-it/5822ea17e9b69b6085905dee/; "Hillary Clinton's Full Concession Speech," nytimes.com, Nov. 9, 2016, http://www.nytimes.com/video/us/politics/100000004708101/hillary-clinton-concession-speech-live-stream.html.

PHOTO CREDITS

p. vi: Michael Ainsworth/*The Dallas Morning News*

PART ONE: p. 2: © Brooks Kraft/Corbis; p. 4: Ron Edmonds/
Associated Press; p. 8: William J. Clinton Presidential
Library; pp. 11, 14, 19: Clinton Family Archives; p. 22:
Clinton Presidential Library; p. 23: Marion S. Trikosko, U.S.
News & World Report Collection, Library of Congress; p. 30:
Courtesy of Wellesley College; p. 36: Rue des Archives/
Granger, NYC—All rights reserved; p. 37: *Southwords*, Dec.
22, 1964, p. 2, courtesy of *Southwords*/Maine South High
School; pp. 41, 44, 48: Courtesy of Wellesley College; p. 52:
Penny Ortner/Courtesy of Wellesley College; p. 56: Clinton
Family Archives; p. 62: Photo by Chalue/Courtesy of
Wellesley College; p. 64: Photo by Stinmell/Courtesy of
Wellesley College; p. 67: Lee Balterman/Life Picture
Collection/Getty Images; p. 72: Courtesy of the League of
Women Voters of the U.S.; p. 76: Clinton Family Archives;
p. 80: Clinton Presidential Library; p. 87: *Yale Law Report*/
Courtesy of Yale Law School; p. 88: Clinton Family Archives;
p. 90: Associated Press; p. 98: Special Collections, University
of Arkansas; p. 100: © Bettmann/Corbis; p. 109: David Hume
Kennerly/Getty Images; pp. 111, 112: Clinton House
Museum—Fayetteville, Arkansas.

PART TWO: pp. 117, 118: Clinton House Museum—Fayetteville,
Arkansas; p. 122: Clinton Presidential Library; pp. 123, 126:
Clinton House Museum—Fayetteville, Arkansas; p. 130:

Associated Press/*Arkansas Democrat-Gazette*; p. 133: Bill
Clinton State Government Project, Butler Center for
Arkansas Studies, Central Arkansas Library System; p. 135:
Arkansas Democrat-Gazette; p. 136: © Mike
Stewart/Sygma/Corbis; p. 139: Bill Clinton State
Government Project, Butler Center for Arkansas Studies,
Central Arkansas Library System; p. 142: Diane Blair papers
(MC1632), Series 5, Box 2, file 16, item #1281, Special
Collections, University of Arkansas; p. 147: Courtesy of
Wellesley College; p. 149: Polaris Images; pp. 150, 151:
Arkansas Democrat-Gazette; p. 157: © Mike Stewart/Sygma/
Corbis; p. 158: Clinton Family Archives; p. 159: *Arkansas
Democrat-Gazette*; p. 165: Kamps Collection, box 1, folder 2,
Bill Clinton State Government Project, Butler Center for
Arkansas Studies, Central Arkansas Library System;
pp. 168, 172: *Arkansas Democrat-Gazette*; p. 173: Author's
collection; p. 176: Associated Press/CBS-TV via Associated
Press; p. 184: Clinton Presidential Library; p. 188: J. Scott
Applewhite; pp. 190, 191: Clinton Presidential Library;
p. 192, photo: Library of Congress/White House photo;
p. 192, button: Author's collection; p. 193: Clinton
Presidential Library; p. 195, top: Bill Clinton State
Government Project, Butler Center for Arkansas Studies,
Central Arkansas Library System; p. 195, bottom: Courtesy
UALR Center for Arkansas History and Culture; p. 196,
top: Michael Crawford/The New Yorker Collection/
The Cartoon Bank, p. 196, bottom: Courtesy of the *Tampa
Tribune*.

PART THREE: p. 201: Associated Press; p. 204: Clinton
Presidential Library; p. 206: FOIA 2006-0810-F, Office of
First Lady's Files on Health Care Task Force/Health Care
Reform, previously restricted documents released on April
18, 2014; p. 209: Clinton Presidential Library; p. 211: Stephen
R. Brown/Associated Press; pp. 217, 219, 226, 227: Clinton
Presidential Library; p. 231: From Ruth Marcus and Charles

R. Babcock, "How $1,000 Stake Netted $100,000," *Washington Post*, March 30, 1994; pp. 234, 236: Clinton Presidential Library; p. 239: Diane Blair papers (MC1632), series 5, box 2, file 42, item #1693, Special Collections, University of Arkansas; p. 242: Clinton Presidential Library; p. 245: John Gaps III/Associated Press; p. 250: Clinton Presidential Library; p. 252: Doug Mills/Associated Press; p. 256: Author's collection; p. 258: Reed Saxon/Associated Press; p. 261: Luc Novovitch/Associated Press/Pool; p. 265: Diane Blair papers (MC1632), series 3, subseries 3, box 1, file 2, Special Collections, University of Arkansas; pp. 266, 267, 271, 272: Clinton Presidential Library; p. 274: Stephan Savoia/ Associated Press; p. 277: Greg Gibson/Associated Press; p. 282: Marty Lederhandler/Associated Press; p. 283: Greg Gibson/Associated Press; p. 285: Roberto Borea/Associated Press; p. 290: Bebeto Matthews/Associated Press; p. 300: Ron Frehm/Associated Press; p. 302: Associated Press; p. 306: Clinton Presidential Library; p. 309: Diane Blair papers (MC1632), series 2, box 5, folder 52, Image #1838, Special Collections, University of Arkansas; p. 312: Author's collection; p. 314: Ron Edmonds/Associated Press; p. 315, top: © Tribune Content Agency, LLC. All Rights Reserved. Reprinted with permission; p. 315, bottom: © 1993 Mike Peters Editorial–King Features Syndicate, Inc.; p. 316, top: Courtesy of The Oklahoman, p. 316, bottom: © Tribune Content Agency, LLC. All Rights Reserved. Reprinted with permission.

PART FOUR: pp. 320, 321: Clinton Presidential Library; p. 329: Robert F. Bukaty/Associated Press; p. 332: Susan Walsh/ Associated Press; p. 337: Associated Press; p. 339: Pat Sullivan/Associated Press; pp. 342, 343: Author's collection; p. 345: J. Scott Applewhite/Associated Press; p. 349: Matt Rourke/Associated Press; p. 350, top: Author's collection; p. 350, bottom: Charlie Neibergall/Associated Press; p. 355: Elise Amendola/Associated Press; p. 360: NBC Universal/

ACKNOWLEDGMENTS

Politics is a team sport, and so is book writing. It just doesn't happen without a gifted team ready to support your cause.

This book wouldn't have happened at all without the brilliance and coaching of my editors Jean Feiwel and Lauren Burniac, who trusted me to tackle this project and kept their cool despite missed deadlines and a monstrously long manuscript. The amazing Deirdre Langeland stepped in to help us cross the first finish line and the fabulous Christine Barcellona guided us through the update and helped me get a grip on the messy 2016 election.

The brigade at Feiwel and Friends had my back in the best possible way. Christine Ma, production editor, somehow kept us on track, and Sherri Schmidt's careful and detailed copyediting greatly improved the manuscript. The design team of Rich Deas, Ashley Halsey, and Kathleen Breitenfeld wrestled an unwieldy pile of pages, photos, cartoons, and back matter into beautiful order.

Kathleen stepped up again, along with production editor Hayley Jozwiak, production manager Kim Waymer, and art director April Ward to create this new and updated edition on a tight deadline.

Glenn Whaley, manager of the Bill Clinton State Government Project of the Butler Center for Arkansas Studies, graciously helped me get access to Bill Clinton's governor archives, giving me a sense of the Arkansas First

Lady's experience. While there, I was lucky to meet Margaret Justus, a Wellesley College student and born researcher who dug into the Wellesley archives for me when she was back at school.

It's impossible to overstate the value of archivists and librarians on a project like this. I owe many thanks for help with documents, facts, photos, and permissions to Jane A. Callahan, Wellesley College archivist; Nancy Lyon, Yale University archivist; Karen Russ of the University of Arkansas–Little Rock's Ottenheimer Library; and Geoffery Stark and the Special Collections team at the University of Arkansas's Mullins Library in Fayetteville.

For help finding and gathering photos, I especially appreciate Kate Johnson of the Clinton House Museum; Walter Hussman, Barry Arthur, and Kristina Hanry of the *Arkansas Democrat-Gazette*; Janet Conroy of the *Yale Law Report*, and Joy Secuban of the Clinton Foundation. John Keller and Herbert Ragan, audiovisual archivists at the Clinton Presidential Library, were beyond wonderful—efficient, thorough, and a pleasure to work with.

I am profoundly grateful to the special group of people who were willing to read the manuscript: David Stern; Jen McCartney; David Redlawsk, chair of the University of Delaware political science department; and political journalists David A. Graham, John Harwood, and Steve Barnes. Their detailed suggestions made this a more thoughtful and more accurate book.

I am deeply indebted to my daughter Abby McCartney. I've never been a student of politics. But after she completed an election project in third grade, I had an in-house expert. As a teen and at college, she campaigned for presidential candidates and canvassed for local ones. When I agreed to do this book, I found not only Bill's and Hillary's autobiographies, but also three other Clinton-era books on her personal bookshelf. She devoted her winter break from a master's program in public policy to reading books on the 2008 election and help me shape those chapters; she also visited the Library of Congress to get Clinton photos. Her critiques and edits were invaluable, and her support means the world to me.

Last, my heartfelt appreciation to my husband, Scott McCartney, for understanding and supporting my work and being my best friend for more than thirty years.

INDEX